Are These End Times?

All You Need to Know About What's Coming Next and How to Prepare for Everything

Dr. Roger G. Ford, Ph.D., P.E.

Dr-Ford.net

Forward by Pastor Mack D. Roller Jr.

ISBN: 9781096393733

DEDICATION

To my Savior and my God, The Lord Jesus Christ,
and to my sweet Mary, my wife of over 50 years

CONTENTS

FORWARD

Those who choose to read this book are among a select few who take prophecy seriously. The "casual Christian" or average church attender, sad to say, fails to see the need and pays the consequences of developing a stagnant faith with little passion for the things of the Spirit. Congratulations; you have self-identified as one who desires to follow the admonition of Scripture. Jesus purposefully trained his disciples as he called them to be watchful and ready (much of the teaching of Jesus focuses on the end times as you will see in this book). The purpose of this book, as stated by the Author, is to bring clarity to a cluttered field of study and to excite the reader to make disciples.

I cannot think of a better person to instruct us in this endeavor than Dr. Roger Ford. I have had the privilege to be his pastor and friend for over a decade. You do not have to spend much time with Dr. Ford before you observe his unashamed love for Scripture and his passion for eschatology. He is a superb teacher who challenges, enlightens, and encourages all those who sit under his teaching. Roger knows prophecy and is able to bring much needed clarity to this subject. You may not agree with every minute conclusion, but you will agree with me that his presuppositions and conclusions are biblically based. Not only does he have a passion for prophecy, but he loves to see people grow in their walk with Jesus. He is committed to the great commission.

Eschatological discipleship is powerful. This is a major part of the model and content of the training of the 12. Most discipleship methods and content focus only on the "here and now" which often leads to a self-centered Christianity. However, when we focus on the complete story of Scripture (particularly the end-times), we anticipate God moving not only in our lives but in the world around us.

The study of prophecy gives us a true biblical perspective and strengthens our passion to make disciples. The joyful anticipation of the return of the Lord is a powerful force in the heart of the church. May God Bless you as you journey through this book, and may God give you a passion for prophecy and for making disciples.

Until He Comes,

Mack D. Roller Jr.
Pastor; Glen Meadows Baptist Church

PREFACE

2 Timothy 2:15, "Study to shew thyself approved unto God, a workman that needeth not to be ashamed, rightly dividing the word of truth."

Colossians 3:16, "Let the word of Christ dwell in you richly in all wisdom; teaching and admonishing one another in psalms and hymns and spiritual songs, singing with grace in your hearts to the Lord."

Nehemiah 8:8, "So they read in the book in the law of God distinctly, and gave the sense, and caused them to understand the reading."

These verses and many others characterize the great need for each and every Christian who is truly a member of the Body of Christ, one with Jesus Christ as Savior and Lord, to know extensively the Word of God, the Bible. Unfortunately, many if not most Christians are not even familiar with the Word of God to the point of knowing that the Old and New Testaments both explain in vivid detail that the only way to God is through faith, not works.

Most who identify with Christ today are very busy, have complicated lives, are striving to live comfortable lives, and are mainly disturbed at the direction in which the nation and the world are heading. Because of their unfamiliarity with God's Word, anxiety and worry have come to be dominating and defining characteristics of American lives, of lives of those in other countries, and, surprisingly and disturbingly, of Christians' lives in general. This is not the way it is supposed to be!

I have been fascinated with Bible Prophecy for decades because I always knew God was in control, there was a life after death, that God was concerned about the way I lived my life, and that God has always had a plan for the human race that was pretty much unknown by everyday people. We often ask questions like, "Why am I here?", or "Why does God allow...?", or "What happens when I die?" The answers to these and many more questions such as these can be definitively answered through God's Word IF we have the desire, the dedication, the conviction, the impulse, the joy, the drive to read the Bible daily and study it in detail.

This is just a word of preparation for why this little book was even conceived of in the first place. I am a teacher, and I am an engineer. My mind works in ways that are not common to most because I am driven to understand, at a detail level, things that many people cannot grasp or do not wish to put in the time to grasp. But I also am a trained problem-solver who has come to the realization that the main reason for difficulties in our lives often centers on our misunderstanding or ignorance of the facts, the details, the instructions, what the True Truth really is about life, and what God expects of us.

Misunderstanding or ignorance is, or can be, caused by just plain old laziness and the lack of desire to do diligent work. Most good things in life come about only by hard work, and that simple fact could be one of the main reasons for anxiety and despair in our lives since we, as a society, are lazy. Understanding comes from knowledge and the application of it, but understanding only comes, from the lowest level, by dedication and hard work. One cannot get understanding by osmosis or expecting someone else to do the work and pour it into our brains for us. We have to dig out the understanding ourselves to know why it is useful to us and how to use it properly. But, sadly, we do not, for the most part. We just bop along in our ignorance expecting others to do and know and act for us. How well is that working out for us? Chaos reigns!

Cognitive processes are what we use to make good decisions and what separates us from the animal kingdom. We are all made in the Image of God and thereby expected by God to learn His ways or get knowledge of them. If we do not know what He says about things, we have no knowledge of His ways, but that is not His fault. It's our fault for not reading His Word!

Then God says get understanding. Proverbs 4:7 says, "Wisdom is the principal thing; therefore, get wisdom: and with all thy getting get understanding." When we initially obtain knowledge of something, we should want to understand. How else can we utilize the knowledge unless we understand how to use, how to incorporate, when to place that knowledge into our lives? The answer is by understanding that knowledge. When our mothers told us that the stove was hot, we did not understand until we touched it and burned ourselves, right?

Proverbs 4:7 tells us to get Wisdom, the Wisdom of God, not man's wisdom which is foolishness. And just how do we do that? By reading, contemplating, studying, and repeating for the rest of our lives through the guidance of the Holy Spirit, the Holy Scriptures, God's Word, the Bible in its entirety!

A last word on my studies of God's Word. I have been a Christian since the summer I turned eleven when I was baptized in Denver, Colorado. My in-depth devotion to the Word of God got its beginnings in high school when the public-school system would still offer Bible classes which happened in Lubbock, Texas, back in the 1960's. After I married Mary, the love of my life now for over 50 years, we began, slowly, to discover the Bible and realize that our two boys needed to be immersed in God's Word. We began our biblical journey along with the boys which led to our daily reading and study of God's Word which has now lasted for many years.

My study of Bible Prophecy began with the gift from my mother-in-law of Hal Lindsey's "Late Great Planet Earth" back in 1972 (HalLindsey.com). Of course, I read all of Hal's books which led me to other noted Prophecy, creationist, and biblical authors such as John MacArthur (GTY.org), John Walvoord (Dallas Theological Seminary), Dwight Pentecost (Dallas Theological Seminary), Tim Lahaye, Henry Morris (ICR.org), J.R. Church (ProphecyintheNews.com), Gary Stearman (prophecywatchers.com), David Jeremiah (davidjeremiah.org), Bruce Malone (SearchfortheTruth.net), Chuck Missler (Khouse.org), Ken Ham (answersingenesis.org), David Reagan (christinprophecy.org), Carl Baugh (CreationEvidence.org), Bill Salus (prophecydepotministries.net), Rapture Ready (raptureready.com), and many others. I recommend all of these because they are believers in the literal Word of God as written and have withstood the tests of time and trials. For over 45 years I have made the study of God's Word my passion, especially Bible Prophecy. It is because of this and the need to try to get all Christians to realize the blessings that God's Word brings that led to this work.

One last item for my readers. I have chosen to use a non-conventional attribution method when I "borrow" from other sources. When I refer to what I have found in other writings, I will place the author's name and sometimes their website so that the original text can be found. I use this method primarily for two reasons: one, the internet is useful and easy to access information, and, two, most Bible writers share in my passion to disperse God's Truth to as many as possible, so the general method of attribution should lead to many searches on their websites and many other examples of their work, not just the specific one I have used.

Of course, the many decades of my study of Bible Prophecy amounts to an accumulation of knowledge that I have gained which cannot all be referenced, nor should it be. I mean to share my accumulated grasp on Bible Prophecy and all the associated and related issues and methods so that many can get the benefit of God's provision, Grace, Mercy, and revelation which brings comfort, counsel, peace, and understanding. May God grant you the calm and reassuring solid foundation of peace and assurance and boldness that only He can grant through the knowledge of His Son's sacrifice and through His unique, inerrant, authoritative, and perfect Word.

INTRODUCTION

A word of introduction to this small literary offering is in order, I think. Just picking up this book will surprise some but possibly and hopefully please others. It will surprise many, challenge many, perhaps offend some, and, again hopefully, answer many questions to those who have contemplated, or were interested, or were fearful of Bible Prophecy.

Reading God's Word reveals many things. As pure literature, the Bible is full of interesting and curious stories about the failures and successes of many individuals, nations, and regimes as well as details of a man who claims to be God in the flesh. As a text on morality, the Bible provides concrete foundational principles on God's morality and His displeasure in mankind's ignoring of it. The instruction of the Bible when dealing with interpersonal relationships is unparalleled even when compared to all the "feel-good" and "self-help" tomes available today from secular writers.

However, the Bible contains subject matter that is unique among ALL literature ever written or that ever will be written. That subject matter is Prophecy in the sense of letting us know what is going to happen in the immediate future as well as in the distant future. This has been true to everyone who ever picked up God's Word from the time it was originally written until today.

Knowing the Bible, God's Word, is knowing that God is the basis of Wisdom. Man's wisdom is foolishness when compared to God's Wisdom. 1 Corinthians 3:19 says, "For the wisdom of this world is foolishness with God…" The alternative to that foolishness is the Wisdom of God. Psalm, 111:10 says, "The fear of the LORD is the beginning of wisdom: a good understanding have all they that do his commandments: his praise endureth for ever." And how do we even appreciate the "fear of the Lord", the Wisdom of God? When we realize that God's Word is premier over man's word. Psalm 118:8, the very middle verse in our Bible, says, "It is better to trust in the LORD than to put confidence in man."

Therefore, when we contemplate our immediate future and our ultimate future in the Lord, where do we turn for enlightenment? To man's explanation for everything – evolution? Certainly NOT! We turn to God's Word because it is the True Truth upon which we can live joyful and meaningful lives, not to mention living according to God's Will for our lives. And what can be more important than that?

This little book is a compilation of the numerous considerations that a thinking and dedicated Christian should know and become familiar with in order to perceive just where we are in God's Plan for the redemption of mankind, where we are in the present in relation to what God has told us will be coming upon the world as a result of its fallen nature, and what glorious and fearful things God has in store for us in the very near future. Read on, dear inquisitor, for many answers are available to the hungry mind and heart all available in God's Word through the illumination of His Holy Spirit!

In this small book is the introduction to many areas of study that surround gaining understanding and wisdom about Bible Prophecy. Some of those include how to read God's Word for understanding, the fundamental concepts to understanding prophecy, Old Testament references to the End Times, New Testament references to the End Times, Pre-Tribulation Rapture defense and justification, resurrections and judgments, and an End Times Timeline. Also, included in the text is the absolute necessity for Christians to reject in its entirety the concept of evolution since any acceptance of evolution is against the Word of God, is insulting to God, and asks for God's Punishment in severe terms. Why speak of evolution at all? Because it is the basis of the enemy's method of leading people away from God's Word, trusting in the absolute Truth of God's Word, and turning to the foolishness known as the wisdom of man. My hope is that this small attempt to offer subject matter to expand understanding of Bible Prophecy will encourage many to open up their Bibles and get started down the narrow road that leads to understanding, God's Wisdom, and the Eternal City of New Jerusalem!

The "End Times". Just what are the "End Times"? The term actually comes from the Bible. The "Time of the End", the "Last Days", the "Latter Days", the "Day of the Lord" all sound alike, but there are differences that every Christian should know and recognize. And, of course, we as Christians in the 21st Century should be on watch for Bible prophecy fulfillment because Jesus IS coming back soon to reign as King of kings and Lord of lords!

These terms referring to the "End" can refer to the Second Coming of Jesus Christ, the end of the Church Age, the Tribulation, even refer to the Church or the Jews since the Bible teaches that the Church, which consists of all Jews and Gentiles that have accepted Jesus as Lord and Savior, and the Jews, or Israel that has not accepted Jesus, will experience different destinies. If we do not understand completely, then we remain confused and unable to explain to others when they ask questions. And questions WILL come because almost everyone senses that there are BIG things on the horizon, the IMMEDIATE horizon, most just do not know exactly what!

I am in the twilight years of my life. Yes, there are fewer years ahead than those behind by a long shot! But that is perfectly OK with me because of the Hope that is within me, Jesus Christ! I am a child of the late '40's, the '50's, and the '60's, and things really are different today than back then. So, why lead off with this? Well, a familiar Bible verse sets the stage, Matthew 24:37-39, 'But as the days of Noah were, so shall also the coming of the Son of man be. For as in the days that were before the flood they were eating and drinking, marrying and giving in marriage, until the day that Noah entered into the ark, and knew not until the flood came, and took them all away; so shall also the coming of the Son of man be.'

This verse points out the utter self-absorption in which mankind dwells virtually constantly, completely unaware of God, His plans, or His coming judgments. Has it always been this way? I submit to you that it has, but in lesser degrees than today. When I was a kid, things were calmer, simpler, less dangerous. No one talked about abortion, or homosexuality, certainly not transgenderism or homeless tent cities. They all existed for sure, but to such a lesser degree that many did not know their true definitions or even cared to. There were Muslims, have been since the 700's, but there was no blatant terrorism, no threats to life and limb in our cities. We, of course, had wars. The Second World War, the Korean War, Vietnam, but these wars were against Nazi or Communist totalitarian regimes that desired dominant military and monetary power.

Today, we have exponentially progressed to wars all around the globe centered on Islam and the Koran, the latter part of the Koran that demands domination, surrender, or annihilation. We still have the totalitarian states, but to a lesser degree, certainly to a less immediate danger aspect. The culture has been led in the direction of godlessness, persecution of Christian beliefs and doctrines to the exclusion of virtually all others, rampant and blatant displays and indoctrination into abhorrent lifestyles, anti-biblical morals, and overwhelming and greatly disturbing acceptance of drug use recreationally as well as performance enhancement. Are things different today as opposed to 50 years ago? Absolutely "Yes" with an addition of increased percentage of the populace participating.

No wonder Matthew 24:37-39 sounds so current to us. People are completely distracted with life, drugs, sex, career, money, fame or the following of same, the internet, cellular phone technology, violent video games, parties of all kinds occurring at least weekly, and many, many others. Do we really have to ask why people are not aware of the times we live in, just how near their eternal destinies lie in wait, how close to either death or eternal life they really are?

Can we be certain of our future? Of course not, except when it comes to Bible prophecy. Any one of us could die tonight or tomorrow. We can't know that. But we can know what lies on the immediate horizon for the world and for Christians and all unbelievers because we serve a loving and gracious, merciful God Who has told us what is to come – soon!

What's Coming

Here is a brief overview of what the Word of God says is coming or is already here. First and foremost, why do we believe that we are living in the last days? Primarily because of two key indicators of the end times that stand out from the rest. The first one is apostasy we have already mentioned. The Bible clearly teaches that society will degenerate in the end times, becoming as evil as it was in the days of Noah (Matthew 24:37-39). If the Lord thought that the antediluvians were evil enough to cause Him to flood the world to destroy all humans except for eight in the ark, what must He think of today, and why is He waiting to bring judgment?

The Apostle Paul, speaking as a prophet, says that society will descend into a black pit of immorality, violence, and paganism (2 Timothy 3:1-5). He asserts that men will be "lovers of self, lovers of money, and lovers of pleasure." People will be "boastful, arrogant, and unholy," and children will be "disobedient to parents." I don't have to point out this is exactly where we, as a society and world today, find ourselves.

The second key end-time sign is the founding of the nation of Israel. On May 14, 1948, against all human reasoning, a nation that had been dead for nineteen hundred years suddenly came back to life. On that day the world unknowingly took a giant step closer to the end of the age, for Israel became a self-governing nation just as the prophets had foretold. Prophecy watchers have pointed to the birth of the Jewish state as the starting point of the End Times. According to Scripture, all prophecy is to be fulfilled within the lifetime of a generation. "Assuredly, I say to you, this generation will by no means pass away till all these things take place" (Matthew 24:34). What is a generation? The Bible refers to a generation as 70 years (Psalm 90:10). Adding 70 years to 1948 and we arrive at 2018. It is never wise to set dates, but isn't it interesting to wonder? I recently saw a calculation that adds to our wondering based on Matthew 1:17. There are 14 generations between Abraham and David, 14 generations between David and the captivity to Babylon, and 14 generations between Babylon and Christ. This equals 42 generations between Abraham and Christ. It can be calculated from the Bible that there are about 2,160 years between Abraham and Christ. 2,160 divided by 42 equals 51.4 years per generation, round to 52 years. Other prophecy watchers contend that, while Israel becoming a nation was extremely important, it wasn't until 1967, when it reclaimed Jerusalem, that it could be considered to have become "official ". Add 52 to 1967 and you get 2019. Am I setting dates? NO! Just sayin'! It is at the very least interesting!

There are many Christians who are unmoved by the warning signs. They often have scorn for anyone who actively promotes Bible prophecy. 2 Peter 3:3-4 says, "...that scoffers will come in the last days, walking according to their own lusts, and saying, 'Where is the promise of His coming? For since the fathers fell asleep, all things continue as they were from the beginning of creation.'" This significant verse shows us that God knew that there was going to be massive doubt surrounding prophecy concerning the End Times. But there are many that will indeed yearn for the Truth of God's Word, the assurance of knowing their future, and the confidence in their destinies. Here's hoping that you are one of those!

As a result of the opening of the fulfillment of End Times prophecy, we come to what I consider the ULTIMATE PROOF of the immediacy of the Rapture and the ASSURANCE of it happening BEFORE any of God's Wrath otherwise known as the Tribulation. In fact, I believe that there are significant wars to come (Psalm 83, Gog Magog – Ezekiel 38,39) that will pre-date the Tribulation and involve nuclear war, but we as believers will not be here for those either. Details to come. What is that "ultimate proof"? 1 Thessalonians 5:1-11!

"But concerning the times and seasons, brethren, you have no need that I should write to you. For you yourselves know perfectly that the Day of the Lord so comes as a thief in the night. For when they say, 'Peace and safety!' then sudden destruction comes upon them, as labor pains upon a pregnant woman. And they shall not escape. But you, brethren, are not in darkness, so that this Day should overcome you as a thief. You are all sons of light and sons of the day. We are not of the night nor of darkness. Therefore, let us not sleep, as others do, but let us watch and be sober. For those that sleep, sleep at night, and those who get drunk are drunk at night. But let us who are of the day be sober, putting on the breastplate of faith and love, and as a helmet the hope of salvation. For God did not appoint us to wrath, but to obtain salvation through our Lord Jesus Christ, who died for us, that whether we wake or sleep, we should live together with Him."

The highlighted parts of this wonderful section of Scripture have special meaning. The "Day of the Lord" is, of course, in this case, referring to the Tribulation that is the Wrath of God on this sinful and evil world. A "thief in the night" is not what we usually think in our day. We usually think of a thief in the night as someone clandestinely breaking in, being very quiet and sneaky, stealing something, then leaving just as quietly. This is not how this was perceived in the time of Jesus on the Earth. A thief in the night was a strongarm break-in, loud and mean, with hostages, bodily harm, demands, possibly even death. The "sudden destruction" is what the thief does when he breaks in to get whatever he wants, and he comes without notice.

The reference to Christians NOT being in darkness is a direct message that we are different than the rest of the world. We are "all sons of light and sons of the day", not "of the night nor of darkness". Being "in the light" is a direct reference to Jesus Christ. John 1:1-5 says, "In the beginning was the Word, and the Word was with God, and the Word was God. He was in the beginning with God. All things were made through Him, and without Him nothing was made that was made. In Him was life, and the life was the light of men. And the light shines in the darkness, and the darkness did not comprehend it." This section at the very start of John's Gospel is the most powerful statement in the entire Bible because we learn that Jesus is the Creator God, He is the Light of men, and that those in the darkness cannot and will not understand any of this. This also means that the darkness, or those who do not know Jesus Christ as Savior and Lord, will be subject to God's Wrath. But those in God's Light, the Light of Jesus Christ, will NOT see or experience God's Wrath!

We go back to Thessalonians where it says, "For God did not appoint us to wrath, but to obtain salvation through our Lord Jesus Christ." We as believers are not to experience God's Wrath because we belong to Jesus and are in His Light, not in darkness. Those in the dark WILL experience God's Wrath, the Tribulation, the Antichrist, the seals, the trumpets, the bowls of Revelation. How do we escape God's Wrath that comes on the entire world in the End Times? The Rapture!

We all know that the word "Rapture" technically does not appear anywhere in the Bible. But, being "caught up" ("harpazo" in the Greek) to meet the Lord in the air is precisely the same as the Rapture! 1 Thessalonians 4:14-18 assures us,

"For if we believe that Jesus died and rose again, even so God will bring with Him those who sleep in Jesus. For this we say to you by the word of the Lord, that we who are alive and remain until the coming of the Lord will by no means precede those who are asleep. For the Lord Himself will descend from Heaven with a shout, and with the trumpet of God. And the dead in Christ will rise first. Then we who are alive and remain shall be caught up together with them in the clouds to meet the Lord in the air. And thus we shall always be with the Lord. Therefore comfort one another with these words."

The Rapture keeps us away from God's Wrath that comes on the entire world to wake up God's Chosen People, the Jews, to their Messiah, Jesus Christ. Throughout the Bible, we see how stubborn, how disobedient, how worldly the Jews have always been. But without the Jews, we would not have a Savior! Jesus was, is, and always will be a Jew! God made covenants with the Jews to always love them, always protect them, and eventually save them. God knows it will take extreme measures to wake the Jews up to the saving knowledge of Jesus Christ, their Savior as well as ours. So, "Jacob's Trouble" (Jeremiah 30:7-11), what we know as the Tribulation and Daniel's 70th week (Daniel Chapter 9), is to get Israel's attention, turn them to Jesus, and to punish the world for its sin and disobedience to God. Then, Jesus can come and reign as King of kings and Lord of lords for a thousand years, the Millennial Kingdom ("Thy Kingdom come, Thy Will be done, on Earth as it is in Heaven." Matthew 6:10).

Certainty or Speculation?

How do we know that all of this is going to happen, that we can be sure of our future, that God's promises will come to pass? The answer to these and other similar questions is found in one place – the Bible. But how do we know that the Bible is trustworthy? How do we assure ourselves that we can trust what the Bible tells us? We all have freedom of choice to do as we please by placing personal preferences above all else, to consider others as more important than ourselves, to learn to do the Will of God, to ignore man's as well as God's law, and so on. We all know that there is a God regardless of what anyone says. Romans 1:20-21 says, "For since the creation of the world His invisible attributes are clearly seen, being understood by the things that are made, even His eternal power and Godhead, so that they are without excuse..." I realize that to accept what the Bible has to say about anything, one has to believe that the Bible is the very Word of God, is inspired by God Himself, is inerrant, infallible, and authoritative. Many do not. Many are wrong. So, how do we actually "know"?

The Bible was written by men chosen by God, supernaturally superintended by the Holy Spirit, to use their own writing styles to author God-breathed messages on doctrine and theology without error. You can find those that agree that the Bible, when it covers Christian doctrine and all things pertaining to God and His Law, is correct and acceptable. But some say the Bible is not scientific and not historical. Yet, we find references to the circle of the Earth, the hydrologic cycle, currents in the seas, as well as references to fulfilled, historical events such as Jesus' virgin birthplace, many of His actions while on this Earth, His death, and His resurrection. Numbers 23:19 says, "God Himself, Who is Truth and cannot lie." And how can the Bible be both true when it comes to theology, but be inaccurate when it comes to science and history? If the Bible is accurate in one respect, it must be accurate in all respects because God cannot lie or be inaccurate.

Some say then, how can we know the Bible is still as accurate as when it was written? Literary confidence is usually tied to the age and number of the oldest known copies of any document. Some ancient texts written by people such as Socrates or Plato no longer exist, so we look for the oldest copies that we can find. Julius Caesar's The Gallic Wars has only 10 manuscripts remaining, with the earliest one dating to 1,000 years after the original. The writings of Plato have remaining only 7 manuscripts dating 1,300 years after the originals. But, the manuscript evidence for the New Testament is dramatic with nearly 25,000 ancient manuscripts discovered and archived so far, at least 5,700 of which are copies and fragments in the original Greek. Some manuscript texts date to the early second and third centuries making them closer to the originals than any other ancient texts, sometimes less than 100 years! Homer's Iliad, the most renowned book of ancient Greece, is the second best-preserved literary work of all antiquity, with 643 copies of manuscript support discovered to date. In those copies, there are 764 disputed lines of text, as compared to 40 lines in all the New Testament manuscripts and these contain no change in meaning to the original text. And, the Old Testament Book of Isaiah was discovered in the Dead Sea Scrolls in 1947, a complete text! It was word for word the same as we have in our Bibles today. So, is the Bible accurate to the original writers and overwhelmingly verified? Of course!

Historically, there has never been any historical reference in the Bible that has been deemed incorrect. There was once a denial that there ever was a tribe known as the Hittites until that name was discovered in an archeological dig in 1876. The name Pilate, the Roman Prefect that washed his hands of the actions taken against Jesus and His crucifixion, was considered false until a stepping stone was turned over in a site in Caesarea by the Sea in Israel. Under the stone was a carved reference to Pilate as Governor of Judea. There are many other examples of the historical accuracy of the Word of God showing us that God's Word is trustworthy. The most important fact of the Bible is that Jesus Christ was indeed alive, died a horrible death on the cross of the Romans in Jerusalem, and was seen by hundreds alive after His resurrection. These are indisputable facts when honestly pursued and studied both within Scripture and outside in works such as writings of Flavius

Josephus (Titus Flavius Josephus (37 – c. 100 A.D.), a 1st-century Romano-Jewish historian of priestly and royal ancestry who recorded Jewish history), Cornelius Tacitus, a Roman Historian who lived from 55-120 A.D., Gaius Plinius Caecilius Secundus, (61 – 112 A.D.) better known as Pliny the Younger, a lawyer, author, and magistrate of Ancient Rome, and many others.

Can we be certain of what the Bible has to say? History has proven the Word of God. Science has proven the Word of God. The Word of God itself refers to the fact that God cannot lie. So, can we be confident in what we read as the Truth? We indeed can and we should. To do otherwise is to cast doubt on the very nature of God Almighty by turning our backs to Him.

Is Prophecy Believable?

Let's suppose that I told you that if you called up a stock broker, bought 100 shares of a certain stock for a dollar a share, waited ten days, then sold the stock, you would receive one hundred thousand dollars for your one dollar stock, and the value of the stock would go back sown to one dollar on the eleventh day. Sounds very improbable or maybe I have illegal insider information or maybe I am a fraud and a swindler or even just enjoy a good joke. But what if you trusted me, did exactly what I suggested, and it was all true? The word would get out and I would be in high demand, right?

The Bible contains prophecy both fulfilled and unfulfilled, and those prophecies are more valuable to us that those many dollars we could have made in the previous illustration. Bible prophecy has been and will be precise and always true whether we believe it or not. Peter said in 1 Peter 1:19, "…no prophecy of Scripture is of any private interpretation, for prophecy never came by the will of man, but holy men of God spoke as they were moved by the Holy Spirit." The Bible, when written, was almost one-third prophecy. According to "The Encyclopedia of Biblical Prophecy" by J. Barton Payne, there are 1,239 prophecies in the Old Testament and 578 prophecies in the New Testament for a total of 1,817. These prophecies are contained in 8,352 of the Bible's verses. Since there are 31,124 verses in the Bible, the 8,352 verses that contain prophecy constitute 26.8 percent of the Bible's volume. But many prophecies were fulfilled during or after the lifetimes of the prophets who gave them—but they were not totally fulfilled. These partially fulfilled prophecies still have an end-time fulfillment.

So what? Perhaps the greatest and most obvious testimony to the accuracy of Biblical prophecy is provided by the people and nation of Israel. The Jews went without a homeland for 1813 years (from 135 A.D. to 1948), just as God had promised numerous times in the Old Testament for judgment on

His rebellious chosen people. Moses warned Israel that if they corrupted themselves, then "the LORD shall scatter thee among all people, from the one end of the Earth even unto the other (Deuteronomy 28:64)". Remarkably, God restored the Jews to their ancient homeland, fulfilling many other specific Old Testament prophesies (Jeremiah 30:3,10,11; 31:8-10; Ezekiel 11:17)

Here are just four of the prophecies in the Old Testament that were fulfilled and referenced in the New Testament:

- Messiah born in Bethlehem (Micah 5:2) — Fulfilled in Luke 2:4–6
- Would teach in parables (Psalm 78:2–4) — Fulfilled in Matthew 13:10–15
- Hands pierced (Psalm 22:16) — Fulfilled in John 20:25–27
- Soldiers gambled for clothing - (Psalm 22:18) — Fulfilled in Luke 23:34

There are over 300 prophecies concerning Jesus Christ in the Bible. Mathematicians have calculated the odds of Jesus fulfilling only 8 of the Messianic prophecies as 1 out of 10^{17} (a 1 followed by 17 zeros). This is equivalent to covering the entire state of Texas with silver dollars 2 feet deep, marking one of them, mixing them all up and having a blindfolded person select the marked one at random the very first time. And, in fact, the prophecies concerning Christ's First Advent (His first appearance on the Earth) have all been fulfilled. Certainly, then, the rest of Jesus' prophecies will come to pass. Fulfilled prophecy is powerful evidence that the Bible is divine rather than human in origin.

God is the only source of prophecy and our knowing the future. God has shown us through His Word that when He predicts the future, we can trust that what He has told us will come to pass.

Conclusion

Are we living in the "End Times"? Without doubt, I believe we are. We need to discover many things to fully grasp and believe that our time on Earth is short. We will cover these in the coming chapters in detail. Things like Biblical Signs of the Times, Dispensationalism, Pre-Millennialism, Pre-Tribulation Rapture, the In-Between Wars, what the Old Testament had to say about the End Times, what the New Testament has to say about the End Times, the End Times Deceivers like is the Earth young or old? Or, is evolution true? or, is the Bible scientific?, and others.

Are These Days the End Times?

CHAPTER ONE

WHAT WE NEED TO UNDERSTAND BIBLE PROPHECY

Introduction

This book came about because of, first, my great desire and joyful love of Bible Prophecy, and second, my realization and concerns that many share my love for prophecy but have questions, or are confused, or are unaware of how or even why Christians today should even be interested in Bible Prophecy. I have taught the Book of Revelation in its entirety before many times. I have taught about how the Bible is literally full, from Genesis to Revelation, of prophecy that has already been fulfilled and also has many, many prophecies yet to be fulfilled. As the result of my concerns, I see the need to attempt to give a complete picture of why we need to be excited to study prophecy today, how to study prophecy so that we see and understand the Lord's revealing of what is to come, and the many varied ancillary details that make prophecy clearer, relate to Israel as well as the Church, and show us how prophecy fits into the overall plan of the Bible to bring mankind into a restored relationship with God Almighty.

What I hope to do with this book is present several ingredients to the formula of understanding Bible Prophecy to clarify, inform, and exhilarate, starting with what we need to understand prophecy overall. Next, we will cover foundational concepts to understanding prophecy like the real age of the Earth and mankind upon it, how evolution is NOT science, all to accomplish why it is vitally important to relate literally everything in life back to the Word of God and NOT to mankind's explanation for "everything". Third, we will look at the Old Testament and the End Times which God spoke of as early as Genesis as well as the sequence of events to come in our lifetimes. Fourth, we will show how New Testament prophecy really cannot be understood completely without linking back to many Old Testament references. Fifth, we will see that the concept of a Pre-Tribulation Rapture is supported from Old Testament verses and many, not just a few, New Testament verses. We will also posit convincing evidence and calculations of the nearness of the Rapture and the subsequent events that the Church will thankfully miss. Sixth, there are many judgments and many resurrections in the Bible. We will cover the ones that have already taken place, but, more importantly, the ones to come since they relate to everyone's eternal destiny, both saved and unsaved, and relate directly to coming prophetic events that are both joyful and terrifying. And finally, we will sum all of this up to a conclusion of, hopefully, a clearer understanding of not only prophecy itself, but how to study it and gain so much more from it. The final reward for completing this book is an "End Times Biblical Prophetic End of Days Current Timeline" which is itself a summation of Bible Prophecy yet to be but soon to be fulfilled in the very near future. We can never be dogmatic and sure of dates, but even Jesus Himself told us we would know the general timeframe.

In my over 45 years studying prophecy, I have encountered many different attitudes, approaches, and objections to Biblical prophecy – even fear of Bible prophecy. I have read literally thousands of articles, multiple dozens of books, pondered and studied so many different viewpoints of prophecy that I am still amazed that there are so many varying ideas, opinions, philosophies, feelings, stances, beliefs, and thinking concerning Biblical prophecy that it literally staggers the mind. It is difficult to find two people that agree completely on Bible prophecy, the sequence of events to come, even the significance of Bible prophecy itself. Why is this subject so controversial, so enigmatic, so confusing to some and indifferent to others? Could it be that we all KNOW that there is something out there after our inevitable death and we are very desirous of knowing what God tells us in His Word; or, are we curious yet fearful, interested but not so much at the present, or deliberately obstinate and uninterested, apathetic to our eventual harm?

This Book's Purpose

The purpose of this book is to clarify some major questions about prophecy and to answer many questions concerning why our time, the present time, is the actual culmination of all of human history as promised in God's Word, why we as Christians should be excited about these times, but also anxious and challenged to do as Jesus commanded, "Go, therefore, and make disciples of all nations, baptizing them in the name of the Father and of the Son and of the Holy Spirit, teaching them to observe everything I have commanded you. And remember, I am with you always, to the end of the age." (Matthew 28:19,20) We all have an inevitable appointment with death some unknown day! We have known that inevitability at all times throughout our lives, we just have chosen to ignore it because we are all going to live a long time, right? Maybe not! We Christians all know that Jesus is waiting for us to join Him some day. Christians all should know that we just might avoid death because of the Rapture since it is so near. Well, the Good News is that that day, the day of the Rapture, could be TODAY because of what we learn from Bible prophecy!

So, what makes Bible prophecy so controversial, seemingly so difficult to interpret, so varied as to how it is explained? Prophecy should be a subject of great anticipation and hope! So, why is Bible prophecy perceived to be so hard to understand (It isn't!), so scary (It is!), so exciting (to the Christian only, not to the unbeliever!)? Why are there so many different opinions, so much confusion on the subject? Why are some people reluctant to read the Book of Revelation especially since Revelation 22:7 says, "Behold, I come quickly: blessed is he that keepeth the sayings of the prophecy of this book."? Revelation is written directly from Jesus to us through John, so Jesus, Himself, spoke of prophetic things! Of course, He did, and also quite a lot of times in Matthew and Mark and Luke. The Bible, the Word of God, is full of End Times prophecy, both Old and New Testaments. Then, why do folks remain confused or, at least, a little hesitant to consider prophetic issues? Don't we trust ALL of God's Word to be true in every subject: for salvation, for faith, for obedience, for instruction? Then why not prophecy?

Let's take a look at the word "prophecy" before we go any further. It has two definitions used in the Bible. But, let's first look at Mirriam-Webster's definition. 1: an inspired utterance of a prophet. 2: the function or vocation of a prophet, specifically: the inspired declaration of divine will and purpose. 3: a prediction of something to come. When you realize that a speaker of God's Word, whether future predictions or just speaking forth God's Will as Scripture, is a prophet, then Pastors and Bible teachers are prophets in that sense. But we all think of prophets as men speaking of things to come inspired by the Holy Spirit. And, since God's finished Word, the Bible, is not to be added to, then there are no more predicting prophets today, just those found in the Bible.

All prophecy comes from God's prophets who are divinely inspired messengers from God. 2 Peter 1:20 says, "Knowing this first, that no prophecy of the scripture is of any private interpretation". This means that the Holy Spirit divinely inspired the writers of Scripture to place in Scripture exactly what God meant without need of anyone to wonder what it means. First, under this definition, all writers of the Word of God can be defined as prophets since they, under the direction of the Holy Spirit, wrote down Scripture, God's message to humans, that we have today known as the Bible.

So, essentially, we are all reading and speaking forth prophecy when we read the Bible! Second, almost all of the writers of the Bible, both Old and New Testaments (or Covenants as they should be called), yes, even Moses, also gave pronouncement of what would, in their near future, come to pass or what would happen to them in their distant future, plus, what will happen in our immediate and distant future. It is this second definition that we most often think of when we hear the term prophecy, and the part of the definition that we speak of today. The theological term for this is eschatology.

3

Perhaps the reason for the hesitancy and fear of prophecy is that it deals with the future, is associated with the unknown, and, in our culture today, the unknown is something to be afraid of or skeptical of. However, Biblical prophecy is neither uncertain nor fantasy. From a believer's perspective, prophecy is the certain future as described by God. To the unbeliever, prophetic descriptions of our future are disturbing and frightening and thought of as mythological and fantasy. Prophecy, however, is a source for believers to enter into discussion of salvation with unbelievers or skeptics to show them the truth of what is to come and why as well as how to escape the judgment that is certain to come!

The Word of God Applied Today

The Bible is unique in being prophetic. There is no religious book, not by Buddha or Krishna or Mohammed or anyone else, ever written which contains actual prophetic events already fulfilled and provable or future prophetic events in such amazing detail from so many different people that were all synchronized in their insight in spite of them living at very different and widespread times. And the prophecies are not general prophecies about the future, but specific prophecies such as the Messiah would descend from the line of David, be born in Bethlehem, be killed by crucifixion (which did not even exist at the time of the prophecy when written), and be raised from the dead three days later. The actual fulfillment of all these prophecies and over a hundred more about Jesus proves the Bible truly is the Word of God and God does not lie, so we can put our faith in what it teaches.

The Prophets and Apostles didn't just relay God's messages about the future, but they also gave powerful messages concerning living morally. When the people obeyed prophetic teachings, they grew spiritually. 1 John 3 declares, "...when He [Jesus] is revealed, we shall be like Him, for we shall see Him as He is. And everyone who has this hope in Him purifies himself, just as He is pure." They became better people, being less self-centered and more God-centered. 1 Peter 4 admonishes, "But the end of all things is at hand; therefore, be serious and watchful in your prayers... have fervent love for one another... minister to one another, be good stewards..."

When a person is more heavenly minded, they'll be more generous because they're investing in eternity. 2 Peter 3 advises, "But the day of the Lord will come... Therefore, since all these things will be dissolved, what manner of persons ought you to be in holy conduct and godliness, looking for and hastening the coming of the day of God..." And, the people became much better at discerning truth from falsehoods. Luke 21 warns, "But take heed to yourselves, lest your hearts be weighed down with carousing, drunkenness, and cares of this life, and that Day come on you unexpectedly…"

Knowing that we're quickly running out of time before Jesus returns, when Christians study Bible prophecy, they become motivated to tell people about the Good News of Jesus Christ. Fulfilled Bible prophecies actually are an excellent apologetics tool (apologetics means defending the Bible as God's Truth) for defending the faith. And, the Gospel is very attractive to people who are actually wanting to know what the future holds. When the world seems to be careening into chaos and you wonder if God's still around, Bible prophecy tells us God certainly is still in control and always has been.

In the light of Bible prophecy, these crazy current events we are experiencing, the inexplicable, irrational, even stupid rantings of today finally make sense. They're all leading up to one big thing — Jesus Christ's return. And when Jesus returns, He wins! And when Jesus wins, believers in Christ win as well! So, when you live a life of anticipating victory, you too can have hope for the future. But we have to fully understand Bible Prophecy to appreciate that future we all anticipate. And, understanding Bible Prophecy means fully understanding ALL of the Bible, both Testaments, as one cohesive text on history, on Creation, on God's Character, on the history of Israel, on the foundations of the Church, and, most importantly, on how we as humans restore our personal relationship with Almighty God!

Start at the Basics

To answer all of the questions about prophecy, its relevance, its meaning, its truthfulness, its reliability, we must start at the basics - how to properly and effectively study all of Scripture. When I say study Scripture, that entails a discipline and a daily joyful and deep concentration on every word in the Bible originating from the very breath of God. The Bible is meant to be understood literally. Almighty God is communicating with us, speaking directly TO us!

The Word of God says what it means and means what it says. To believe otherwise, to assume other meanings or hidden meanings, to repeat that the Bible is vague and unclear is actually accusing God Himself of being vague and unclear and that He is not Who He says He is. Proper interpretation (hermeneutics in theology speak) is to be accurate in understanding what the writer and the Holy Spirit were conveying to us when the text was written – not what we think it means now because we live in a "different world", or what it should mean to us today, or what we should look below the surface to find. Some "modern" scholars want us to interpret Scripture from our perspective, from current mores and social behaviors. The true interpretation of anything written is to study the author and his or her background and education, the culture in which the text was written, and the effort to discern the author's intent in writing the text. Through this method and this method only can the true interpretation of a text be properly understood without "modern" bias which would lead to major error and loss of meaning.

There is no middle ground in God's Word, no ambiguities, not any gray areas. God speaks clearly and trying to smooth out a difficult or sensitive area to make it more palatable is to question the Almighty God we are supposed to be worshipping. The Bible is not a buffet line where we can choose a little here, a little there, and even skip some of that. The Word of God is a totality, an infallible, complete, very clear, very frank, truthful message from the Creator of the Universe to each and every one of us. And every word is meant to be read, studied, and applied by each of us individually to our individual lives, not collectively, not corporately, not jointly, but individually. God has a message to each of us and that message is, "Turn away from selfishness and sin, return to me by listening to the Gospel of Jesus Christ, and believe and accept it!"

Two "Modern" Heresies

Today there are two heresies that are being taught in some mega-churches and many smaller ones. The first is the most outrageous false teaching that can be imagined concerning the entire Bible. It is being taught that the Old Testament is no longer applicable to us today, in our "modern" era, so we should ignore it altogether. The second heresy that is being taught is that Bible Prophecy is unimportant to the "modern" Christian because it no longer applies and takes our concentration away from the here-and-now to what "just might be coming but probably isn't".

The first heresy relegating the Old Testament to the trash heap is amazingly stupid, to begin with, and demonstratably refutable through Scripture itself! First and foremost is Hebrews 13:8, "Jesus Christ is the same yesterday, today, and forever." Since Jesus Christ is God Incarnate (John 1:1), what He had to say in both Testaments through His Holy Spirit is relevant, powerful (Hebrews 4:12, "For the word of God is quick, and powerful, and sharper than any two-edged sword, piercing even to the dividing asunder of soul and spirit, and of the joints and marrow, and is a discerner of the thoughts and intents of the heart."), and applicable to any human ever born or ever will be born – and that certainly applies to the Old Testament! The moral foundation of all law and our very Constitution is based on the Law of Moses or the Ten Commandments from the Book of Exodus (which is in the Old Testament). Is the Old Testament relevant? It was to our nation's Founding Fathers! So, it should be to us as well, even in our "modern" world!

The second heresy points to the history and the love that God has for the people He chose to bring forth the Savior of the World, the Jews being in the Old Testament. Many of the over 300 prophecies of Jesus Christ being the promised Savior and concerning His First Advent or First Coming to the Earth as Suffering Servant have come to pass exactly as foretold, and the rest of those 300 prophecies are about His Second Advent or Second Coming. If all of the prophecies about His First Coming happened exactly as the Bible said they would, then why should we not believe or, as many are saying today, ignore the rest of the prophecies about His Second Coming? That would be foolish (in the sense that anyone who does not believe them is a fool), ill-advised, and irresponsible because our very destiny in eternity hangs in the balance, or, in the case of deceived Christians, our very service to our Lord and Savior is destroyed. Prophecy plays a huge role in the Bible directly referencing both Advents of Jesus Christ, the first completed and the second to come soon. So, prophecy should most certainly NOT be ignored.

There is an interesting story that Jesus was telling His disciples in Luke Chapter 16 starting at verse 19. It is about a certain rich man and a beggar named Lazarus. It seems that in life, the beggar had it very rough, even stooping to eating crumbs from the rich man's table, while the rich man was privileged beyond measure. They both died, and since this was all happening (or actually did happen) prior to Jesus' Resurrection, they both went to the place of the dead, hell, or Sheol, or Hades. At that time, there was a place for the righteous dead and a place for the unrighteous dead separated by a "great gulf" as Abraham told us in the story. [As a side note, when Jesus died on the cross, He descended to hell. Ephesians 4:8-10 says, "Wherefore he saith, When he ascended up on high, he led captivity captive, and gave gifts unto men. (Now that he ascended, what is it but that he also descended first into the lower parts of the Earth? He that descended is the same also that ascended up far above all heavens, that he might fill all things.") He took the people in Abraham's Bosom, the "good" side of Hades or the side with the righteous dead, to Heaven and left that side of Hades empty. He then was resurrected.]

Apparently, the rich man, who was agonizing in the suffering and unrighteous dead side of hell, could see across the "great gulf" separating the two sides of hell. Characteristically, the rich man kept his arrogance and spoke to "Father Abraham" asking him to send Lazarus, who was on the righteous dead side, to come and cool the rich man's tongue with water.

But Abraham told the rich man that their destinies had been determined, Lazarus was comforted while the rich man was tormented – plus, there was that "great gulf" between them that could not be traversed. So, the rich man begged Abraham to send Lazarus back to Earth to his five brothers to tell them of his fate and to warn them so that they would not also end up being tormented as he was in hell. To this, Abraham replied, rather significantly, that his brothers have Moses and the Prophets (read the Law and the Major and Minor Prophets of Scripture), so let them confer there to learn of the warnings of a future destiny of torment. Undaunted, the rich man retorted back to Abraham that if a man returned from the dead, his brothers would listen and repent thus not suffer as he was suffering.

This is the point that most Christians read verse 31 of Luke 16 and take it, as they should, at face value. That verse reads, "And he said unto him, 'If they hear not Moses and the Prophets, neither will they be persuaded, though one rose from the dead.'" What this tells us is that if the Word of God does not sway, even someone rising from the dead, like Lazarus, would certainly not sway. But, let's look deeper and realize what else is taking place here, and this goes to many today who do not give the Old Testament the respect that it deserves.

Go back to Luke 16:1 and we see that this story is coming from Jesus speaking to His disciples. Now, look at Luke 16:14, "And the Pharisees also, who were covetous, hearing all these things, and they derided Him." Wow! The Pharisees are listening to Jesus, and this is when the Lord says very interesting things. Luke 16:16,17 says, "The Law and the Prophets were until John (The Baptist); since that time the kingdom of God is preached, and every man forces his way into it. And it is easier for Heaven and Earth to pass, than one tittle of the Law to fail." It is at this point that Jesus relates the rich man and Lazarus story.

With all of this in mind, return to verse 31. Jesus is speaking to Pharisees who, supposedly, knew the Old Testament Scripture backward and forward. They certainly knew what the Law of Moses was, and also the Prophets. They should have been expecting the Messiah to come as a Suffering Servant, to die for the sin of the world, then to rise on the third day to everlasting glory since all of those things are foretold in the Old Testament– but they did not, they chose to ignore, even deride Jesus Who was standing before them, the Almighty Creator God! Here, also, Jesus said if the Pharisees did not know Who He was from reading and perceiving the Law of Moses and the Prophets of the Old Testament (of course, they did not use the term Old Testament since what they had were the books we know as the Old Testament – they called all of those books the Torah, the Law, Poetry, and the Prophets), then they would not listen to Him when He would soon be resurrected from the dead.

The lesson here is that Jesus wanted the Pharisees and His disciples to read the Law and the Prophets to know His Father and Him since the Old Testament is the Word of God. Nothing has changed for us today. If we diminish the Old Testament, we are diminishing the very Word of Almighty God. Simply excluding the Old and reading the New is also diminishing the Word of God. Lesson? Read all of the Bible! Every word is inspired by the holy Spirit and profitable for doctrine, reproof, for instruction in righteousness (Hebrews 4:12), and that includes both Testaments!

Read the Word for Yourself!

Did you know that when we listen to others talk about prophecy, we can be misled or confused if we do not read the Word of God for ourselves? Opinions or teachings from others are basically without merit unless they are based directly upon the written Word of God. When we read and study Scripture ourselves, we can develop our own confidence in Scripture, being led by the Spirit, and easily recognize error and lie when we hear it from others. Simply accepting the teachings of another without having the knowledge of the Truth is dangerous in that there are many false teachers alive today, as has always been. Matthew 24:24 says, "For false messiahs and false prophets will appear and perform great signs and wonders to deceive, if possible, even the elect." 2 Timothy 4:3,4 says, "For the time will come when people will not put up with sound doctrine. Instead, to suit their own desires, they will gather around them a great number of teachers to say what their itching ears want to hear. 4 They will turn their ears away from the truth and turn aside to myths."

When we read God's Word, we see many references to God revealing His plan for people through prophecy. And, when we read Bible prophecy, it always happens or will happen exactly as God says. God cannot lie! (Titus 1:2, "In hope of eternal life, which God, who never lies, promised before the ages began."; Hebrews 6:18, "So that by two unchangeable things, in which it is impossible for God to lie, we who have fled for refuge might have strong encouragement to hold fast to the hope set before us.") Therefore, we should pay attention to unfulfilled prophecy when we find it and search out the meaning so that we can grasp what God is saying and doing. By doing that, we find out amazing things to come which add to our ability to share God's incredible Word when speaking with others.

Everything we may hear concerning TRUE prophecy should always point back to Scripture because Scripture is the actual Word of God for our human understanding. Ask yourself these revealing questions: Have you ever read every word in the Bible from beginning to end? Every single word? How many times? Do you skip around in the Bible really never reading the Word of God sequentially? Do you seem to concentrate on one or the other Testaments? Do you skip reading all of the names in the Book of Numbers? You just might be missing many blessings hidden within the names. Also, many of the names have Hebrew meanings, so you just might be uttering blessings upon yourself when you attempt to read the names!

Example! The Pre-flood names in the Bible from Genesis Chapter 5 show the genealogy of man from Adam to Noah. The period of time covers 1,656 years from Creation to the Flood of Noah, and each man lived many years beyond what is "normal" today because of the canopy of water above the Earth and the difference in atmospheric pressure on the Earth before the Flood. (Ever hear of a hyperbaric chamber and the healing capabilities of two atmospheres of pressure?) Back to the names. Here are the ten names given in Genesis 5: Adam, Seth, Enosh, Kenan, Mahalalel, Jared, Enoch, Methuselah, Lamech, and Noah (from Chuck Missler and Khouse.org). Most of us read these names since there are only 10. But, for instance, the Book of Numbers has hundreds of names that we often skip or say they are too difficult to pronounce. Well, skipping reading the names is a mistake. Why? Because look at this! Here are the meanings of those 10 names in Genesis 5, in order: Adam = Man, Seth = Appointed, Enosh = Mortal, Kenan = Sorrow, Mahalalel = The Blessed God, Jared = Shall come down, Enoch = Teaching, Methuselah = His death shall bring, Lamech = The despairing, and Noah = Rest, or comfort. So what, you say? Put all of those meanings into a sequential sentence and you will see just why I am saying that we should all read the names in the Bible because we may be uttering a blessing when we do! "Man is appointed as mortal and has sorrow, but the Blessed God shall come down teaching that His death shall bring to the despairing, rest or comfort." Reads like the very Gospel of Jesus Christ found in the 5th Chapter of Genesis! Now, just try to skip reading all those names! Bet you can't!

Is the Book of Job boring to you? Are there too many Psalms to stay focused? Is Hebrews too deep to understand? Does the Book of Ecclesiastes sound too negative when you read it? (It's not!) Have you ever read Revelation in its entirety? Have you referenced back to the Old Testament and the prophecies found there when you were reading through Revelation? Did you know that those who read Revelation are promised a special blessing? The point here is that in order to understand prophecy, one must have a complete view of the Word of God in order to grasp how prophetic glimpses into the future helped those in the past, and how those prophetic glimpses into our future from the Bible can help us in our day and time.

To the Christian, the true believer in the sacrificial death, burial, and resurrection of our Lord and Savior Jesus Christ, reading God's Word daily is essential to our walking with Christ on the road of sanctification leading to our glorification with Him in Heaven. Repenting of our sins daily, praying for forgiveness daily, asking for wisdom daily, and reading God's Word daily is the rock-solid foundation of our faith and our glorious hope in our eternal future with Christ as well as abundant life while we wait. Anything short of those things results in the world gaining advantage over our spirits, distractions from what we should be about, saved or not. How can we be about God's plan for our lives and the good works He expects of us if we do not fully understand His Word in its entirety? Remember, we are not citizens of Earth! We are citizens of Heaven! Even NOW!

We Are Blessed!

Did you know that we are blessed? Every one of us saved believers? Did you know our church is blessed since we all should be in a church that is a Bible-believing and Bible-teaching church? Why, you ask? First and foremost because the Holy and Omnipotent God of the Universe, the Only Wise God, loved us all so much that he gave us His Word – both Jesus Christ and the written Word of God! Second, we are blessed because we believe and practice and learn from the Word of God, the Bible, in its entirety from our Pastor and our teachers, not some man-made doctrine or contrived variation, watered down, dumbed down version of God's Word made popular by false teachers. We learn straight from the Bible, God's Word, without man's interpretation, without man's philosophy, knowing that we are all sinners in God's sight in need of salvation through the shed blood of Jesus Christ.

So, to fully know what God has done, why God has done it, and what God will do, we MUST read and STUDY God's Word – DAILY! That enables us to know and understand Bible Prophecy! God's Word has to be the priority in our lives. What do I mean by that? Show God that His Word is of the highest priority, the highest importance to you in your life by putting reading and studying His Word daily, preferably early. What better way to start the day than to spend time with God? Is another half-hour to one hour of sleep in the morning that precious making it more important than God? Don't you want to know God's Will for you daily? The only way to do that is read His Word and pray before any activity of the day. Trust me! It makes all the difference.

Most so-called Christian churches today, some have said as many as 95%

of them in the United States never study prophecy or hear Biblical prophecy from the pulpit. That seems almost impossible considering that almost a third of the Bible was prophetic when written! That's right. At the time of the writing of the Scriptures, almost a third of the entire Bible was about the future. There are some who say the Bible is a book of myths, not to be believed since there are so many things that happened that stagger our imagination, such as: a global flood, the sun moving backwards, a man swallowed by a fish for three days and living, a group of cities destroyed by fire from the sky, a sea parting to let millions cross ten miles of deep water on dry ground, a talking burning bush, a man walking on water, miraculous healings of blind-from-birth eyes, restoration of legs that had never stood, raising from the dead, and many, many more. Did all these really happen? When it was prophesied that entire nations would be defeated, taken into captivity, totally wiped out years before it actually happened, do you believe this to be so? Do you know that every one of these and many more DID actually happen exactly as the Bible says? God knows the future as well as He knows the past and the present so that He can tell us what will happen with 100% accuracy? The Bible tells us these things. So, can we trust that what God says about our future will come to pass? How do we know? The answer is faith, but it is pleasing to hear of man's validation of the Bible when it happens.

Biblical Archaeology

Biblical archaeology has confirmed many things thought to be errors or inaccuracies in the Bible. Do we need proof of the accuracy of God's Word? Of course NOT! But it IS highly satisfying and joyful when someone finds something that aligns precisely with what God had someone write down some 2,000 to 4,000 years ago! For centuries, no one believed that there ever was a people called the Hittites mentioned several times in the Old Testament. But, (1), in 1834 the first discovery of the Hittite civilization was found in Turkey confirming their existence. (2) Until 1993 there was no physical proof of the existence of King David! Imagine that! (3) It wasn't until 1955 that we confirmed the existence of Sennacherib as King of Assyria and his march toward Jerusalem in 701 B.C. where He lost 185,000 troops in one night at the hand of one angel. (4) Did you know that Jesus' virgin birth in Bethlehem, death on a cross, and resurrection three days later were all Old Testament prophecies written hundreds of years before they happened? (5) Workers repairing a sewage-pipe break in 2005 uncovered the Pool of Siloam in Old Jerusalem. This pool was a major gathering site for the Jews and is central to the account of the miracle of Christ healing a blind-from-birth man. (6) The establishment of the nation of Israel after over 1,800 years of total absence on the world scene is a miracle of the first order, but it happened some 70 years ago in 1948! From 135 A.D. until 1948 Israel was non-existent as a nation. Then in 1948 arising from a now very antagonistic League of Nations known as the U.N. today, Israel was allowed to rise as a nation once again from the history books. No other nation has ever even come close to this amazing miracle of God!

We could spend hours relating all the many ways that man has proved that the Bible is inerrant in its prophetic statements. But that is not necessary since the Bible has never been proven wrong! Therefore, we should be interested in what the Bible has to say about our immediate future, right? Don't you think it is valuable to know what our future holds for us? We trust in God's Word, so let's get excited about what He says is going to happen very, very soon!

Background Essentials

The Bible is a comprehensive and sequential history book about God's plan to restore mankind to spiritual life with Him. God originally made man perfect, He also made the world and the universe perfect. Remember when He said upon completing the Creation that it was not only good, it was very good? In God's eyes His Creation was very good! That means Creation was perfect in every way which included man's ability, his gift from God, to be a free thinker - able to make his own choices, not just some robotic invention of a selfish deity wanting companionship.

But God knows the future, remember? He knew that His first creation of angels would be fragmented because of the enemy's rebellion due to angels having freedom of will. In fact, a third of the Heavenly Host chose to follow narcissistic Satan rather than God. Do you suppose that they also believed Satan's deceptions when they chose to follow him instead of God? Did they make a free choice even though it meant an eternity in the Lake of Fire since angels have no possibility of salvation? Don't you think this applies to the human race as well? We will discover the truth someday soon.

However, in God's plan for mankind, He, of course, knew that man would fall, would choose his own way instead of God's, would choose to disobey God and be selfish, to sin which is to willfully and knowingly disobey God, to be Selfish In Nature (SIN). But God started putting into place His plan from the Garden of Eden for the salvation of man. God pre-programmed into the very DNA of all of Creation His Plan B. Plan A was to have man obey God. But God knew we would not follow through and turn to our own way and sin (Isaiah 53:6). So, he had a plan B. Before the Fall of Adam, all animals ate plants and grass, even lions and bears - even dinosaurs.

Yes, dinosaurs roamed the Earth while man did the same because evolution is false science – but that's another cause for examination! (More on this later.) There was no death before Adam since death entered because of sin. Originally there was no sin, so no death and eating of slain animals for meat.

But, when man sinned, Plan B went into effect. God kicked Adam and Eve out of the Garden because of their sin, cursed the ground, and instituted His Plan B. Adam and Eve were instantly ashamed of their nakedness and covered themselves, all as a result of becoming aware that they were sinners before a Holy God. And what about the animals? Some had their DNA switched to becoming meat eaters instead of herbivores. Some insects turned to needing blood to get protein instead of getting it from plants. There are a few plant species that need insects to survive instead of getting their needs from the soil. Some plants became thorns and thistles instead of being beautiful and edible. And Creation itself began deteriorating, degrading, spiraling downward in a Second Law of Thermodynamics pathway to loss of energy and beauty and function. Today, there are over 4,000 genetic disorders suffered by newborn humans because of the degradation of our DNA over time. Ever wonder why there seems to be more and more evidence of birth defects from autism to auto-immune disorders to spina bifida, Down Syndrome, congenital heart defects, and many others? How long can the human race last with this rapid deterioration of the Human DNA? This leads us to the next topic.

Creation Versus Evolution

There is much controversy over the origin, the history, the real story of the human. People say they believe in God, yet they also say they trust "science". Others say the Bible is full of unbelievable myths and swear to their belief that evolution is a so-called "fact". Have you ever heard of an oxymoron? By definition, an oxymoron is a figure of speech, usually one or two words in which seemingly contradictory terms appear side by side, such as bittersweet, jumbo shrimp, clearly misunderstood, or, my favorite, intelligent liberal. When I speak of an oxymoron in relation to evolution versus the Bible, I am referring to an "evolutionary scientist", a significant oxymoron since science, by definition, is the field of study concerned with discovering and describing the world around us by observing and experimenting and being able to reproduce observations and experiments over and over in order to prove their existence and plausibility.

Evolution, contrary to the very definition of science, is unobservable in the macro sense, and never has been or ever will be repeatable. There is adaptation within species for variations in the environment, but changing from one species into an entirely different one (like dinosaur lizards into birds, for instance) never has happened because there is no evidence in the fossil record or in nature of this ever happening. Besides, it defies logic and mathematical probability – it is impossible as well as blasphemous! Solid bones "evolving" into hollow bones? Completely different lung functions? Feathers from scaly skin? Impossible! Belief in evolution is entirely based in faith not fact whereas belief in creation is also belief BUT is demonstrably irreducibly complex, without man's ability to duplicate indicating Creation came from God and from nowhere or no one else. A "simple cell" was thought by Darwin to be just protoplasm with a cell wall and a nucleus. Today, we know that a cell is anything but simple. It contains DNA, which itself is unimaginably complex containing billions of bits of information IN EACH CELL, and proteins that transport oxygen and nutrients within the cell and carry out waste, as well as proteins that fight intruding attacks within the cell itself. This all happened by accident and chance over millions of years? Nonsense! Nothing cannot make something, nothing cannot make living tissue, and nothing cannot ever make irreducibly complex things such as the "simple cell" and DNA!

Evolution has another problem in the timing of the appearance of plants, insects and birds on the Earth. The Bible says that plants were created on Day 3, and Fish and Birds on Day 5. The Bible does not tell us when insects were created, but it is reasonable to assume they came along with either the plants as pollinators on Day 3 or with the winged creatures or birds on Day 5. Evolutionists say plants evolved along with insects about 300 million years ago, but birds waited around until about 150 million years ago to arrive. But there is a problem. What eats and controls the insect population today? Birds for the most part. And that is a very big job. It has been demonstrated that in one growing season, one pair of potato beetles if left unchecked (read no birds or pesticides) would produce 60 million offspring. In just one summer, a pair of flies left unchecked would fill 144,000-bushel baskets (Bruce Malone and SearchfortheTruth.net). So, my question is, how did the Earth's plants, trees, grasses, and other green things survive for 150 million years with no birds to check the ferocious growth rates of insects on the Earth? Wouldn't ALL the green things have been consumed in a much shorter time by the proliferation of the bugs? Then, what would the animals eat?

Evolutionists say mankind arose from the slime, became a fish, which evolved into an animal, then a monkey, then man over some six million years. Imagine the amount of death happening over millions of years, yet the Bible says death entered into existence with Adam only some 6,000 years ago. Both cannot be correct. If evolution were even close to being true, the Earth would have been overrun with population by now because of reproduction rates, and human development would be totally corrupted because of DNA genetic defects. The Bible says mankind came from His direct creation of two people, significantly in our time, a man and a woman, because that is the only way to be "fruitful, multiply, and fill the Earth". And, just when did this happen? About 6,000 years ago as the Bible tells us.

Answers in Genesis (answersingenesis.org) does a very interesting calculation. "In the beginning" there was one male and one female – Adam and Eve. Now let us assume that they have children and that their children have children and so on realizing that at least initially brothers and sisters had to marry. When you think about it, initially, the DNA would have been perfect because God does not make anything that is not perfect. But, the Fall of Man with Adam's sin made the Creation cursed and error began to be seen in our DNA because of the entry of death because of sin. So, after some time, intermarrying of siblings would have to be prohibited because of increasing defects, and that is exactly what happened when God forbid marrying siblings with the Mosaic Law. Back to the numbers - let us assume that the population doubles every 150 years. Therefore, after 150 years there will be four people, after another 150 years there will be eight people, after another 150 years there will be sixteen people, and so on. It should be noted that this growth rate is actually very conservative. In reality, even with disease, famines, and natural disasters, the world population currently doubles every 40 years or so according to the U.S. Census Bureau.

After 32 doublings, which is only 4,800 years, the world population would have reached almost 8.6 billion. That's almost 2 billion more than the current population of 7 billion people. This simple calculation shows that starting with Adam and Eve and assuming the conservative growth rate previously mentioned, the current population can be reached well within 6,000 years. Mathematics, and especially geometric sequencing, is fascinating, interesting, revealing, fun, and accurate. Evolutionists should try using it sometime to realize that their so-called "facts" just do not stand up to scrutiny!

Evolutionists say that humans have been around for hundreds of thousands of years at least. So, assume that humans have been around for 50,000 years and using the calculations above, there would have been 332 doublings, and the world's population would be a staggering figure, 1×10^{100}, a one followed by 100 zeros; 10,000,000,000,000,000,000,000,000,000,000, 000,000,000,000,000,000,000,000,000,000,000,000,000,000,000,000, 000,000,000,000,000.

Such a number is unimaginable but look at it this way. It has been estimated that there are 1×10^{80} total atoms in the entire universe! If that is true, then the evolutionists claim of man being in existence for just 50,000 years would amount to more people than there are atoms in all the solar system, the Milky Way Galaxy, and all the other billions of galaxies in the entire universe! Such a calculation makes nonsense of the claim that humans have been on Earth for tens of thousands of years. Such a claim makes evolutionary theory laughable!

Simple, conservative arithmetic reveals clear mathematical logic for a young age of the Earth. From two people, created around 6,000 years ago, and then the eight people who survived the Flood on the Ark about 4,500 years ago, the world's population could have grown to the around 7 billion we see today. So, the Bible gives us a chronology of men and their ages before and after the Flood of Noah going back to Creation itself so that we can at least approximate the time the Earth has been in existence. And that number is a very young 6,000 years, not the 4.5 billion that the evolutionists claim.

All of this, of course, is if one believes the Bible to be the true, inerrant, authoritative, accurate, and sufficient Word of God, perfect in every word, syllable, letter, paragraph, book, in its entirety. If you believe that, along with 2 Timothy 3:16 and 17, "All Scripture is God-breathed, inspired by God, and is profitable for doctrine, for reproof, for correction, for instruction in righteousness; that the man of God may be perfect, thoroughly furnished unto all good works", then you believe Genesis Chapter 1 that says God created everything in six literal 24-hour days and rested on the seventh thus giving us a pattern for our lives to live week by week. God could have created everything in a millisecond or less, but He chose to set a pattern for our lives. Marxists (actually Stalin) have tried to change that pattern to one of a base-10 pattern where we work for 9 days and rest the tenth, but that failed miserably because people got tired and complacent and productivity fell dramatically. This, of course, proves God's plan is best for us – the 7-day week.

The Bible chronology of man's days on the Earth as well as the age of the Earth and the universe is that they are in total 6,000 years old. This is very interesting when examined carefully (from ICR.org):

> (1) The oceans are salty, as everyone knows, but how salty would they be if the Earth was 5 to 6 billion years old as evolutionary scientists say?

> (2) Would the planets that are farther from the sun than the Earth still be hot after billions of years? Certainly not, they would have long ago cooled off. But spacecraft flying by the outer planets have found

them to be putting out more heat than the Sun provides to them. This is truly amazing since the outer planets (Jupiter, Saturn, Uranus, Neptune) are all enormous distances from the Sun (Jupiter 484 Million Miles, Saturn 551, Uranus 1,784, Neptune 2,794) while the Earth is 93 million miles from the Sun.

(3) The Earth's magnetic field protects us from the Sun's rays as well as deflects many space objects like meteorites from entering our atmosphere. Would our magnetic field still exist after the supposed age of Earth at 5 billion years based on its deterioration that we observe today? The answer is that we would have no magnetic field at all after even 100,000 years.

(4) Don't the rocks tell scientist that they are millions of years old? Scientists use more than 10 different radiometric tests, all of which give widely varying results. Some scientists base the age of rocks on the fossils they contain, and some scientists base the age of fossils on the age of the rocks which is all circular reasoning without evidence.

(5) If they have found dinosaur DNA in fossils, and they have found DNA starting in 2005, and since DNA cannot exist more than 10 to 20,000 years at most, then "Houston, we have a problem".

(6) Creation scientists have conducted radiometric dating just like the evolutionary scientists and found significantly younger ages for rocks. In fact, their research has determined the rock layers we see today with their knife-edges showing no erosion between layers were laid down during Noah's Flood and worldwide.

(7) There are now over 4,000 genetic defects possible in babies due to the deterioration of the human DNA over the last few decades. How many genetic defects would the human race have developed after 5 million years? How could we be healthy humans with so much time for our DNA to degrade as it is today?

There is so much to consider when realizing that what we have been told about the age of the Earth or even the universe by so-called expert scientists and researchers is blatantly illogical, unreasonable, and absurd!

The Age of the Earth

So, what do the creation scientists and the Biblical scholars, the Biblical scholars that truly believe the Bible to be inerrant, say about the age of the Earth? Why is the age of the Earth important? Because it gives us insight into God's design, into His Plan for mankind, into His future for us. We can use what is written in God's Word, take it as the True Truth, and obtain very interesting, yet very different conclusions from what evolution tells us.

Noah's Flood came about 1656 years after Creation based on the ages of the antediluvian forefathers in Genesis Chapter 5. The years from the Flood to Abraham were only 344 years since Abraham lived around 2000 B.C. That makes from Creation to Abraham 2000 years, and from Abraham to Jesus another 2000 years. How long has it been from Jesus until now? Another 2000 years. Hmmm. That's 6000 years from Creation until now. Interesting.

It says in the Bible that a day is as a thousand years and a thousand years is as a day, right? (Psalm 90:4 and 2 Peter 3:8) What does that really mean? First, it means that we are not like God. He sees things differently than we do. He is eternal, we are not. God lives outside of time – He made time so He can see past, present, and future all at the same time (to us). We ARE made in His image, but we are not God, are we? But, look at those verses another way. Maybe God is trying to tell us something and we are not quite getting it. Hosea 6:2 says, ""He will revive us after two days; He will raise us up on the third day, that we may live before Him." The reviving could be the Rapture, and the third "day" the Millennium. Psalm 90:4 says, "For a thousand years in thy sight are but as yesterday when it is past, and as a watch in the night." 2 Peter 3:8 says, "But, beloved, be not ignorant of this one thing, that one day is with the Lord as a thousand years, and a thousand years as one day." So, could that very intriguing verse in Hosea be referring to two periods, one of 2,000 years and another of 1,000 years? Let's examine this possibility.

So, if God made Heaven and Earth 6,000 years ago according to the Bible's genealogies and Biblical scientific observation, Creation was 1,656 years before the Flood of Noah, the Flood was about 344 years before Abraham (1,656 + 344 = 2,000), and Abraham was 2,000 years before Jesus, that leaves just 2,000 years from Jesus until now (the Church Age or Age of Grace or Dispensation of Grace) when "we may live before Him" for 1,000 years in His Millennial Kingdom of Rest. Total those four periods together and you arrive at 7,000 years, 6,000 years until now and then the Millennium of 1,000 years. These 7 periods of 1,000 years each also mimics the Creation Week where God created all things in 6 days and rested on the 7th day.

Hosea has a prophecy that says after two days (read 2,000 years), something happens so that God's people will "live before Him" for another day (read 1,000 years or the Millennium). "Him" is God and specifically Jesus and God the Father. It has been about 2,000 years (again, the Church Age) since Jesus' Resurrection in 27 A.D. (more on this later), so we must be on top of the time when this happens since it is 2019, right? Where do we "live before Him" for that 3rd day or the 1,000 years? That 3rd day of Hosea's verse corresponds to the 7th 1,000-year period from Creation which corresponds to the 7th day of rest in Creation otherwise known as the rest of the Millennial Kingdom of Christ. This is the "kingdom come" we all pray when we say the Lord's Prayer.

To sum this up, the six days of Creation and the 7th day of rest is our model from God for our work week. Remember the work week? 2 Thessalonians 3:10, "…that if any would not work, neither should he eat." And that model for the week came from Creation Week which is also a model for the existence of mankind on the Earth (7,000 years) and the time it would take for man to restore his relationship to God and be sinless, holy, and live eternally with God. God is the same yesterday, today, and forever, right? Then, it should come as no surprise when we see parallels in God's Word and His plan for mankind. A seven-day workweek with a day of rest after six days? That is the manner in which God created the heavens and the Earth. Could He have created everything in a microsecond? Of course! But He created everything in an explicit order that defies man's ideas (evolution), and He did it in six literal days again defying man's ideas (evolution again). So, when God planned for the salvation of mankind, He used the same model but this time He used a thousand years as a substitute for a day. The model for the total time existence of man is based on the 7 days of Creation with each day of Creation being 1,000 years on Earth. Man would struggle after sin was introduced for 6,000 years, then rest with Jesus reigning on the Earth for a thousand years called the Millennium. We are at the 6,000-year mark RIGHT NOW meaning that Christ's Millennial Reign has to be very, very near! But a trumpet call has to sound BEFORE that Millennial Kingdom can start. That trumpet along with a shout of "Come up here" is what we as Christians are longing for since we desire righteousness and to be with our Lord and Savior. That trumpet call is the sound of the Rapture calling us home to be with Jesus forever and ever!

The Rapture

The Bible, specifically the New Testament, is about 2,000 years old, or, in other words, it was written by men, inspired by the Holy Spirit, that lived that long ago. The concept of the "Great Escape" to come was there in those sacred scriptures. In fact, Paul's reason to inform the Thessalonians of the "catching away" was to allay their fears that they might have missed Christ coming to "take" them to be with Him. Consequently, isn't it interesting that the first best–selling Bible prophecy book in history was "Jesus is Coming", written by William E. Blackstone and published in 1878. Blackstone was an American Evangelical and Christian Zionist. The book sold multi–millions of copies worldwide and was translated into 48 languages. It is still in print today. In the book, Blackstone affirmed his belief that the Jews would be gathered back to their homeland, and he endorsed the concept of a Pre-Tribulation Rapture or occurring before the Tribulation even starts.

The Scofield Study Bible, first published by the Oxford Press in 1909 became the most popular such book in the world, and it continues to be distributed worldwide today. Scofield was an ardent advocate of the Pre–Tribulation Rapture. And then there are the sermons by Harry Ironside at the Moody Church in Chicago and W. A. Criswell at First Baptist Church in Dallas. Both taught the Pre–Tribulation Rapture, and their books have been greatly blessed with widespread distribution. Other giants of Pre-Tribulation Rapture teaching are men I have met in my life, Dwight Pentecost and John Walvoord of Dallas Theological Seminary and John MacArthur of Grace Community Church and Grace To You (GTY.org). Then there is David Jeremiah of Turning Point. All of these share the Pre-Tribulation view of the Rapture. With so great an assembly of godly men known for their devotion to the Truth of the Word of God, perhaps we should strongly consider the evidence or at the very least give it another look.

Consider the fact that Hal Lindsey's Pre–Tribulation book, "The Late Great Planet Earth" (which was the book that started my studies of prophecy back in the early '70s), was the number one best-selling book (except the Bible) for ten consecutive years (1970–1980), only to be outdone by the "Left Behind" series of books by Tim LaHaye and Jerry Jenkins which have sold more than 60 million copies. I think the Lord is trying to provide hope to His people in the midst of a rapidly darkening world by assuring them that they will escape the Tribulation that is on the horizon, no, is at the door!

Some use the term "Great Escape" for the Rapture. That term upsets Post–Tribulation and Mid-Tribulation and Pre-Wrath advocates because they think that Christians are called to suffer for the Lord during the Tribulation. But Jesus Himself is the one who used the word "escape" when He said that when we see all the end time signs converging, we are to pray that we might "escape all these things that are about to take place..." (Luke 21:36). Paul told us in 1 Thessalonians 5:9, "For God did not appoint us to suffer wrath but to receive salvation through our LORD Jesus Christ." This seems unmistakable evidence of a Pre-Tribulation Rapture.

When?

It is true that the Bible does not provide us with a declarative statement about the timing of the Rapture. Its timing is something that must be determined by inference or deduction. But the idea that the Rapture will occur before the beginning of Daniel's 70th Week of Years is not something that was manufactured out of nothing. It is biblically based. Simply stated, the Church is promised immunity from the wrath of God (1 Thessalonians 1:10, "...and to wait for his Son from Heaven, whom he raised from the dead-Jesus, who rescues us from the coming wrath."), and scriptures in both the Old and New Testaments describe Daniel's 70th Week of Years as a time for the pouring out of God's wrath upon the unbelieving world primarily for His Chosen People the Jews (Jeremiah 30:4–7 and Revelation 6:17).

Further, there is no purpose for the Church in the Tribulation. This is true because the entire seven years of the Tribulation are part of the 490 years (Daniel's 70 Week Prophecy) God has set aside for achieving His purposes among the Jewish people (Daniel 9:24–27). The Tribulation is the time of Jacob's Trouble, not the Church (Jeremiah 30:7, "Alas! for that day is great, so that none is like it: it is even the time of Jacob's trouble; but he shall be saved out of it.") And, when you read Revelation you find that the remnant of believing in Christ Jews protected by God through the last half of the Tribulation are "saved out of it".

Then there is the important issue of imminence. The scriptures urge us to live looking for the coming of the Lord and that His appearance could occur at any moment (Matthew 24:36, 42, 44). Why should I be looking for the Lord if there are many prophecies that must be fulfilled before He can return, as is the case when you place the Rapture after the beginning of the Tribulation or combine it with the Second Coming at the end of the Tribulation or even in the middle? Why should I be looking forward to "escaping" the Wrath of God if I know I will be facing that very same Wrath if the Rapture is in the middle or at the end of the horrible Tribulation?

How Close?

How close are we to that trumpet call otherwise known as the Rapture? No one knows the exact date, but we can come very close because of Scripture and a little deduction. Jesus was about 15 to 18 months old when the Magi came to worship Him in Bethlehem. They DID NOT come at the time of His birth as so many of the Christmas stories tell us (read Matthew and Luke carefully). Magi came from the East, actually from the old Babylonian area, because they were recognized as "king makers" by those in that time and greatly respected. It is interesting to think that these Magi came from the advisors to Nebuchadnezzar of Babylon who were greatly influenced by Daniel over his 70 or more years as one of the highest leaders in the land.

These Magi, numbering perhaps 20 or more – not just three (the Bible never mentions the number of Magi, we just assume there were three because there are three gifts mentioned) - first went to Herod the Great, Israel's Idumean king (NOT a Jew) because they supposed he would know about this newborn king. Herod was suspicious of them and he did not know of this new born king. He became jealous and enraged that a usurper was born to replace him, not excited to welcome a savior who would become king. As a result, Herod found out that this new king was to be born in Bethlehem from Scripture, so he had all the newborn boy babies in Bethlehem under age 2 killed. Jesus and his parents had fled to Egypt before this massacre because it was announced to Joseph by the angel Gabriel what was about to happen, and they stayed in Egypt until Herod's death, probably a couple of years.

History tells us that Herod died in 4 B.C., and that presents a chronological problem for those that think Jesus was born with our calendar or at 1 A.D. Herod the Great's death in 4 B.C. has to put Jesus' birth around 6 B.C., not at the time of the beginning of our calendar, the start of 1 A.D., as we assume. Since maturity for priests starting their service was considered to be 30 years of age, we assume Jesus started His earthly ministry at 30 since the Bible does not tell us He was 30, then died when he was about 33 making His resurrection date about 27 A.D. (remember, there is no year zero between B.C. and A.D.). Add 2,000 years to that and you get 2027, and we are in 2019. The difference – 8 years give or take. Now, considering errors of calendars, errors in specific times of years (Spring versus Fall for example), this date of 2027 could be sooner or later, but very near the 2,000-year time that completes the total of 6,000 years for man on Earth before Christ's Kingdom comes. What does this calculation imply, and I stress "imply" since we cannot nor should we even try to set specific dates? That Jesus' Second Coming could be as close as 2027 which means that the Rapture happens 7 years prior to that! Can we know exactly? No! But we see that we are close indeed! No date setting here, but you see what might be!

However, Jesus did say we would not know the day or the hour, but He did suggest we would know the "general" time. Matthew 24:33,34 says, "So likewise ye, when ye shall see all these things (the signs of the times), know that it is near, even at the doors. Verily I say unto you, this generation shall not pass, till all these things be fulfilled." I suggest to you that since we see a convergence of End Time signs, we are in the general time, that generation, for the Rapture, certainly, and the other End Time Prophecies that we will cover in detail.

Conclusion

We will soon cover other topics such as dispensations, the Feasts of Israel, the timing of the significant End Times events, and what events probably happen immediately after the Rapture and before the start of the Tribulation and why. All of this is certain because of Israel being a restored nation which recently celebrated its 70th anniversary – a very significant number indeed and the reason for us to be very sure and excited about the times we live in – or at least live in a while longer before we get snatched in the Rapture! Israel is the key to End Time Prophecy, so next time we will dig deeper into the reason why we should be expecting that Shout and Trumpet call to, "Come up here!"

CHAPTER TWO

FOUNDATIONAL CONCEPTS TO UNDERSTANDING BIBLE PROPHECY

Introduction

In the first chapter, we covered many essential things such as the right way to study God's Word, the meaning of prophecy and why prophecy is controversial, why prophecy is important, why man's ideas about how we arrived at this point in time compared to what the Bible tells us are different, the time that has elapsed from Creation to now (about 6,000 years), and an introduction to what should come next in the biblical timeline (the Rapture).

It is very important for all of us to fully understand the Word of God and the prophecy He has in store for us all. Why? So, we can accomplish God's will in our lives and answer the age-old question, "Why am I here?" In order to fully understand the Bible, we need first and foremost the Holy Spirit Who enlightens us with His Wisdom to understand His Word. And, you only receive the Holy Spirit when you accept the Lord Jesus Christ not only as Savior/Redeemer, but as Lord of your life. But, secondarily, we must read God's Word as what it is – the Truth, the TRUE Truth, and not spend time trying to read into the Bible what we want it to say. We have to take God's Word as it appears, clear, without error, and profitable for us in our lives. To try to overlay our own preconceived notions over the Word of God is to blatantly deny God Himself and call into question what He has to tell us. It is blatantly saying that we know and are more savvy than God Himself!

We found out that about a third of the Bible was future, unfulfilled prophecy, when it was written, and there is a significant amount of Bible prophecy that is still in our future today. Many of the Old Testament prophecies have, indeed, come true, such as, for example, of the 300 or so prophecies that referred to the first coming of Jesus Christ as Suffering Servant. Now, in order to discern what the remaining unfulfilled prophecies mean to us, we have to add to our understanding certain things we will cover at this time. Isn't it amazing and incredibly wonderful that our God loves us so much that He wants us to know His plan for our and humanity's future?

We now will see what foundational concepts need to be fully understood in order to be able to not only read prophecy from God's Word with understanding, but to grasp the reasons why God is telling us what is to come in our immediate future. I know that presentations about the details of prophecy (like what's next) are exciting, even awesome, and we will get to more of them in due time, but we first need to know many things in order to know the truth of how God wants us to be enlightened. We will now look at very interesting subjects that are needed to fully grasp what God has to say to us about what is next for us, for the Jews, and for the rest of the world.

We will look at the order of Creation versus Evolution to see that we have been deceived into worldly thinking – not biblical thinking. Next, we will look again at the age of the Earth because, again, what we are taught does not line up with the Bible. From the true age of the Earth we see how God has used certain times across the centuries, ages, dispensations, to prove to us as humanity that we need Him not only for salvation, but for everyday existence. Then we will see the hidden meanings in the Feasts of Israel as they relate to Jesus Christ, and finish with the significance of the restoration of the Nation of Israel and how that fits into the End Times prophecies.

Order of Creation vs. Evolution

God tells us in Genesis 1 and 2 that He created the heavens and the Earth in six literal days and rested the seventh day. (Much of this information comes from the Institute for Creation Research or ICR.org) These are days, "yom" in Hebrew, which always refers to literal days when associated with "the evening and the morning" as Genesis states, not eons of millions or billions of years as the evolutionists, the God-deniers, want us to believe. And, yes, I said "believe" simply because nothing is a "fact" unless it can be proven. The evolutionists claim that evolution is a fact, even a "proven" fact, but nothing could be further from the truth! To prove something by repeatable demonstration is the definition of scientific fact, and evolution has never been proven, shown to have happened even once or shown to be repeatable at any level making it a belief not a fact. There exists micro-evolution which we would call adaptation and inner-species variation. This happens all the time. Consider how many breeds of dogs exist all due to selective breeding. But they are all still dogs, aren't they? But there has never been any animal that turned into a completely different animal over eons of time. That is called macro-evolution or rising higher in complexity from one lower species to a completely different species like a monkey to a man, or a dinosaur into a bird as the evolutionists want us to blindly accept. Macro-evolution has never happened – in fact, it could never happen, and we will discuss why not.

Evolutionists want us to believe that life sprang forth from non-life – that somehow distinct inorganic elements along with some unusual event, such as electrical or thermal or magical, came together and formed a living cell or a one-celled animal. From that initial form of life, evolution took over and produced everything that we see around us, but that process took millions upon millions of years of death, random events, failed and successful mutations and genetic formation, then some truly marvelous mutations that first, violated the Second Law of Thermodynamics (nothing can improve, all things degrade), then proved beneficial to natural selection, the survival of the fittest, and the ascending process of higher forms of life began. From Goo to You by way of the Zoo! Understand that all of this violates every single law of physics that exists, but evolutionists have to say these things, even claim they are "facts", because they have no other explanation since they will NOT admit that God is the Creator with Whom we ALL have to deal!

The basic problem with evolutionary theory is that life comes from life, not from inorganic substance or from nothing at all (the Big Bang), it can come from no other source! God gave life through His Omnipotent power. Inanimate matter cannot come to life nor emerge from nothing! The next problem with evolutionary theory (again, it is a belief, NOT a "fact" as claimed) is that it is thoroughly, demonstrably, conclusively NOT "scientific"! Why, you may ask? Because it violates the definition of science. Mirriam Webster defines science as "knowledge or a system of knowledge covering general truths, or the operation of general laws especially as obtained and tested through scientific method." And what is the "scientific method"? "A method of research in which a problem is identified, relevant data are gathered, a hypothesis is formulated from these data, and the hypothesis is empirically tested." Did you get that? Any theory must be thoroughly actually real-world tested over and over with repetitive positive results. In fact, the scientific method REQUIRES these steps:

1. Make an observation or observations.
2. Ask questions about the observations and gather information.
3. Form a hypothesis — a tentative description of what's been observed and make predictions based on that hypothesis.
4. Test the hypothesis and predictions in an experiment that can be reproduced.
5. Analyze the data and draw conclusions; accept or reject the hypothesis or modify the hypothesis if necessary.
6. Reproduce the experiment until there are no discrepancies between observations and theory. "The reproducibility of published experiments is the foundation of science. No reproducibility – no science."

Hmmmmmm! If a "theory of evolution" cannot be tested and repeated thus proving its validity, then it is not "scientific" nor a "fact", it is just a theory that must be believed on faith or rejected based on the lack of proof.

Some will say Creationism cannot be repeated either, it must also be believed. That statement is true. But, and here I say this with pointed exclamation, Creation itself is so irreducibly complex that scientists cannot even explain how a human cell can be so complex, or how the Sun can continue to produce energy through nuclear fusion (a process scientists have tried to master and cannot even though we have tried for decades to do so), energy seemingly unwavering, consistent, and producing continuously without sign of being used up, or how do we explain how a tiny hummingbird that weighs a couple of grams can fly across the Gulf of Mexico, some 1,500 miles, and survive. Man cannot explain either of these phenomena much less anything else in detail in the universe like how a leaf can use photosynthesis to produce food for the tree through photosynthesis (an incredible 70 chemical reactions done in precise order) using the carbon dioxide in the air and release oxygen for us to breathe (information from SearchfortheTruth.net). To me, that proves that there is a Master Designer/Creator whose name is God. Proof positive!

What is also fascinating to me is the order of evolution versus the order of Creation. It's as if God wanted to show us just how absurd evolutionary theory really is and test us at the same time as to whether we believe Him or some men who tell us evolution caused the universe as we see it. Evolutionists say that, for example, birds evolved from reptiles, from dinosaurs, over millions of years. Yes, that's right. From scales to feathers, from lungs to air sacs, from solid bones to hollow bones, from walking skeleton structure to flight skeletal structure. Seems implausible, and it absolutely is because it didn't happen that way at all. Feathers are completely different than scales since scales are just hard skin and feathers have pinions that are attached to bone! But the most amazing thing is that in God's creation order, birds are first, then mammals. On day five, God made birds and sea creatures. God made mammals on the sixth day showing us that what evolution says is incorrect. And, fortunately, God had made plant life on the third day of Creation so the birds and sea creatures could eat. It is as if God purposely planned the order just to spite man's evolutionary ideas.

Evolutionists say the stars formed out of the chaos known as the Big Bang, gases swirled together and compressed into stars and planets. But, again, there are problems. First and foremost, nothing can never turn into something. So, if there ever was a "cosmic egg" that blew up and caused everything from the "Big Bang", then where did the "cosmic egg" come from? From nothing? But nothing can do absolutely nothing. Nothing is the absence of everything – no matter, no space, no energy, no nothing.

Ridiculous! Isaiah 45:18 says it all, "For thus saith the LORD that created the heavens; God himself that formed the Earth and made it; he hath established it, he created it not in vain, he formed it to be inhabited: I am the LORD; and there is none else."

Then, there are laws of science that have never been seen to be violated. One of those laws is Boyle's Law which states that gases in the vacuum of space would disperse not compress (again, ICR.org). So, according to evolution, the origin of all the stars and planets was a miniscule speck of unimaginable energy coming from no one knows where instantly and for some unknown reason exploded, thus creating the universe, then gases swirled together billions and billions of times forming stars and planets and solar systems. But, according to accepted scientific laws, gases in a vacuum cannot compress! In fact, gases in a vacuum disperse! This completely destroys the evolutionary position that somehow stars compressed from the gases from the Big Bang. God, on the other hand, started, not with gasses and a Big Bang, but with the Heaven and the Earth and water. He didn't even make the Sun and the Moon until the fourth day! At that time, He also made the stars, all at once in a single day, billions of galaxies, each one containing billions of stars! Who should we believe, the evolutionists with their implausible and irrational theories or the ever truthful, faithful, omnipotent God? And, yes, Earth IS the center of the universe since God made the Earth BEFORE HE made the rest of the universe! Read it! It's in Genesis Chapter One!

Evolutionists say insects came before birds which came after lizards and dinosaurs. Consider this. If that were true, there would not have been any plant life left for the dinosaurs and lizards to eat. If insects came before birds, and evolutionists say they preceded birds by millions of years, the Earth would have been destroyed by unimaginable numbers of insects without anything to control their reproductive rate. Insects reproduce at unimaginable rates. One pair of potato beetles over one season can produce 60 million offspring. There are supposedly over a million species of insects, so imagine how many would cover the Earth without birds to eat them?

Probably the most egregious claim of evolution is that changes over millennia of time has resulted in increased complexity, the evolution of lower forms of life into higher forms, and the sudden appearance of all kinds of life without any evidence of transitional forms. Why is this so egregious, so absurd? Because of the violation of the Second Law of Thermodynamics. I know this sounds very ominous and something most people could care less about, but these three laws are not that hard to understand:

1. The First law of thermodynamics states that energy can neither be created nor destroyed. It can only change forms. In any process, the total energy of the universe remains the same.

2. The Second law of thermodynamics says that entropy of an isolated system not in equilibrium will tend to increase over time, approaching a maximum value at equilibrium, and entropy is the measure of disorder and randomness in a system. In other words, disorder and deterioration increase over time, order does not. Chaos rules!

3. And the Third law of thermodynamics says that as temperature approaches absolute zero (minus 460 degrees Fahrenheit, zero degrees Kelvin), the entropy of a system approaches a constant minimum. In other words, all activity stops.

The most tested foundational laws of science clearly show the impossibility of the Big Bang as an explanation for everything including our very existence. Yet these laws are perfectly compatible with recent creation of the universe by God, which is exactly what the Bible teaches! Do we not observe the deterioration of everything as time advances? Have you ever seen anything, anything at all, IMPROVE with age such as hundreds of years? Of course not. Ever see a cow skeleton in a field last a million years, slowly get covered up by dust blowing in, then be preserved as a fossil? NO! The skeleton would disintegrate long before it could ever be covered up.

What this simply means is that the Second Law, which is totally accepted by all scientists, evolutionists or creationists, says over time that everything degrades, nothing improves. Can we say it more clearly? Evolution from lower forms of life to higher forms of life does not nor ever has happened! Look around you in the here and now. How many things have you ever seen that get better over time? Be honest! Nothing, right? Everything rusts or dissolves or decomposes or gets dirty or starts stinking or falls down. So how can a life form IMPROVE or even change into something larger, more powerful, even develop intelligence like monkey to man? The answer? It CANNOT! It NEVER has! It NEVER will!

The point of all of this is to show that when man tries to explain life as we see it, he comes up with absurd theories that are often disproven by the very laws that science knows to be true and unwavering. Why? Because of some of mankind's inability or choice to believe in an all-powerful, all-knowing Creator God! Trusting in God and His Word makes explanations about the universe easy, understandable, and believable. Evolution, at its very foundation, is an inconsistent belief, not fact, easily disproved and thoroughly unsatisfying due to the incomprehensible claims that cannot be proven and are blatantly absurd in their assumptions.

Death versus Development

There is a grave danger in accepting what evolutionists shovel at us, specifically that the Earth is billions of years old and death and destruction have been occurring since the formation of life itself - that countless millennia have passed in the "development" of man and our world today. In fact, accepting the error of evolution as "fact" destroys the basis for Christianity! How, you say? Because evolution requires millions and millions of years of death, decay, and disorder for mutations to emerge into higher and more complex levels of creatures resulting in what we see today.

Belief in evolution requires the acceptance of billions of years of death and impossible increasing complexity of life over time or a development of higher forms of life over time which violates every scientific law imaginable. In reality, evolution is a record of death – NOT development! Evolution is a continual screeching of nails on a blackboard or incessant blaring of a thousand sirens in a Christian's ears because it is a lie straight from the corrupted mind of the enemy himself and a mortal and spiritual danger to Christianity!

Why is evolution a danger to Christianity? Because the Bible says death came about because of the first man's sin, his disobedience to God through a willful act in defiance of God's Word. Adam and Eve were created perfect in the Garden of Eden, capable of living forever with only one stipulation. Genesis 2:16,17 says, "And the LORD God commanded the man, saying, Of every tree of the garden thou mayest freely eat: but of the tree of the knowledge of good and evil, thou shalt not eat of it: for in the day that thou eatest thereof thou shalt surely die." So, death entered into creation through disobedience of God.

Man was originally created as an eternal being, both spiritually and physically. In fact, man was created in the image of God with three components, body, mind, and spirit (or body, soul, and spirit) indicating that each of us is totally unique and individual because each of us has our own soul/mind completely separate from everyone else who has ever been born. But Adam disobeyed God and caused a change in man's existence. When Adam disobeyed God, he not only placed a limitation on his physical life meaning his body would age and eventually perish, but his spirit, his spiritual life would also "die" meaning he was separated from God eternally as well. When Satan tempted Eve with the famous line in Genesis 3:4,5, "And the serpent said unto the woman, Ye shall not surely die: for God doth know that in the day ye eat thereof, then your eyes shall be opened, and ye shall be as gods, knowing good and evil", he deceived her because he was speaking of immediate physical death, not eternal spiritual death!

We also know that "The wages of sin is death." (Romans 6:23) Therefore, sin and death entered into existence when Adam disobeyed God in the Garden of Eden some time after Creation which, according to the Bible's genealogies, was a brief 6,000 years ago, not billions of years according to evolution. We must always remember too that, "It is better to trust in God, than to trust in man." (Psalm 118:8) God told us through Paul in the Book of Romans, "By one man sin entered into the world, and death by sin." (Romans 5:12)

So, from all of this, we can conclude that evolution's fairy tale about eons upon eons of death and mutation leading to our present day could not be true because sin caused death and the original sin was committed by Adam only about 6,000 years ago according to biblical genealogies. So what, you say? What does that have to do with evolution and Christianity? Something very simple yet devastating to our faith. If evolution is true, then the Bible is false! If evolution is true, then God is a liar! If evolution is true, then salvation through faith in Jesus Christ's death on the cross of Calvary in payment for our sins is meaningless and He died in vain! One CANNOT accept evolution as "fact" and believe in God's Word at the same time! To do so is to poke God in His eye and diminish Him.

To believe in evolution is to deny the Holy Spirit's leading which is the very definition of the unforgivable sin. The unpardonable/unforgivable sin or "blasphemy of the Holy Spirit" is mentioned in Mark 3:22-30 and Matthew 12:22-32. Jesus said, "Truly I tell you, people can be forgiven all their sins and every slander they utter" (Mark 3:28), but then He gives one exception: "Whoever blasphemes against the Holy Spirit will never be forgiven; they are guilty of an eternal sin" (verse 29). What does it mean to blaspheme the Holy Spirit? There is no pardon for a person who dies in his rejection of Christ. The Holy Spirit is at work in the world, convicting the unsaved of sin, righteousness, and judgment (John 16:8). If a person resists that conviction and remains unrepentant, then he is choosing hell over Heaven thus blaspheming the Holy Spirit and committing the unpardonable sin.

Christianity depends on trusting in and living for God and God's Word. To accomplish that lofty goal, we must accept the free gift of salvation through the shed blood of Christ and make Him Lord of our life. To turn from what the Word of God very clearly tells us is to deny the Truth, and that is precisely what we do when we acknowledge the lie of evolution. Remember that the foundation of evolution is the attempt to explain everything **without** God! We have God because we know His Son. So, why believe in evolution's lies in any way? None of it is true. Trust the Word!

Age of the Earth vs. Evolution

Those of us that believe the Bible is inerrant and, therefore, that the Earth is quite young rather than very, very old, would have a much easier time if we just gave in to evolutionists and start using the millions and billions of years arguments for the way things really are. But the problem with that is that those extreme year descriptions have no basis in fact, but, and more importantly, actually bring into question and doubt the very fundamental beliefs of Christianity. If we say that it makes no difference when God (or even IF God) created the Heavens and the Earth, as many Christians and some churches have given in to saying, then we sound either insincere or unsure when we say we believe that God is Creator God or Jesus is the Word and He made all things (John 1:3).

The evolutionary time periods for the Earth and the universe, 4.6 and 15 billion years respectively, most certainly did not come from the Word of God. Those enormous time periods came from man's so-called wisdom born out of skepticism that there is even a God at all. We are all bombarded with evolutionary thinking in schools, in museums, on television, when we search on-line, literally everywhere, with these ridiculous timeframes for the appearance of life on Earth, even the formation of the topography of the Earth. So, even Christians want to "get along" in society by acquiescing to using the long ages instead of staying biblical. Some Christians start doubting God's Word by inferring that the "days" of Genesis are not real 24-hour days but eons of millennia to conform to evolutionary numbers.

But this "giving in" to false data is dangerous when examined in the long term. Henry Morris, Founder of the Institute for Creation Research in Dallas (ICR.org) points to a cascading set of conclusions that lead Christians away from the Truth of the Bible if and when they turn to modern claims of so-called "science" that has never been proven to be fact and is in essence just a fairy story – evolution. Dr. Morris lists the following downward trending conclusions that result when the Bible is abandoned, and evolutionary thinking is adopted:

1. God cannot be a God of Mercy and Grace after all since literally billions of years of death and destruction had to have taken place for mankind to evolve from a lower form of life.
2. The Bible cannot be authoritative since science contradicts so much of the Word causing us to question other things in the Bible like salvation,

Heaven, and everlasting life.

3. Death must not be the wages of sin as the Bible says because violence, pain, and death ruled on the Earth long before sin came in through Adam. Plus, the Earth was "very good" when God finished with it implying God is sadistic and cruel, taking pleasure in observing the suffering and death of His creatures.

4. Jesus is our Creator and He was Creator before He became our Savior. But Jesus told us in Mark 10:6 that He created Adam and Eve, male and female, "from the beginning". Evolution says the race of men took millions upon millions of years for man to rise from the ooze making the Bible a myth.

5. If death was not an important part of the penalty of sin for so many millions of years, then Jesus' death on the cross accomplished very little indeed.

6. The, if Jesus' death on the cross was not significant, then we have no real Savior. We still have sin and death today, so what the Bible tells us about the promises of future salvation is questionable. And if eternal life in the future is in question, why should we care anything about prophecies of the future?

7. Finally, why should we believe in God at all, what the Bible makes Him out to be, the holy, personal, loving, omniscient, omnipotent, righteous God that died for our sins?

If we compromise our faith in any way, we open the door wide for the enemy to shovel in the wisdom of man, his pseudo-science, and the questioning of whether God matters in our lives. It may seem convenient to adopt the old-Earth philosophy, make us look acceptable to the world out there, look more "intelligent" to the unbelieving world, but a traitor to the Truth, a Judas to the Savior, a false believer calling into question our faith and our ability to witness and proclaim the Gospel.

The Truth is that the Bible is the inerrant, infallible, inspired, authoritative Word of the One True God, the Omnipotent Creator, the King of kings and the Lord of lords, Jesus Christ. The real and truly unquestionable facts of science and history, of many of the original scholars of science in the past like Louis Pasteur (1822-1895), Isaac Newton (1642-1727), Johann Kepler (1571-1630), Robert Boyle (1691-1726), Charles Babbage (1792-1871), Isaac Newton (1642-1727), James Clerk Maxwell (1831-1879), Michael Faraday (1791-1867), and a hundred more, support the Word of God in its entirety, without question, boldly, and completely. It has been reported that there are over 1,000 present-day scientists and engineers that attest to the validity of Scripture and against evolution, but the media will not report such facts. On the other hand, all the media will promulgate is that "all" reputable scientists "know" that evolution is "fact" when there is absolutely NO genuine scientific, repeatable, proven evidence for evolution at all. We do well to believe in God's Word as written, without parsing, without question, with no personal interpretation. God does not lie, mislead, or deal in myths. To believe so is just poking Almighty God in His eye!

We can look and not see. By this I mean not examining God's Word to appreciate His Truth. My favorite, obscure testimony to the veracity of God's Word is found in the Book of Job written, perhaps, before any other book in the Bible since Job lived contemporaneously with Abraham some 2,000 years before Christ. Back then, I believe men were smarter than today since we started with a perfect Adam before the Fall and have degraded every year since, but technology had not progressed to the point that it has today either. The Book of Job tells us many things of God, especially in Chapters 38 through 42. One reference to God and His Creation is in Job 38:31, "Can you bind the sweet influences of Pleiades or loose the bands of Orion?" These two names represent star constellations in the night sky easily seen from our Northern hemisphere perspective, especially Orion with its three straight-line-arranged formation – Orion's Belt. But what we miss if we are not careful and what even Job could not know is hidden in the descriptions of the two constellations. Only in this modern age starting in the 1800's have we determined that, indeed, the stars in Pleiades (the Seven Sisters) are moving toward each other be it ever so slowly ("bind") and the stars in Orion are, indeed moving away from each other ("loose") in an unnoticeable way. God made the heavens, so He knows their motion. He told us these constellations from our perspective were moving and how they were moving in respect to each other 4,000 years ago. If that doesn't impress you, then your heart is in need of warming up!

It helps to show the absurdity of what evolution requires us to accept without inquiry, without thinking, without evidence. Evolutionists will have you believe that the Earth is 4.3 to 4.54 billion years old. Let's see, there is a significant and unexplained gap there, a gap of 0.24 billion years or 240 million years – quite an error factor wouldn't you say? So, is this believable? Where did that error come from? Does it make any logical sense, or is it just a SWAG, a Scientific Wildly Assumed Guess!

Here are some examples of the obvious errors of evolution that really make no sense (taken from ICR.org and AnswersinGenesis.org):

1. The Earth has a magnetic field due to its magnetic molten core that repels the Sun's incoming solar and stellar radiation that continually bombards Earth and does great damage to life, causing

harmful mutations and likely contributing to the aging and death of living things. Indeed, if these rays were not impeded and filtered by Earth's magnetic field, life here would be impossible. According to evolutionists, the Earth's magnetic field is about 4 ½ billion years old. The strength of the magnetic field has been reliably and continually measured since 1835. From these measurements, we can see that the field's strength has declined by about seven percent since then, giving a half-life of about 1,400 years. This means that in 1,400 years it will be one-half as strong, in 2,800 years it will be one-fourth as strong, and so on. There will be a time not many thousands of years distant when the field will be too small to perform as a viable shield for Earth.

However, and more interestingly, calculating back into the past, and assuming a constant half-life which may or may not be true, the present measurements indicate that 1,400 years ago the field was twice as strong. It continues doubling each 1,400 years back, until about 10,000 years ago it would have been so strong the planet would have disintegrated--its metallic core would have separated from its mantle. The inescapable conclusion we can draw is that the Earth must be fewer than 10,000 years old. Without millions and billions of years, evolutionary history completely falls apart.

2. Far from proving evolution, carbon-14 dating actually provides some of the strongest evidence for creation and a young Earth. Radiocarbon (carbon-14) cannot remain naturally in substances for millions of years because it decays in relatively short time periods. For this reason, it can only be used to obtain "ages" in the range of tens of thousands of years. Scientists from ICR (The Institute for Creation Research) examined diamonds that evolutionists consider to be 1–2 billion years old and related to the earth's early history. Diamonds are the hardest known substance and extremely resistant to contamination through chemical exchange. Yet the scientists discovered significant detectable levels of radiocarbon in these diamonds, dating them at around 55,000 years—a far cry from the evolutionary billions!

3. The gravitational pull of the moon creates a "tidal bulge" on Earth that causes the moon to spiral outwards very slowly. Because of this effect, the moon would have been closer to the Earth in the past. Based on gravitational forces and the current rate of recession, we can calculate how much the moon has moved away

over time. If the Earth is only 6,000 years old, there's no problem, because in that time the moon would have only moved about 800 feet. But most astronomy books teach that the moon is over four billion years old, which poses a major dilemma because less than 1.5 billion years ago the moon would have been touching the Earth!

4. In recent years, there have been many findings of preserved biological materials in supposedly ancient rock layers and fossils. Consider that geologists determine the age of rocks from the fossils found in those rocks and paleontologists determine the age of fossils from the age of the rocks they find them in. In other words, circular reasoning without foundation. One such discovery of fossilized material that has left evolutionists scrambling is a fossilized Tyrannosaurus rex femur with flexible connective tissue, branching blood vessels, and even intact cells! According to evolutionists, these dinosaur tissues are more than 65 million years old, but laboratory studies have shown that there is no known way for biological material to last more than thousands of years. Evolutionists are completely wrong about how recently these dinosaurs lived.

5. It's amazing what basic mathematics can show us about the age of the Earth. We can calculate the years of human existence with the population doubling every 150 years (a very conservative figure) to get an estimate of what the world's population should be after any given period of time. A biblical age of the Earth (about 6,000 years) is consistent with the population of the Earth today. In contrast, even a conservative evolutionary age of 50,000 years comes out to a staggering, impossibly high figure of 10 to the 99th power which is greater than the number of atoms in the universe! Clearly, the claim that humans have inhabited the Earth for tens of thousands of years much less millions of years is completely absurd!

6. When solid rock is bent, it normally cracks and breaks. Rock can only bend without fracturing when it is softened by extreme heating (which causes re-crystallization) or when the sediments have not yet fully hardened. There are numerous locations around the world (including the Grand Canyon) where we observe massive sections of strata that have been tightly folded, without evidence of the sediments being heated. This is a major problem for evolutionists who believe these rock layers were laid down

gradually over vast eons of time, forming the geologic record. However, it makes perfect sense to creationists who believe these layers were formed rapidly in the global, catastrophic Flood described in Genesis.

Does the age of the Earth really matter? While each of these evidences reveals reasons why the Earth cannot be billions of years old, the real issue is not the age of the Earth. Instead, the real issue is authority. God's infallible Word must be our ultimate authority, not the unstable foundation of evolutionary human reasoning. Are we trying to fit our interpretations of the world (evolution) into Scripture, or will we simply let God speak for Himself through His Word?

If we can't trust the first chapters of Genesis, why should we believe when Scripture says that faith in Jesus Christ as the only way of salvation? (Romans 10:9; Acts 4:12; John 14:6) But when we take Scripture as written, it's clear that the Earth can't be more than a few thousand years old. And from a biblical worldview, the scientific evidence agrees!

Dispensations

We have covered how God has always had a plan for the redemption of mankind to bring us back into fellowship with Him as it was in the Garden of Eden. God's gift to us of His written Word dramatically shows His Compassion, His Mercy, His Grace, His Love for us. His plan for our salvation has always been working, but the Savior did not appear for 4,000 years after Creation. Why wait so long to deliver the Savior promised so early in Genesis 3:15 while Adam and Eve were still in the Garden? Could it be that God's Plan is segmented into stages to demonstrate to mankind that there is only one way to God? That man's mind and man's ideas of how to approach and please God will NOT work back in the past, today, nor in the future. There is only one way to God and that is through His Son Jesus Christ.

We are familiar with the two Testaments of the Bible, so we already are familiar with two ages or times that are different from each other in many ways, but each demonstrates to us that God is forever the same, faith is the only way to God, but our circumstances as humans can vary greatly. In the Old Testament, mankind had to come to God through faith while in the New Testament the same was and is true with the exception that in the New, Jesus is known and in the Old He was not – just hoped for.

When we examine the two Testaments more closely, we can see more times or ages emerge that directly answer questions that man has for God as to whether we can please Him by doing things, living our lives our own way. Those times or ages are referred to as "dispensations" by theologians.

Often, when one is asked about the Dispensations of God, the response is, "What is a dispensation?" The easiest answer is an age or a length of time that God has used to teach mankind a lesson. Formally, the dictionary refers to dispensation in a number of ways from a special permission or release from a rule or a law to an act of providing something to people, dispensing something. It can mean a general state or ordering of things; specifically, a system of revealed commands and promises regulating human affairs or a particular arrangement or provision especially of Providence (God). The best way to look at a dispensation is that it is a scheme over a period of time according to which God carries out his purposes towards men. Systematic Theology, whose author was the founder of Dallas Theological Seminary Lewis Sperry Chafer, views Scripture as an unfolding revelation and doctrine or as a process of on-going "dispensing" of God's message of redemption to man. As the best example of a dispensation of God is the "Age" we currently live in – the Church Age, also known as the Dispensation of Grace.

Hebrews 1:1-2 says, "In many separate revelations (dispensations) – each of which set forth a portion of the truth – and in different ways God spoke of old to our forefathers in and by the prophets. But in the last of these days He has spoken to us in the person of a Son..."

The Greek word "oikonomia" signifies a disposition of affairs entrusted to someone. Thus 1 Corinthians 9:16,17 says, "For though I preach the gospel, I have nothing to glory of: for necessity is laid upon me; yea, woe is unto me, if I preach not the gospel! For if I do this thing willingly, I have a reward: but if against my will, a dispensation of the gospel is committed unto me," or "I have stewardship entrusted to me." In Ephesians 1:10, God's own working is spoken of as dispensation. "Having made known unto us the mystery of His will, according to his good pleasure which He hath purposed in Himself: that in the dispensation of the fullness of times He might gather together in one all things in Christ, both which are in Heaven, and which are on Earth; even in Him."

Later in Ephesians, Paul emphasizes the complete fulfillment of His will in Ephesians 3:1, 2, "For this cause I Paul, the prisoner of Jesus Christ for you Gentiles, if ye have heard of the dispensation of the grace of God which is given me to you-ward". Finally, Paul refers to his ministry as administration of God passed to him and intended to be given to a lost humanity in Colossians 1:25, "Whereof I am made a minister, according to the dispensation of God which is given to me for you, to fulfill the word of God".

There are actually seven dispensations that each answer a different situation or question or excuse that prove beyond a shadow of a doubt that we cannot please God on our own. We as a human race have tried many times to please God through our own efforts, failing miserably each and every time. Some in each age or dispensation have come to faith in God which was counted as righteousness for salvation, but the huge majority in each age were lost as it is today. So, why do we fail so miserably in each age? Because we are sinners, we are born that way – completely sinful with the penalty of death hanging over our heads like the Sword of Damocles. But Jesus was not a sinner. He lived a perfect life, sin-free as a human, so He could sacrifice His perfect human life for us thereby satisfying the Law, becoming the perfect sacrifice for sins forever, and covering our many sins with His shed blood, for the Bible says in Hebrews 9:22 that there is no forgiveness of sins without the shedding of blood. And, since Jesus' blood was sin-free, His sacrifice covered all sin, past, present, and future for all men, for all time. The only act on our part is the act of the humility of repentance and acceptance of Jesus' sacrifice for our sins. Then we know that Jesus was raised from the dead and sits on the right of the Father in Heaven until He comes back for us in the Rapture (1 Thessalonians 4:13-18).

Belief in God, faith in God, submission to God in our lives has always been the only way to God. But God has also known that we are hard-headed as humans determined to do things our own way. That's why God allowed different ages to occur to show us, demonstrate to us through our own actions under different circumstances, that our way will not work when trying to please God. The universally accepted number of seven dispensations is spread out from Eden through today and on to the Millennium. Those seven dispensations are the dispensations of Innocence, Conscience, Human or Civil Government, Promise, Law, Grace, and the Millennial Kingdom.

The questions from God to mankind and God's answer for each of the dispensations are the following: (1) Dispensation of Innocence (Garden of Eden) – With only one rule (do not eat of the Tree of the Knowledge of Good and Evil), can I trust you to obey me?; (2) Dispensation of Conscience (from the Fall to the Flood) – Now that you know that I expect you to obey me, can I now trust you?; (3) Dispensation of Human Government (from the Flood to the Tower of Babel) – Can you govern with a ruler and do well without me?; (4) Dispensation of Promise (from Abraham to Moses) – If I promise to bless you Israel, will you trust in me?; (5) Dispensation of the Law (from Moses to the Resurrection) – If I define sin to you, will you cease to sin without me?; (6) Dispensation of Grace (from Pentecost to the Rapture – Your sins are forgiven through Jesus' shed blood, will accept the gift on faith?; and (7) Disposition of the Millennium (from the Second Coming to the Great White Throne Judgment) – If I am visible and you can hear me, will you obey? Of course, the answer to all of God's questions was and will be "NO!" We cannot make it without God in any way because we are born sinful, prideful, arrogant, and obstinate. The dispensations actually prove that we cannot please God on our own, no matter what we try or how hard we try, without Jesus and we will continue to prove this until the New Heavens and New Earth.

Understanding the dispensations and their order, especially the future, the actual end of Dispensation 5 (otherwise known as the Tribulation) and the Millennium that follows, gives us insight into prophecy and how everything fits together. Without this knowledge of the ages and man's failures to please God on our own, we cannot fully see why we are at the end of times, more specifically the Last Days of the Last Days!

Feasts of Israel

Now we come to a subject that is obscure to say the least to our modern, non-Jewish minds, but exceedingly important to understanding and accepting prophecy. What are the Feasts of Israel? They are given to us in the Old Testament as requirements for the Jewish people to celebrate throughout the year. In fact, three of the seven feasts were to be celebrated personally in Jerusalem by each and every Jew meaning three times per year everyone had to "go up" to Jerusalem and celebrate the feasts. (To "go up" to Jerusalem applies to elevation since everywhere in Israel Jerusalem is higher than all surrounding land, and that's why regardless of where anyone was, they always "went up" to Jerusalem.) I would guess that when seeing this topic, most would wonder why look at the Feasts of Israel when studying prophecy. The major reason is, frankly, because they are Jewish, found in the Old Testament, and they all have great prophetic meaning to us today which we will soon see.

"Let no one act as your judge in regard to food or drink or in respect to a festival or a new moon or a Sabbath day: things which are a mere shadow of what is to come; but the substance belongs to Christ." (Colossians 2:16-17) This statement by the Apostle Paul refers to the Jewish Feasts as a "mere shadow" of things to come, the substance of them being found in Yeshua, Jesus, the Messiah. What Paul is saying here is that the feasts were prophetic types, or symbols, that pointed to the Messiah and which would be fulfilled in Him. So, if the feasts point to Jesus Christ, and Jesus is not finished with us because He has not returned yet in the Second Advent, then there could be meaning in the feasts for our future since some of the feasts were fulfilled in Jesus' First Advent but not all of them. (Some of this information comes from Lamb and Lion Ministries headed by Dr. David Reagan with the website christinprophecy.org. David is a wealth of Prophecy information and strongly recommended. The rest of the information comes from a man I have personally met, but he has gone on to be with the Lord – Zola Levitt.)

Origin and Timing of the Feasts

The feasts were a part of the Mosaic Law that was given to the Children of Israel by God through Moses (Exodus 12; 23:14-17; Leviticus 23; Numbers 28 & 29; and Deuteronomy 16). The Jewish nation was commanded by God to celebrate seven feasts over a seven-month period of time, beginning in the spring of the year and continuing through the fall. The first three feasts Passover, Unleavened Bread, and First Fruits occur in rapid succession in the Spring of the year over a period of eight days starting in March/April. They came to be referred to collectively as "Passover."

The fourth feast, Harvest, occurs fifty days later at the beginning of the Summer, roughly in June, and occurs at the time of the major harvest of the year. By New Testament times this feast had come to be known by its Greek name, Pentecost, a word meaning fifty which is the time between Passover and Pentecost, a total of fifty days.

The last three feasts - Trumpets, Atonement, and Tabernacles - extend over a period of twenty-one days in the Fall of the year, roughly in the September/October timeframe. They came to be known collectively as "Tabernacles." There is an eighth feast known as Hanukkah which Jesus celebrated which arose in 165 B.C. associated with the Maccabean Revolt against Antiochus Epiphanes IV.

The Nature of the Feasts

Some of the feasts were related primarily to the agricultural cycle. The feast of First Fruits was a time for the presentation to God of the first fruits of the barley harvest in Spring. The feast of Harvest, Pentecost, was a celebration of the major harvest of the year or the wheat harvest in Summer. And the feast of Tabernacles was in part a time of thanksgiving for the harvest of olives, dates, and figs in the Fall.

Most of the feasts were related to past historical events. Passover, of course, celebrated the salvation the Jews experienced when the angel of death passed over the Jewish houses in Egypt before the Exodus that were marked with the blood of a lamb. Unleavened Bread was a reminder of the swift departure from Egypt that was so swift that they had no time to put leaven (yeast) into their bread and allow the bread to rise before baking.

Although the feasts of Harvest and Tabernacles were related to the agricultural cycle, they both had historical significance as well. The Jews believed that it was on the feast day of Harvest, Pentecost, that God gave the Law to Moses on Mt. Sinai. And Tabernacles was a yearly reminder of God's protective care as the Children of Israel tabernacled or lived in temporary tents in the wilderness for forty years.

The Spiritual Significance of the Feasts

All the feasts were related to the spiritual life of the people. Passover served as a reminder that there is no atonement for sin apart from the shedding of blood. Unleavened Bread was a reminder of God's call on their lives to be a people set apart to holiness and leaven (yeast) was a symbol of sin. They were to be unleavened that is, holy and sinless before the nations as a witness of God. The feast of First Fruits was a call to consider their priorities, to make certain they were putting God first in their lives. Harvest or Pentecost was a reminder that God is the source of all blessings, even produce.

The solemn assembly day of Trumpets was a reminder of the need for constant, ongoing repentance. The Day of Atonement was also a solemn assembly and a day of rest and introspection, a day to contemplate personal sin. It was a reminder of God's promise to send a Messiah whose blood would cover the failure to meet the demands of the Law with the mercy of God. In sharp contrast to Trumpets and Atonement, Tabernacles was a joyous celebration of God's faithfulness, even when the Children of Israel were unfaithful, and His dwelling with mankind once again someday. Hanukkah was a celebration of the oil lasting eight days to keep the menorah lit in the newly re-captured Temple in Jerusalem while more oil was prepared – something that should not have happened since there was insufficient oil to last that long.

The Prophetic Significance of the Feasts

What the Jewish people did not seem to realize is that all of the feasts were also symbolic types. In other words, they were prophetic in nature, each one pointing in a unique way to some aspect of the life and work of the promised Messiah:

1) Passover (Pesach) - The Messiah as our Passover Lamb shed His blood for our sins. Jesus was crucified on the day of preparation

43

for the Passover at 9:00 A.M., and died at the same time, 3:00 in the afternoon, the time of the evening sacrifice at the Temple that the lambs were being slaughtered for the Passover meal that evening.

2) Unleavened Bread - The Messiah's sinless life, like bread without yeast, which is the biblical symbol for sin, made Him the perfect sacrifice for our sins. Jesus' body was in the grave during the first days of this feast, like a kernel of wheat planted and waiting to burst forth as the Bread of Life.

3) First Fruits - Messiah's resurrection is the first fruits of the righteous. Jesus was resurrected on this very day, a Sunday, which is one of the reasons that Paul refers to him in I Corinthians 15:20 as the "first fruits from the dead." Jesus' Resurrection was the First Phase of Three Phases of the Resurrection of the Righteous. The Second Phase is the Rapture, and the Third Phase is the Resurrection of the Old Testament Saints along with the Tribulation Saints.

4) Harvest or Pentecost (Shavuot) – The Festival of Weeks (Shavuot) is a metaphor for the great harvest of souls, both Jew and Gentile, that would come into the kingdom of God before and during the Church Age. The Law on Mount Sinai is celebrated by the Jews as being given to Moses on Pentecost. The Church was actually established on this day also when the Messiah poured out the Holy Spirit and 3,000 souls responded to Peter's first proclamation of the Gospel. Pentecost (which means fifty) occurs 50 days after Passover when the High Priest held two leavened loaves aloft as a wave offering to the Lord symbolizing the Jews and Gentiles who came to faith.

The long interval of three months between Harvest and Trumpets pointed to the current Church Age, a period of time that was kept as a mystery to the Hebrew prophets in Old Testament times. The actual time of Pentecost 50 days after Passover is mysterious because of the determining of the actual start of the new moon. So, the festival is called the "festival without a date." The Jews observe Pentecost over two days because of this mystery.

Jesus' Resurrection marked His appearing to many people proving His coming back to life was, indeed, true. He remained on the Earth after Resurrection for forty days (Acts 1:3) meaning He arose about 10 or so days before Pentecost. Some believe that since the Church began on Pentecost with the arrival of the Holy Spirit, it just might end on Pentecost as well with the Rapture. But, what if the Rapture happens somewhere around 10 days BEFORE Pentecost corresponding to Jesus ascension into Heaven some 10 days prior to Pentecost? We would still not know EXACTLY when the Rapture would occur since the exact date of Pentecost is a mystery each and every year, and we are not setting dates, just posing a small interval when the Rapture could happen. Interesting thought.

That leaves the three Fall feasts which are yet to be fulfilled in the life and work of the Messiah. Because Jesus literally fulfilled the first four feasts and did so on the actual feast days, it is safe to assume that the last three will also be fulfilled and that their fulfillment will occur on the actual feast days. We cannot be certain how they will be fulfilled, but most likely they will have the following prophetic implications:

5) Trumpets (Rosh Hashana) – Could be the Rapture when the Messiah will appear in the heavens as a Bridegroom coming for His bride, the Church (that is, if the Rapture does not happen around Pentecost!). The Rapture is always associated in Scripture with the blowing of a loud trumpet which could point to the Rapture or to the calling of the Jews to their Messiah coming better known as the Second Coming (1 Thessalonians 4:13-18 and 1 Corinthians 15:52)

6) Atonement (Yom Kippur) -The Second Coming of Jesus when He will return to Earth. That will be the Day of Atonement for the Jewish remnant when they "look upon Him whom they have pierced," repent of their sins, and receive Him as their Messiah (Zechariah 12:10 and Romans 11:1-6, 25-36).

7) Tabernacles (Sukkot) - Refers to the Lord's promise that He will once again tabernacle, be present and live, with His people when He returns to reign over all the world from Jerusalem for a thousand years (Micah 4:1-7) called the Millennial Kingdom.

8) Hanukkah – The Feast of Dedication. Hanukkah (sometimes transliterated Chanukah) is a Jewish holiday celebrated for eight days and nights. It starts on the 25th of the Jewish month of Kislev, which coincides with late November-late December on

the secular calendar. In Hebrew, the word "Hanukkah" means "dedication." The name reminds us that this holiday commemorates the re-dedication of the holy Temple in Jerusalem following the Jewish victory over the Syrian-Greeks in 165 B.C. Could this be fulfilled when Christ's Millennial Temple is dedicated perhaps at the end of the Great Tribulation leading into the Millennium?

So, could the Feasts of Israel be a clue as to when Jesus fulfills what is coming in Bible Prophecy? If past fulfillment centered on the first four of the seven, eight including Hanukkah, prophetic fulfillment which happened exactly ON the feast days, it could be that the Rapture, the Second Coming, the Millennial Kingdom, and the dedication of the Millennial Temple all come to pass on future feast days. What year? Signs point to a year very, very soon.

Restoration of Israel

The last subject to cover is the most significant happening in the history of man. Why do I say this? Because the restoration of the Jewish nation on May 14, 1948, marks the starting date for the End Times! The idea of a "latter day" restoration of Israel is integral to the dispensational premillennial view of the Lord's Second Coming. To better understand the issues involved, let's first take a look at several arguments for a latter-day restoration of Israel:

From the Old Testament

God has promised to restore His people to Israel (Jeremiah 29:14) from all over the world to wherever the Jews had dispersed, not just Assyria and Babylon. Ezekiel Chapter 37 prophecies the reunification of Israel and Judah in the dry bones prophecy which certainly has not ever happened in all of history since the divided kingdom in 931 B.C. Israel is back in their land today and growing steadily ever since the Nation of Israel was once again established on May 14, 1948! The return prophecies made to those from Israel who had been restored are found in Zechariah 8:1-8.

People who had come back from Babylonian captivity to Jerusalem in 536 B.C. did not have peace and safety, so Zechariah must be referring to later events which translates to events occurring today. The expression "in the latter days" found in Jeremiah 30:24 confirms that there will be a final return of the Jews to Israel just before the Second Coming. There is the promise of physical and economic restoration in Isaiah 35:1; and 61:4, not just political and religious restoration, but also the land itself along with ancient ruins.

Amos 9:14,15 says that along with promise of victories over their enemies, the Jews will no longer be pulled up from the land suggesting victory over any who would try including their close-in enemies, which during the Psalm 83 war God will eliminate, and the Ezekiel 38 and 39 war in which God will eliminate Israel's far-out enemies including Russia and all of the Islamic nations that are Israel's enemies. This should be very good news for the Jews in Israel today with all of the dangers that are presenting themselves.

From the New Testament

The return of Jerusalem to the custody of the Jews found in Luke 21:24 starts with the city to be trodden down by the Gentiles until the time of the Gentiles are fulfilled. This "trodden down of the Gentiles" ended on May 14, 1948, with the Jewish nation coming to life after over 1800 years since 135 A.D. and Hadrian's destruction of Jerusalem and Israel and re-naming the country Syria Palaestina and Jerusalem Aelia Capitolina. (Note: The land of Israel was NEVER Palestine when Jesus walked the Earth!) The re-establishment of the Hebrew language has also happened after being dormant for decades. Then, in 1967, the Jews regained complete control of Jerusalem indicating the fulfillment of End Times prophecy.

Something very interesting (prophecyinthenews.com) is also seen in the time differential between when Israel ceased to be an independent and sovereign nation, then became one again. When Nebuchadnezzar destroyed the Temple in 586 B.C., he ended Israel's existence and took the last of the exiles of Israel (actually Judah) to Babylon for their 70 years of captivity prophesied in Jeremiah 29:10 which started in 606 B.C. with the first captives taken to Babylon which included Daniel and Hananiah, Mishael, and Azariah. Then, when the Medo-Persian Empire took control from the Babylonians, Cyrus, the new king, allowed the Jews to return to Jerusalem in 536 B.C. but did not give them back their sovereignty! The Jews got back their sovereignty as a nation on May 14, 1948! So, how many years from Nebuchadnezzar's ending Israel's sovereignty until they got it back? From 586 B.C. to 1948 A.D. is 2,534 years. Allowing for some error to be present because 586 B.C. was so long ago and ancient history is, well, ancient, we can say the time is approximately 2,520 years. Why is this number significant? Israel had to suffer at least 2,520 years before their status as a sovereign nation was restored. No other nation in world history has ever been restored after having been totally destroyed as Israel was. Then to be brought back to life after at least 2,520 years is truly a miracle of God! But here is the amazing thing. Israel must suffer for another period of time that relates to the number 2,520. How long is the Time of Jacob's Trouble otherwise known as the Tribulation? It's seven years, a time, times and half a time twice according to the Word of God, two periods of 3 ½ years, 42 months twice, a total of 84 months, or 2,520 days! The Jews must suffer the exact number of days corresponding to the number of years that they were not a sovereign nation! 2,520 years and 2,520 days! Incredible! Is God remarkable, amazing, and wonderfully consistent, worthy of glorious praise? Amen!

The Apostles came to Jesus and asked Him about the end of the world, and how would people living then know it was happening. Matthew 24: 2-6 says, "And as he sat upon the mount of Olives, the disciples came unto him privately, saying, Tell us, when shall these things be? and what shall be the sign of thy coming, and of the end of the world? And Jesus answered and said unto them, Take heed that no man deceive you. For many shall come in my name, saying, I am Christ; and shall deceive many. And ye shall hear of wars and rumors of wars: see that ye be not troubled: for all these things must come to pass, but the end is not yet."

So, Jesus begins to tell them about how things will gradually heat up and increase until we reach the time that we call the Last Days. The Book of Matthew continues, giving more and more details and time clues until we reach the "big clue", the biggest one of them all. Stating in Matthew 24:32, Jesus says, "Now learn a parable of the fig tree; When his branch is yet tender, and putteth forth leaves, ye know that summer is nigh: So likewise ye, when ye shall see all these things, know that it is near, even at the doors. Verily I say unto you, this generation shall not pass, till all these things be fulfilled."

He tells them that the generation of people that will be alive on the Earth when the Last Days come about, would witness what He called the "fig tree" blooming, and putting forth it's leaves. And He equated that with the fulfillment of His End Time prophecy. Throughout recorded history, some biblical history as well, nations have always been typified by "types and figures" to describe them. Russia is the "bear", America is the "eagle", England the "lion", and Israel the "fig tree". Yes, Israel is referred to as a fig tree in the Bible. In the Old Testament, figs were identified with the nation of Israel by the prophets. Hosea wrote: 'I found Israel like grapes in the wilderness, I saw your fathers as the first ripe in the fig tree in her first time" (Hosea 9:10). Jeremiah received the vision of two baskets of figs, which represented Israel: "Like these good figs, so will I acknowledge them that are carried away captive of Judah" (Jer. 24:5).

So, Jesus was saying that when you see ISRAEL re-blooming, that generation would be the one that would be on the Earth and living when the Last Days would occur. Israel's Temple was destroyed in 70 A.D., the entire nation disappeared in 135 A.D., and Israel bloomed again on May 14, 1948,

1,813 years after their destruction at the hands of the Romans. The generation that witnessed the re-birth of Israel, the WWII generation, still have not passed away. They are still alive and with us today, and we are the people that Jesus said would be alive on the Earth when the Last Days would happen. That time is right now. The time of the "last days" that Jesus referred to, is not "in the future" and it's not "coming soon". It is here right now. Ever since 1948 all the major players have been taking the stage and playing the parts that God said they would.

Also, very significant is that the restoration of Israel into being a sovereign nation again happened 70 years ago, the very definition of a generation. Psalm 90:10 says, "The days of our years are threescore years and ten; and if by reason of strength they be fourscore years, yet is their strength labor and sorrow; for it is soon cut off and we fly away." Couple this generation definition with Matthew 24:30-36, "And then shall appear the sign of the Son of Man in Heaven: and then shall all the tribes of the Earth mourn, and they shall see the Son of man coming in the clouds of Heaven with power and great glory. Now learn a parable of the fig tree; When his branch is yet tender, and putteth forth leaves, ye know that summer is nigh: So likewise ye, when ye shall see all these things, know that it is near, even at the doors. Verily I say unto you, this generation shall not pass, till all these things be fulfilled. Heaven and Earth shall pass away, but my words shall not pass away. But of that day and hour knoweth no man, no, not the angels of Heaven, but my Father only." Combine these prophecies and the inescapable conclusion from them and you determine that our generation, the one alive today seeing all of the signs of the End Times, will be the terminal generation, the generation that gets raptured, the generation who knows that Jesus is about to appear in Glory on the Earth!

The rebuilding of the temple will occur so that the Antichrist can enter it and demand worship of himself (2 Thessalonians 2:4). I believe that because of Matthew 24:1,2, "And Jesus went out, and departed from the temple: and his disciples came to him for to shew him the buildings of the temple. And Jesus said unto them, See ye not all these things? verily I say unto you, There shall not be left here one stone upon another, that shall not be thrown down", that the location of the new Tribulation Temple is NOT where the Dome of the Rock stands.

Daily sacrifices numbering in the hundreds were performed in the Temple in Jesus' day. Massive amounts of water were needed to take care of all of the sacrificing, and the Gihon Spring is located down the hill from the "Temple Mount" of today, placing the location of Herod's Temple to the SOUTH of the Dome of the Rock and even South of the El Aksa Mosque. Josephus, first century writer, detailed that the Antonian Fortress which held a legion of Roman troops (6,000) "looked down" onto the Temple in Jerusalem with a large distance between them. That places the Temple somewhere South of the southern wall of the so-called Temple Mount of today in the ancient City of David.

What this also does is dispel the belief that the Wailing Wall that the Jews have prayed at for so long is in reality just the Western wall of the old Antonian Fortress, not the Temple. Remember, Jesus said "not ONE stone would be left upon another" (Matthew 24:2). When Titus came to destroy the Temple in 70 A.D., he had given orders NOT to destroy it! But, one of his soldiers set fire to the temple (its roof was wood). The fire melted all of the gold plating on the walls and ceiling, and the gold ran down between the stones. The Romans tore the Temple down to the last stone getting to the gold thus fulfilling Jesus' prediction. All of this means that as soon as the Jews realize that the Temple was not on top of Mount Moriah where the Dome of the Rock is located today, they can begin building their Temple to the South NOW, TODAY! What this analysis shows, if true and it sure seems as if it is, is that the Jewish Temple could go under construction any day, or, as I believe, the setting up of a tabernacle, a tent like Moses did, will be done even more quickly. If we are that close to the Tribulation Temple, how close is the Rapture?

Conclusion

We have covered many foundational concepts that are absolutely necessary to completely understand Bible Prophecy and to be able to discern how prophecy relates to our lives in the here and now. We covered the order of Creation as stated in the Bible versus evolution's lame explanations for our world today. We looked at the real age of the Earth at 6,000 years based on the Bible and scientific facts and how the evolutionists hope we will continue to believe millions of years have passed since the so-called Big Bang.

The definition and relevance of dispensations, which is a biblical word, was covered so that we can understand that our Gracious Lord has been very patient with us as a human race allowing us to try to prove that we can be good and earn salvation on our own. The next subject was the Feasts of Israel and how they are a picture of God's salvation of man starting with Jesus' sacrifice on Passover all the way to His Second Coming and Millennial Kingdom as the Feast of Tabernacles represents.

The last and really the most important subject we covered is the amazing restoration of Israel to nation status after being completely non-existent for over 1800 years and not even a sovereign nation for over 2,520 years! This restoration is the very start of the End Times, the start of the birth pangs, the beginning of the culmination of man's existence on the Earth prior to Christ's Millennial Kingdom. Add to that the passing of 70 years since the May 14, 1948, date, the knowledge that 70 years is a generation, and the statement of Jesus Himself that the generation that sees the signs of the times is THE terminal generation, and you should conclude that we are about to be raptured off this planet to be with our Lord and Savior Jesus Christ!

CHAPTER THREE

OLD TESTAMENT REFERENCES TO THE END TIMES

Preliminary Discussion

Why do Christians become anxious about what the future holds when God knows exactly what each person's future holds to the finest detail? What do the Scriptures tell us to do? Psalm 27:14 says, "Wait on the Lord; be of good courage, and He shall strengthen your heart; wait, I say, on the Lord!" Personal prayer to be in the Will of God in our individual lives should, along with daily reading of God's Word, give us confidence of our immediate and distant future. Add to that God's willingness to reveal what He has planned for His Church in all of our futures through Bible prophecy, and anxiety or fear should decrease dramatically.

Of course, there are some who claim that Bible Prophecy is too hard to understand or demand proof of the validity of Scripture in order for them to understand it. To these folks there are also very easy answers. First of all, everyone who is a born-again believer in Jesus Christ as Savior and Lord has the Holy Spirit guiding, directing, advising, interceding, and testifying to them every second of every day. Any claim to not understanding any part of the Bible results from the lack of trying, the unfortunate disregard of giving God time in order to read His Word, or evidence of lack of the Spirit because of unbelief or of present unforgiven sin. Otherwise, God's Holy Spirit will lead you to read, study, and search for meaning until success is achieved. "Seek and you will find…"

To the question of wanting proof, let me quote from A.W. Tozer, "What God declares, the believing heart confesses, without the need of further proof." But we can take that rather matter-of-fact statement further. Scripture compared with other scriptures reveals true meaning because God repeats what He wants us to know in both Testaments and multiple times on top of that. Searching will reveal truth and spiritual confidence which is much better than "proof"! And, there will always be what Peter called "scoffers". Scoffing at the Word of God comes from unbelief, personal or private interpretation, or lack of understanding because of willful neglect of Bible study. Number one, we as humble servants of God Almighty must NEVER sit in judgment on the Word of God! Our human reason and logic actually condemn us and judge us because when the Truth is discovered, we will always find that our judgment is flawed and in error, where God's Word is always true. 2 Peter 3:3 and 4 says, "Knowing this first, that there shall come in the last days scoffers, walking after their own lusts, and saying, 'Where is the promise of His coming? For since the fathers fell asleep, all things continue as they were from the beginning of Creation.'" Peter goes on to say that those he heard that statement from did not even recognize the Flood of Noah which was the Judgment of God on a very sinful world. There are many such people today, both believers and unbelievers, who deny or question what God has told us.

The current popular phrase, "See Something; Say Something!", certainly applies to us as true Bible-believing Christians today. When we see error, when we witness unbelief, when we hear scoffers, when we hear misunderstanding of God's Word, are we prepared to defend His Word? When we hear false claims or blatant misrepresentation of the prophecies in God's Word, are we ready to give a proper interpretation based upon Scripture itself? Do we feel confident to answer questions from inquiring minds of unbelievers about the Bible? Can we feel compassion for hearts that are searching for a Savior and then provide verses in the Bible, books appropriate to their hungry souls? How do we get this confidence in God's Word? How do we understand Bible Prophecy? The surprising answer (to some) is just get into His Word! Everyone can know these things. What it takes is dedication, commitment, and the love of God's Word enough to read it daily, study it constantly, and talk about it and apply it to every aspect of our lives! To use a metaphor from a noted Bible teacher and author, Gregory Koukl, Bible study and Bible Prophecy is like a puzzle with many pieces. You cannot put it all together in quick fashion, it takes time and study to fit the proper pieces together. And, if we have some puzzle pieces mixed in that do not belong to the real puzzle, then we will be confused until we eliminate the rogue pieces. How do you identify the rogue pieces? It takes effort and dedication and hard work through reading, studying, meditating, and applying what God has deemed to let us know straight from the Mind of Christ!

One last thing before we move into the main topic. Jesus identified two levels of His Church in His self-sacrificing love discussion with Peter after the Resurrection. He told Peter to feed His lambs, then He told Peter to feed His sheep two times. Feeding lambs involves easy-to-digest milk and not much more. Feeding sheep, on the other hand, requires solid food to maintain health. It is the same for Christians. New, baby Christians need the milk of the Word or just the major doctrines with little else. Lambs need more shepherding and gathering and guarding by a shepherd. Prophecy can be a little hard for immature Christians to just jump into the deep end. More mature Christians, however, the sheep, must be fed the full Word of God to be spiritually nourished, to be on the growth pathway to increasing sanctification, becoming more and more like Christ. For this reason, Bible Prophecy should greatly appeal to mature Christians and they should desire to know Bible prophecy in its fullest manifestation. True spiritual joy comes from knowledge of God's Word which increases day by day, and prophecy (eschatology) details God's Plan for our future still here on the Earth and beyond after the Rapture, then into the Millennium, then on to the New Heaven and the New Earth. That is the reason for this book.

Introduction

So far, we have covered what we need to understand Bible Prophecy and foundational concepts to understand Bible Prophecy in the first two chapters in this book titled, "Are These Days the End Times?" In this third chapter, we will show many of the Old Testament references to the End Times. Yes, there are many prophecies about the very times we live in today located in the Old Testament. Kind of makes the Old Testament take on a new significance, doesn't it? First, however, we must examine our true beliefs and the basis for those beliefs.

Is there any way of knowing who the true God is? Is there any way of knowing whether the Bible is the Word of God? Are we simply to accept these things 'by faith' without any evidence? The answers to these and many other such questions are found in God's Word, if you read it. Let's talk about some of the basics.

For God to be God, He is outside of His Creation, He knows all things, He is Sovereign over everything. There are no other gods, no one to challenge Him, no competition. The God of the Bible says this about Himself. Isaiah 46:9-10 says, "I am God, and there is no other; I am God, and there is none like me. I make known the end from the beginning, from ancient times, what is still to come. I say: My purpose will stand, and I will do all that I please."

So not only does the God of the Bible know all things, but He has chosen to reveal our future near and far away in a very special way, through the Bible! In an interesting perspective on God's totally unneeded defense of His Sovereignty, God challenges any other gods. Isaiah 41:21-23 says, "'Present your case,' says the LORD. "Set forth your arguments," says Jacob's King. "Bring in your idols to tell us what is going to happen. Tell us what the former things were, so that we may consider them and know their final outcome. Or declare to us the things to come, tell us what the future holds, so we may know that you are gods.'"

Yahweh, the God of the Bible, issues this challenge easily simply because He knows that there are no other gods of any kind. He alone is God, and therefore, He is the only One who accurately and consistently declares the end from the beginning! In view of the knowledge that God is the only God, it is no surprise that there are no detailed prophecies in the Koran (Islam's holy book), the Hindu Vedas, the book of Mormon, or the sayings of Buddha for the simple reason that these works are works of men and not God. And, prophecy is only known to God because He alone can see the future as clearly as we see the present or remember the past. So, when we read of things to come, we are getting a glimpse of what God already knows to be true, and we can rely on it to happen with no error and no discrepancies.

By far, the greatest number of prophecies in the Bible concern the nation of Israel. In fact, many have said that if you want to know what time it is on God's clock, then look at the nation of Israel, for she shall be the center of attention in the fulfillment of Bible prophecies in these last days. Today we live in an age when the entire focus of the world is upon a tiny strip of land in the Middle East called Israel. We also see the way the world treats Israel, the anti-Semitism that exists today, and the threats and actions of war and conflict that could mean death and destruction to millions.

Old Testament End Times Prophecies

The Bible, when written, was close to a third prophecy. Many of those prophecies dealt with Israel, many with Jesus' First Advent or First Coming, and many with Jesus' Second Advent or Second Coming. The prophecies of Jesus' First Coming have already come to pass with many of the over 300 prophecies fulfilled exactly. The probability of only 8 of those 300 coming true, fulfilled in just one God/man, Jesus Christ, has been calculated to be one chance in ten to the seventeenth power or equivalent to covering Texas with two feet of silver dollars, putting a red "X" on just one of them, mixing them all up and re-spreading them across the entire state, and having one person pick just one silver dollar and it being the one with the red "X". In other words, impossible. And, that is only 8 out of 300 proving without question that Jesus is the Christ, the Son of the Living God! Therefore, Jesus fulfilled all prophecies concerning the First Coming of God to the Earth in the form of a sinless man so that He could die for the sins of everyone and defeat death by resurrecting from the dead. This also should show everyone that the prophecies concerning His Second Coming will also be fulfilled, each and every one.

Many of the prophecies concerning Israel are End Times prophecies. In fact, the determination of the actual start of the End Times relies on Israel being restored to their land which happened 70 years ago in 1948. More on that later. The prophecies concerning the Second Coming of Jesus Christ as King of kings and Lord of lords are on the doorstep of being fulfilled as we will see as we progress.

Many of the Old Testament prophecies have a partial fulfillment in the past with a complete fulfillment in the End Times, our immediate future. These types of prophecies are sometimes called "dual mountain" prophecies where we look to the future initially and cannot see the second large mountain because it is obscured by the closer, smaller mountain. This is exemplified by, as one of many occurrences, Isaiah 30:19 says, "For the people shall dwell in Zion at Jerusalem; You shall weep no more." This refers to the Jews being exiled from Jerusalem in their near future by the Babylonians (606, 597, and 586 B.C.) and then returning 70 years later in 536 B.C. at the decree of Cyrus, king of the Medo-Persian Empire. But this also refers to the future, today, when the Jews "returned" to their land, Israel, in 1948 and/or captured their capitol city, Jerusalem, in 1967 as a sign of the End Times being about to take place. Any of these dual prophecies can have spiritual applications at any time for all believers before their complete fulfillment at the end of the age.

We must begin the Old Testament prophecies of the End Times with Genesis 3:15, or the "Protoevangelium" which means literally "first gospel". "And I will put enmity between you and the woman, and between your seed and her Seed; He shall bruise your head, and you shall bruise His heel." The capitalization is not by accident. Seed, He, and His all refer to Jesus Christ, Jesus being the Seed of Mary since God is Jesus' Father, and no woman has "seed" – that comes from man. Therefore, Jesus was born of a virgin who knew no man prior to Jesus' birth making the prophecy of the Savior "born of a virgin" (Isaiah 7:14). The reference to "you shall bruise His heel" is fulfilled when Jesus died on the cross and Satan and his fallen angels rejoiced greatly for three days. Of course, when Jesus rose from the dead on the third day, the evidence that Satan only "bruised" Jesus was evident. "He shall bruise your head" is a mortal wound. The power of Satan is crushed by the cross of Christ. At the cross, Jesus dealt Satan a fatal blow. There, He paid for the penalty of sin fully.

There are many Old Testament prophecies that relate to the End Times. We will not be able to cover them all in this venue, but we will cover a significant number of them. We start with the Pentateuch, Moses' first five books in the Old Testament.

Specific Old Testament End Times Prophecies

Leviticus 26:14-45 contains the promises of blessings on Israel's obedience and warnings for her disobedience. A seven-fold judgment on

Israel's rebellion is promised by God in order to "break the pride of her power". This judgment will come to fullness in the End Times, the Tribulation, so that Israel will confess her iniquity and a remnant will be saved because God never goes back on a promise that lasts forever, in this case the Abrahamic Covenant (Genesis 12:1-3, 13:15). The Jews will have their land in its entirety in the Millennium ruled by Jesus, their Messiah, in person.

Numbers 23 and 24 contain four prophetic oracles from Balaam to Balak, the king of Moab. Some of these prophecies were fulfilled by King David, but the fullness of them does not occur until the end of the Tribulation when Jesus returns as "A star shall come out of Jacob; a scepter shall rise out of Israel" to crush Israel's enemies (Who the Jews were looking for at Christ's First Coming).

Deuteronomy 32 contains the Song of Moses sung after the Israelites crossed the Red Sea. A song modeled after the Song of Moses will be sung, according to Revelation 15:2-4, in Heaven by martyred saints just prior to the beginning of the terrible bowl judgments of God that occur very near the end of the Tribulation. Israel will be delivered from ALL her enemies and Israel will join in with Gentiles in rejoicing. "For all nations shall come and worship before you, for Your judgments have been manifested" (Revelation 15:4).

There are a number of times that Israel's destiny is described in the Psalms with the eventual result of Israel being reigned over by Jesus in the Millennial Kingdom.

In Psalm 2, David prophesies the rage of the nations against Jesus, God's Anointed, which will fully manifest in the battle of Armageddon. Psalm 14 prophesies about the fullness of sin and oppression of God's people that occurs in a great falling away. Psalm 24 speaks of King Jesus making triumphal entry into Jerusalem after defeating the kings of the Earth. Psalm 46 tells us of the ultimate victory over all nations and the forever reign of God.

Psalm 83 depicts the victory of Israel over her close-in enemies (the modern areas of Jordan, Syria, Lebanon, Gaza, and down south toward Egypt) which will occur, probably, before the start of the Tribulation but after the Rapture – an "In-Between" war. This war happens to set up the larger war of Ezekiel 38 and 39 which we will discuss a little later. Prophecy tells us that the Antichrist comes to power over the entire Earth. The fifth empire of Nebuchadnezzar's huge statue was represented as the feet of mixed iron and clay signifying fragile strength. These feet are attached to the legs of the fourth kingdom or the Roman Empire, so this fifth kingdom is called by the unbiblical name, the Revived Roman Empire. Today, it seems that the European Union will someday rise in power and assume that fifth empire of Daniel. But, until that day happens, and the Antichrist becomes world leader of a globalist utopia, Islam stands in the way. Psalm 83 shows us how God gives peace to Israel for a short time by removing the close-in Islamic threat, and how God reveals to the nations that He is in control. Unfortunately, not everyone will believe it quite yet. Much more will come to convince even the skeptical!

Today, no one man regardless of his power could overcome the two billion people who call themselves Muslim. The radical Muslims would fight to the death, and, considering the over 16-year war in Afghanistan we have been fighting, it would take an Antichrist quite some time to rid the world of radical Muslims. The majority of Muslims are not radical, but they still believe in the supremacy of their religion and would not give their allegiance to a Gentile leader like the Antichrist. Something must happen and happen quickly to remove the Muslims from the world stage. The first step of that removal is the Psalm 83 war in which Israel and Israel's God defeat the afore-mentioned close-in enemies of Israel and they are removed as any kind of threat. It is then that Israel can say that they will "dwell safely" (Ezekiel 38). This war probably happens immediately after the Rapture.

Psalm 96 shows that Jesus at His Second Coming is coming as Judge to judge the whole Earth. Psalm 110 describes Jesus' reign in the Millennium and His End Time judgment of the nations. There are others in the Psalms, so, when you read them, be aware of predictions of Israel's future!

The Bible divides the prophets into two categories: major prophets and minor prophets. The only reason for this is that the major prophets (Isaiah, Jeremiah, Ezekiel, and Daniel) wrote books of greater length than the minor prophets (Hosea, Joel, Amos, Obadiah, Jonah, Micah, Nahum, Habakkuk, Zephaniah, Haggai, Zechariah, Malachi). There is nothing "minor" about what these prophets had to tell us. In fact, some of the "minor" prophets speak stronger words than the "major" ones do (Zechariah 14:12, "…their flesh shall dissolve while they stand on their feet, their eyes shall dissolve in their sockets, and their tongues shall dissolve in their mouths.")

Each of the Major prophets has a lot to say concerning the End Times. Isaiah uses the "dual Mountain" prophetic method often to show an early fulfillment of prophecy to the Jews (Isaiah wrote in about 730 B.C. over a hundred years before the Jews were sent into exile), the exile of the Jews to Babylon (606, 597, 586 B.C.), and their release 70 years later to go back to Jerusalem (536 B.C.), and a late fulfillment of the Jews going through the

Tribulation ending in the Millennial Kingdom. Here are a few of Isaiah's prophecies concerning the End Times:

Isaiah 2 is all about the Millennial reign of Jesus. Isaiah 4 calls Jesus "The Branch", which Jeremiah uses in Jeremiah 23, Who rules over the Millennial Kingdom. Isaiah 11 tells of the peace in the Millennium when ruled over by the Branch or Jesus. This is also where "the wolf shall dwell with the lamb…and a little child will lead them". The Lord will gather His people (The Jews) from the four corners of the Earth and all the nations will be subdued before them. Isaiah 13 covers the fall of Babylon which fell to the Medo-Persians in the 6th century B.C., but also refers to the Day of the Lord when the Lord will bring His wrath upon the Earth during the Tribulation. Isaiah 14 is the ultimate defeat of Satan and the Antichrist again in the Day of the Lord.

Isaiah 17 is a prophecy clearly relevant to today. The chapter is generally a prophecy against Syria and their capitol city Damascus. But, verse 1 says, "The burden of Damascus. Behold, Damascus will cease from being a city, and it will become a ruinous heap". It goes on to say that the remnant of Syria will be the glory of Israel says the Lord of Hosts. These prophecies are not fulfilled today, but we all see how close they are to becoming reality. Assad of Syria is gassing his own people and Israel as well as the United States are certainly not going to let that stand. Plus, Assad is very close to Israel with Damascus being only a hundred miles from Jerusalem. Threats from Assad towards Israel as well as Assad's barbaric actions using chemical weapons could very well lead to the very destruction of Damascus and, possibly, Israel gaining at least some of the land of Syria. The total fulfillment of this prophecy against Syria could occur in the "In-Between" time after the Rapture and before the Tribulation.

Isaiah 34 is about the Day of the Lord when He will judge the nations with the result of that judgment violently portrayed. Isaiah 40 is obviously prophetic because "all flesh" has not seen the Glory of the Lord which only happens at the Second Coming of Jesus Christ. Isaiah 44 promises that the Spirit of the Lord will be poured out on Israel and that Israel is NOT forgotten. Isaiah 60 shows God's blessings on Israel in the Millennial Kingdom as many nations bring wealth to her. Isaiah 65 promises the New Heaven and the New Earth after the Millennium created anew with great rejoicing, no crying, no more danger. Isaiah 66 is a prophecy of Israel being re-born as a nation in one day (May 14, 1948), the judgment of the nations, and the vindication of Israel.

Isaiah prophesied at the end of the Northern Kingdom of Israel, and

Jeremiah prophesied at the end of the Kingdom of Judah about a hundred years later. Jeremiah 30 tells of The Lord's restoration of both Israel and Judah to their Promised Land which happened beginning in 1948. But this chapter goes on to predict the time of Jacob's Trouble (30:7), the Tribulation, which will result in God's punishment on Israel, but not total destruction (30:11). The final condition of God's people is their complete restoration in the Millennial Kingdom. Jeremiah 33 describes the fullness of God's promises to Israel and Judah, honored above ALL nations, in the Millennium. Jeremiah 50 and 51 first foretells the destruction of ancient Babylon at the hands of the Medo-Persians in 539 B.C. But, the future judgment of Babylon described in Jeremiah 51 is also the future judgment of the kingdom of the Antichrist from Revelation is found in Revelation 18.

We finish with Ezekiel, a Levite, who was captured in 597 B.C. by Babylon and Nebuchadnezzar as a young man. He joined Daniel, Hananiah, Azariah, and Mishael as exiles in Babylon and probably lived out his life in Babylon. Ezekiel prophesies about Israel in the latter days, some of which we are seeing come to pass in our lifetimes, and some that are yet to happen although their fulfillment is imminent. Ezekiel 11 prophecies that God will restore all of Israel to their God-given land, put a new spirit in them, and cause them to be obedient to the Lord. This another of the "dual mountain" prophecies since this one was fulfilled after the Babylonian captivity in 536 B.C. but also in 1948, and fully in the Millennium.

Ezekiel 37 is the famous "Dry Bones" chapter where the valley of the dry bones is suddenly infused with life by God, the Jews are raised from obscurity as a nation once again in 1948, and Israel will be fully restored and blessed at the Second Coming of Jesus Who reigns from Jerusalem for a thousand years.

Probably two of the most exciting chapters pertaining to the End Times are Ezekiel 38 and 39. What is described here is the second "In-Between" war occurring after the Rapture and before the start of the Tribulation. The first war of Psalm 83 was to remove the close-in enemies of Israel so that Israel can "dwell in peace" as a requisite for the Ezekiel 38 and 39 war. Ezekiel 38:11 speaks of Gog, the leader of Rosh or Russia says, "I will go up against a land of unwalled villages; I will go to a peaceful people, who dwell safely, all of them dwelling without walls, and having neither bars or gates – to take plunder and to take booty…". This means that the present conditions in Israel make the timing of the Ezekiel 38 and 39 war come after the Psalm 83 war.

Psalm 83 refers to a confederacy of nations that come against Israel. These nations are the biblical names of the tents of Edom and the

Ishmaelites(Central Jordan, Northwestern Arabia, and, perhaps, Palestinian tent cities), Moab and the Hagrites (Northern Jordan), Gebal (Syria), Ammon (Southern Jordan), Amalek (Eastern Egypt), Philistia (Gaza and Hamas), the inhabitants of Tyre (Sidon and Lebanon with Hezbollah backed by Iran), and Assyria (Iran and Russia controlled Iraq. The descendants of Lot settled in Northern Syria.

Psalm 83 refers to a confederacy of nations that come against Israel. These nations are the biblical names of the tents of Edom and the Ishmaelites(Central Jordan, Northwestern Arabia, and, perhaps, Palestinian tent cities), Moab and the Hagrites (Northern Jordan), Gebal (Syria), Ammon (Southern Jordan), Amalek (Eastern Egypt), Philistia (Gaza and Hamas), the inhabitants of Tyre (Sidon and Lebanon with Hezbollah backed by Iran), and Assyria (Iran and Russia controlled Iraq), and the descendants of Lot settled in northern Syria.

Why form this confederacy? Verse 4 says that "they have said, 'Come, and let us cut them off from being a nation, that the name of Israel may be remembered no more." This is a direct confession that this confederacy of the nations listed want the land that Israel has, and that Israel disappear. Sort of throws the "Two-state solution" idea into the trash, doesn't it? We are dealing with radical thinking enemies of Israel that want them all dead, not neighboring countries that want to co-exist! So, the Psalm 83 war eliminates this confederacy, and Israel then dwells safely, without walls because they are no longer needed to keep the radicals out and ceases to need bars and gates since the close-in enemies are gone! The perfect set-up for Ezekiel 38 and 39.

There is an additional prophecy in Ezekiel 28:24 referring to Sidon which is essentially Lebanon along with Tyre, both part of the Psalm 83 confederacy. This verse adds confirmation of the result of the Psalm 83 war when it says, "And there shall no longer be a pricking brier or a painful thorn for the house of Israel from among all who are around them, who despise them. Then they shall know that I am the Lord God." This is in a direct prophecy against Sidon, but this particular verse points to all of Israel's enemies being no longer a threat to them.

Ezekiel 38 then sets up the war that will eliminate five-sixths of the Muslims in the world that want Israel gone. (Ezekiel 39:2 KJV) These enemies of Israel are those that are far-off; first Russia (Leader Gog of the country Magog with Rosh (Siberia), Meshech or Moscow (Western Russia), and Tubal or Tobolsk (southern central Russia) which locates these people firmly in Russia today – they came from the sons of Japheth after the Flood of Noah in Genesis 10:2; then Persia (Iran); then Ethiopia (south of Egypt);

then Libya (northern Afrika); Gomer (Eastern Europe); and last, Togarmah (Turkey). On a map, it is easy to see that this confederation of countries contains all of the distant countries that despise Israel, most of which are Muslim countries.

Notice that Saudi Arabia is not listed. Neither is Egypt. Today, these two countries are very friendly to the United States and with Israel due to their fear and anxiety over Iran and their nuclear weapon capabilities. Saudi Arabia is in negotiation with Israel and the U.S. currently to partner and somehow resolve the Iran problem. Interestingly, and in exact parallel with what is happening in the world today, Ezekiel 38:13 refers to Saudi Arabia as well as the merchants of Tarshish, which alludes to Great Britain and the "young lions" that many say could refer to the U.S., wondering why Russia is coming to Israel. Ezekiel 38:13, "Sheba, and Dedan, and the merchants of Tarshish, with all the young lions thereof, shall say unto thee, Art thou come to take a spoil? hast thou gathered thy company to take a prey? to carry away silver and gold, to take away cattle and goods, to take a great spoil?" They seem to be perplexed as to why they would come except to "take a spoil" or to conquer Israel to take their wealth such as the natural gas fields found recently or the oil that is soon to be discovered (Deuteronomy 33:24, "And of Asher he said, Let Asher be blessed with children; let him be acceptable to his brethren, and let him dip his foot in oil.")

There is a prophecy in Jeremiah 49:34-39 concerning Elam and its scattering to the winds with great disaster still future. Elam is located on the Persian Gulf in southern Iran where their nuclear facilities are located. Perhaps the coalition of the U.S., Israel, and Saudi Arabia have something to do with that? It is not hard to imagine Israel taking out Iran's nuclear threat overnight leaving the destruction that these verses seem to describe, scattering all of Southern Iran to the distant lands. That would remove the imminent threat to Israel from the world's prominent supporter of terrorism, Iran, but probably ensure Iran's coalition with Russia later fulfilling Ezekiel chapters 38 and 39.

Back to Ezekiel 38, the pre-requisite for the invasion of Gog and his partners is Israel dwelling safely in the "latter days". (Ezekiel 38:15-17) Then, God says that His fury and wrath accompanied by a great earthquake will come down on these invaders. They will turn against each other, not to Israel. Great hailstones, fire, and brimstone will rain down on them, the result of which will glorify God and will show to the rest of the nations that God Almighty has done this. Then Ezekiel 39 tells us that the weapons of this war will be burned by Israel for seven years. This fact firmly places this war in the "In-Between" time after the Rapture and before the start of the Tribulation because in the last half of the seven-year Tribulation, the Jews will have fled Jerusalem because of Satan's possession of the Antichrist to be divinely protected by God for the last three and one-half years of the Tribulation, or the Great Tribulation, and they cannot burn those weapons of war because they are hiding from the Antichrist!

The end of Ezekiel 39 and the next nine chapters tell of the restoration of Israel to their promised land, the Millennium for them, and the building of the Millennial Temple from which Christ will reign in Jerusalem.

Conclusion

Old Testament prophecy, as we have seen, is very timely for us today since there are many prophecies that have been partially fulfilled in the past but remain to have their ultimate fulfillment in our immediate future. The plan of God to reconcile mankind to Him is coming to a close. But, as we are beginning to see, God's desire to have as many Gentiles and Jews come to know and accept His Son as their Savior and Lord will have to be dramatically demonstrated through His Wrath on unbelieving humanity. We get into the global government that the Antichrist reigns over in the next chapter. Remember that we believers alive today are not subject to God's Wrath because of our Savior and Lord Jesus Christ. We do see tribulation or stress or persecution in our lives even as Christians, but we will not see THE Tribulation because of the imminent and sudden Rapture, set to occur at any time. There is absolutely NOTHING that has to happen before the Rapture can happen, unlike so many of the coming prophecies concerning the End Times. Actually, the Rapture is the starting point of virtually ALL of the events of the End Times, even though we are experiencing what Jesus called "birth pains" or precursors and warnings of the very bad things to come to wake up God's people, the Jews, and the rest of humanity to our loving but vengeful God.

An Example of One Old Testament Prophecy That Already Happened

"About the time of the end, a body of men will be raised up who will turn their attention to the Prophecies, and insist upon their literal interpretation, in the midst of much clamor and opposition." (Sir Isaac Newton 1642-1727)

"All things are mortal, except the Jew. Other forces pass but he remains. What is the secret of his immortality?" (Mark Twain 1835-1910)

Sir Isaac Newton was a strong Christian and Mark Twain was not. But both men knew that the Jewish people were special, different, blessed, and what God said about them was unusual. There is a special term located in Leviticus 25:8-13 called the Jubilee. This was a special year of celebration to occur after seven sets of seven years that ruled Jewish Old Testament life. Crops were sown every year for six years, but the seventh year, the Sabbath Year, was to be a year of rest for the ground to allow it to regain its nutrients and assure six more years of productive growth and provision of grain. At the end of seven such seven-year cycles, there occurred a 50th year called the Jubilee Year. This Jubilee Year was when all land ownership returned to its original Jewish owner, all debts owed were forgiven, and celebration was dominant throughout the year. So, every 50 years, the economy was essentially re-set.

To illustrate deep Bible study and the amazing benefit and joy of doing it, we will examine Jeremiah's prophecy of the 70 years of exile for the Jews in Babylon and how it relates to Sabbath years and Jubilee years. In Leviticus 25, the Israelites were told to observe a Sabbatical year once every seven years to let the land rest. In addition, every 50th year they were to observe another Sabbatical year, called the Jubilee year. The Jews followed the decree of God to let the land lie fallow or resting every seventh year to observe the Sabbath year requirement.

For many years from Joshua to King Saul (about 400 years), the Jews complied but then stopped because of disobedience and disregard for God. And, because of this disobedience, the prophet Jeremiah prophesied that the Jews would go into exile for 70 years to make up for the 70 unobserved Sabbath years and Jubilee years they failed to observe from King Saul, approximately, in about 1000 B.C. until the actual exile began in 606 B.C.

Sabbatical Year – Every 7 years

Leviticus 25:2-4, "Speak to the sons of Israel and say to them, 'When you come into the land which I shall give you, then the land shall have a sabbath to the Lord. Six years you shall sow your field, and six years you shall prune your vineyard and gather in its crop, but during the seventh year the land shall have a sabbath rest, a sabbath to the Lord; you shall not sow your field nor prune your vineyard."

Jubilee Year – Every 50 Years

Leviticus 25:8-11, "You are also to count off seven sabbaths of years for yourself, seven times seven years, so that you have the time of the seven sabbaths of years, namely, forty-nine years. You shall then sound a ram's horn abroad on the tenth day of the seventh month; on the day of atonement you shall sound a horn all through your land. You shall thus consecrate the fiftieth year and proclaim a release through the land to all its inhabitants. It shall be a jubilee for you, and each of you shall return to his own property, and each of you shall return to his family. You shall have the fiftieth year as a jubilee; you shall not sow, nor reap its aftergrowth, nor gather in from its untrimmed vines."

Jeremiah was called to be a prophet from his birth (Jeremiah 1:5) and prophesied to the nation of Judah from 627 B.C. (Jeremiah 25:3) until its destruction in 586 B.C. Remember that before Christ (B.C. – before Christ), we count years counting DOWN to Christ's birth, where after the birth (A.D. – Anno Domini, which means "in the year of our Lord"), we count the years UP as we move forward through time. He lived during the dawn of one of the greatest empires of ancient history, Babylon, and during the reign of its equally infamous king Nebuchadnezzar. It was Nebuchadnezzar who, after Judah successfully held off Assyrian forces in 701 B.C., laid siege and first conquered Jerusalem in 606 B.C. where he took captives to Babylon among who were Daniel, Hananiah, Mishael, and Azariah (their Babylonian names were Shadrach, Meshach, and Abednego). Nebuchadnezzar came back to Jerusalem in 597 B.C. and again took captives among whom was Ezekiel. Then in 586 B.C., Nebuchadnezzar came back a third time and destroyed the Temple and razed Jerusalem. It was Jeremiah who prophesied and recorded these events in the book of Jeremiah written some 120 years or so before they actually happened.

There is direct evidence of Jeremiah's actual existence. Several seals have been found inscribed "Baruch, scribe of Jeremiah" (Jeremiah 36:26) and dated to the time period that Jeremiah lived. In addition, pottery fragments called the "Lachish Letters" document a prophet in Jerusalem who encouraged the submission of Jerusalem to Babylon. The prophet was almost certainly Jeremiah. His message to Judah not only included a call for repentance and warnings of future subjection to the nation of Babylon, but a message of hope in the return of Israel from captivity. Modern archeology verifies that Jeremiah existed, and even modern scholarship suggest that he had a hand in forming the Old Testament as we know it today.

Jeremiah 25:8-12, ""Therefore thus says the Lord of hosts, 'Because you have not obeyed My words, behold, I will send and take all the families of the north,' declares the Lord, 'and I will send to Nebuchadnezzar king of Babylon, My servant, and will bring them against this land and against its inhabitants and against all these nations round about; and I will utterly destroy them and make them a horror and a hissing, and an everlasting desolation. Moreover, I will take from them the voice of joy and the voice of gladness, the voice of the bridegroom and the voice of the bride, the sound of the millstones and the light of the lamp. This whole land will be a desolation and a horror, and these nations will serve the king of Babylon seventy years. Then it will be when seventy years are completed, I will punish the king of Babylon and that nation,' declares the Lord, 'for their iniquity, and the land of the Chaldeans; and I will make it an everlasting desolation."

God does not simply rain down judgment upon an individual or nation without cause. Like the prophecy of the Great Tribulation and Daniel's 70 Weeks, there is a definite pattern of sin followed by judgment. The interpretation of Jeremiah's 70 years is the 70 years desolation of the land. Earlier, in the book of Chronicles, it was found why the time length was set to 70 years.

2 Chronicles 36:20-21, "And them that had escaped from the sword carried [Nebuchadnezzar] away to Babylon; where they were servants to him and his sons until the reign of the kingdom of Persia to fulfill the word of the LORD by the mouth of Jeremiah, until the land had enjoyed her sabbaths: for as long as she lay desolate she kept sabbath, to fulfill seventy years."

The observance of this Levitical law of observing every seventh year as a Sabbatical year cycle started when the Israelites crossed over the Jordan River into Canaan. It was the fact that the Israelites did not observe the Sabbatical and Jubilee year sometime later around the time of Samuel the Prophet and King Saul, Israel's first king, that determined the length of the 70-year captivity and desolation of the land.

Like the prophet Jeremiah, Ezekiel lived during the time of the Babylonian Captivity and was both a prophet and priest. Unlike Jeremiah, who escaped captivity in Babylon, Ezekiel was taken during the second deportation in 597 BC. There he was called to prophesy in 593 BC (Ezekiel 1:1-2) and continued to prophesy for at least 22 years (Ezekiel 29:17). His life is typically divided into two periods. From the time he was called to be a prophet to the final siege of Jerusalem, Ezekiel prophesied the coming judgment of Judah and Jerusalem. After the destruction of Judah, he preached a message of hope and resurrection. His prophecies, both the message and the method, were often so extreme that he was labeled neurotic or even schizophrenic. In one of these prophecies, Ezekiel was to act out a scene that represented the coming siege of Jerusalem. He was told to engrave a picture of Jerusalem on a brick and lay it in front of him. He was then to use an iron pan as a wall between him and the city, as he "lay siege against it."

Ezekiel lay on his left side for 390 days to represent 390 years of Iniquity of the House of Israel and again on his right side for 40 days to represent 40 years of Iniquity of the House of Judah. These two periods correspond to years and add to 430 years representing the time that both Israel and Judah did not observe their Sabbath years.

Ezekiel 4:1-8, "Now you son of man, get yourself a brick, place it before you and inscribe a city on it, Jerusalem. Then lay siege against it, build a siege wall, raise up a ramp, pitch camps and place battering rams against it all around. Then get yourself an iron plate and set it up as an iron wall between you and the city and set your face toward it so that it is under siege and besiege it. This is a sign to the house of Israel. As for you, lie down on your left side and lay the iniquity of the house of Israel on it; you shall bear their iniquity for the number of days that you lie on it. For I have assigned you a number of days corresponding to the years of their iniquity, three hundred and ninety days; thus, you shall bear the iniquity of the house of Israel. When you have completed these, you shall lie down a second time, but on your right side and bear the iniquity of the house of Judah; I have assigned it to you for forty days, a day for each year. Then you shall set your face toward the siege of Jerusalem with your arm bared and prophesy against it. Now behold, I will put ropes on you so that you cannot turn from one side to the other until you have completed the days of your siege."

We have 430 years the Jews, both Israel and Judah, have not observed the Sabbath years or the Jubilee years. God does not like disobedience, and continued disobedience is almost a guarantee of God's anger. Punishment often follows willful disobedience, and this example is no exception! How many Sabbath years in 430 years? 430 divided by 7 is 61 plus a remainder of three. 61 Sabbath years missed. 61 years the land did not get its rest. How many Jubilees in 430 years? Every 49 years is a Jubilee, the 50th year, so in 430 years there are at least 8 (430 divided by 50 equals 8.6), so, if there were Jubilees on each end of the 430 years, there would be 9 Jubilees in the 430-year period. 61 missed Sabbath years plus 9 missed Jubilee years adds up to 70, the exact number of years of exile from the land the Jews had to endure in Babylon to allow the land to "catch up" and rest making up the years that the Jews were disobedient. Wow! See what some time and willingness and study can bring? So, the Jews had a 70-year obligation to go into exile in Babylon some 120 years in their immediate future so that they could satisfy God's requirement to let the land rest to cover for the many Sabbath years and Jubilee years that they neglected to observe. They would fulfill the 70 years of Babylonian exile from 606 B.C. until 536 B.C.

An Example of One Old Testament Prophecy That Has Not Happened Yet

One of the most remarkable and important prophecies in the Bible is found in Daniel 9:24-27. It is the cornerstone of Messianic prophecy because it establishes the timing of both the First and Second Advents of the Messiah. The prophecy is usually referred to as "The 70 Weeks of Years." This name derives from the opening words of most English translations: "Seventy weeks have been decreed" (Daniel 9:24).

Just as the English word "dozen" can refer to a dozen of anything, the Hebrew word "shavuim", meaning "sevens," can refer to seven of anything. Its exact meaning is dependent upon the context. In this key passage from Daniel, the context makes it clear that he is speaking of years - seventy sevens of years, which would be a total of 490 years. It is therefore appropriate to refer to the prophecy as "The 70 Weeks of Years" even though those exact words are not found in the passage itself.

Another important thing to keep in mind about the context of the passage is that it is directed to the Jewish people. The opening words of the prophecy make this clear: "Seventy weeks have been declared for your people and your holy city..." (Daniel 9:24). The focus of the prophecy is the nation of Israel and the city of Jerusalem.

The prophecy begins by stating that six things, six consequences, will be accomplished regarding the Jewish people during a period of 490 years:

1. "Finish the transgression"
2. "Make an end of sin"
3. "Make atonement for iniquity"
4. "Bring in everlasting righteousness"
5. "Seal up vision and prophecy"
6. "Anoint the most holy place"

1. The first, "finish the transgression," refers to the Jew's rejection of God. The Hebrew word translated "transgression" means rebellion, and the rebellion of the Jewish people is their rejection of Jesus as their Messiah. Jesus said He would not return until the Jewish people are willing to say, "Blessed is He who comes in the name of the Lord" (Matthew 23:37-39). The Jews will open their hearts to their Messiah before Daniel's 490-year period ends which will be during the 70th week that we call "The Tribulation". Those last seven years have to be lived out by the Jews to fulfill

all 490 years of the "70 weeks of years".

2. The period will also witness an "end of sin" for the Jews. The word translated "sin" refers to the sins of daily life - sins of dishonesty and immorality. This end of sin will occur at the time the Jews accept their Messiah and His earthly reign of righteousness begins called the Millennium.

3. An atonement for Israel's sins is the third thing that will happen during Daniel's 70 weeks of years. This atonement occurred, of course, when Jesus shed His blood on the Cross for the sins of the world. But that atonement will not actually be applied to the Jews until they appropriate it by accepting Jesus as their Messiah.

4. The 490-year period will also "bring in everlasting righteousness." This undoubtedly refers to the establishment of the Messiah's earthly reign when the Earth will be flooded with peace, righteousness and justice as the waters cover the sea.

5. The fifth achievement will be the fulfillment of all prophecy concerning the Messiah. The Apostle Peter referred to two types of Messianic prophecy - those related to "the sufferings of Christ" and those concerning "the glories to follow" (1 Peter 1:11). The suffering prophecies were all fulfilled at the Cross. The prophecies concerning "the glories to follow" are yet to be fulfilled. Just as Jesus humbled Himself in history, He is going to be glorified in history. This will occur when the Jews accept Him, and He returns to reign over the world from Mt. Zion in Jerusalem during the Millennium.

6. The final goal to be achieved at the end of the 70 weeks of years is "the anointing of the most holy." Most English translations say, "the most holy place." The Hebrew simply says, "the most holy." Commentators therefore differ as to whether this is a reference to the anointing of the Messiah as King of kings or whether it is talking about the anointing of the Millennial Temple described in Ezekiel 40-48. Either way the anointing will not take place until the Lord returns in response to the national repentance of the Jews.

Old Testament Prophecies

We last covered Old Testament prophecies about the End Times from

Genesis to Ezekiel. Now, we start with Daniel and progress through the Minor Prophets all at the end of the Old Testament. And, please realize what I am praying and hope to make you intently aware of – that the Bible, Old and New Testaments alike, are alive, inerrant, pertinent, accurate, and applicable to us now and in our future for daily life, for loving one another, for becoming more like Christ, and for learning of what God has in store for His Church, His people Israel, and for the unbelieving rest of the world today what is very soon in store for them. Now is the time to be excited and watchful because God is about to bring to a close His Plan for the salvation of man.

Daniel's Prophecies

Daniel Chapter 2 tells us of Daniel's interpretation of Nebuchadnezzar's statue, the great image (90 feet tall or as tall as a nine story building) that represents the four successive great empires starting with Babylon followed by Medo-Persia, then Greece, and then the two legs of the Roman Empire that, indeed, had two capitols – Rome (West) and Constantinople (East). The feet of the statue were composed of both iron and clay representing the fifth empire of the future Antichrist, the Revived Roman Empire as we refer to it today, that will be crushed and destroyed by the stone cut out without human hands which represents Jesus Christ's Second Coming and the establishment of His Millennial Kingdom.

Daniel Chapter 7 is Daniel's vision of four beasts representing those same four successive empires (Babylon, Medo-Persia, Greece, and Rome) plus the Antichrist's empire emerging at the end of the age or End Times. Daniel sees a heavenly courtroom where the Father as the Ancient of Days gives the Son Jesus power over all the nations and decrees judgment over Antichrist to be fulfilled at the Second Coming of Jesus Christ at the end of the Tribulation. This still future Revived Roman Empire will consist of ten worldly areas or groups of nations with a king over each, all of which will give their allegiance to the Antichrist. It is very interesting to note that the United Nations has divided the world into areas, distinct areas combining countries and borders, and allegiances to form exactly ten global communities, regional groupings, where the United States and Canada form the North American community with one king over all countries. The groups are as follows:

1. North America including the United States and Canada
2. Western Europe
3. Japan
4. Australia, South Africa, and the rest of the market-economy of the developed world.

5. Eastern Europe, including Russia
6. Latin America including Central America and South America
7. North Africa and the Middle East
8. Tropical Africa
9. South and Southeast Asia
10. China

Of course, this has not gone into effect as yet, but it does show the intent of the globalists to accomplish exactly what Daniel predicted some 2600 years ago in Babylon.

Daniel Chapter 8 describes the rise of Medo-Persia (the ram with two horns representing the Medes and the Persians) and Alexander the Great of Greece represented by a goat with a prominent single horn who is, of course, Alexander the Great. The Grecian Empire is broken up into four kingdoms at the demise of Alexander in Daniel 8:8, and these four were Alexander's generals who did not have great power as Alexander did. Daniel 8:15-26 is interpreted by Gabriel because Daniel did not understand the symbolic animals. Gabriel then describes a "Dual Mountain" prophecy that was partially fulfilled by Antiochus Epiphanes in about 167 B.C. and will be completely fulfilled by the Antichrist in the Tribulation to come.

Daniel 8:23-26 tells us of these two men, first Antiochus Epiphanes who was a Greek tyrant that captured Jerusalem and the Temple, tried to claim that Zeus was to be worshipped, but then he was defeated by the Maccabean Revolt Led by Judah Maccabee that restored the Temple and Temple worship to the Jews and also saw the feast of Dedication or Hanukkah begin to commemorate the miraculous preservation and continual burning of the oil in the Menorah for eight days until new oil could be made.

Then, in the middle of the Tribulation, Satan himself possesses the Antichrist, who is a man, and enters the third Temple in Jerusalem, proclaims himself as God, and demands worship across the planet. The Jews at this time have been warned by God to flee to a safe place, probably Petra in Edom, where God supernaturally will protect them until Jesus' Second Coming. This enrages Satan/Antichrist to the point that he knows he cannot get to the Jews, so he goes after the new Christians that have believed during the Tribulation to kill them all. Revelation 15 refers to these martyred Christians pleading with God to pour out His Wrath on the beast.

Daniel Chapter 9 contains the "70 Weeks" prophecy that so many have misunderstood for so many years. Daniel 9:24-27 speaks of 70 "weeks" ("heptads" in Greek or "shavuim" in Hebrew) which are interpreted as 70 "weeks" of years. Since the Hebrew word for "weeks" means "sevens", we see that Gabriel is telling Daniel about a period of time lasting 70 "weeks" of years, or 70 times 7 years, or 490 years. This prophecy is for the Jews and for Jerusalem and its result will bring the end of sins, reconcile the Jews to God, and to bring in everlasting righteousness.

This time of 490 years was to show the Jews and Jerusalem that God never goes back on a promise. This time, the promise was the Abrahamic Covenant which comes from Genesis 12:2, 3. The provisions of the Abrahamic covenant are outlined in their main factors in Genesis 12:2, 3, "I will make of thee a great nation, and I will bless thee, and make thy name great; and be thou a blessing: and I will bless them that bless thee, and him that curseth thee will I curse: and in thee shall all the families of the Earth be blessed." As many writers have indicated, this covenant includes seven provisions: (1) the promise of a great nation through Abraham; (2) personal blessing on Abraham; (3) the name of Abraham shall be great; (4) Abraham is to be a blessing to others; (5) blessing will rest on those blessing Abraham; (6) a curse will rest on those who curse Abraham; (7) all nations of the Earth will be blessed through Abraham.

Four things stand out in the original covenant: (1) the national promises given to Israel; (2) the personal promises given to Abraham; (3) the principle of blessing or cursing upon nations other than Israel based on their attitude toward Abraham and his seed; (4) the promise of universal blessing through Abraham, fulfilled through Christ. However, in order for the Jews to actually receive the fulfillment of this covenant, they have to experience Daniel's 70 Weeks. The 490 years start from verse 25 where it states, "that from the going forth of the command to restore and build Jerusalem until Messiah the Prince (Jesus) thee shall be seven weeks (49 years) and sixty-two weeks (434 years) for a total of 483 years. Notice the difference in 483 years and 490 years.

We have three groups of years within the 490 years: 49 years, 434 years, and 7 years. During these 490 years, six things are to take place, all listed in Daniel 9:24, "to finish the transgression, to make and end of sins, to make reconciliation for iniquity, to bring in everlasting righteousness, to seal up vision and prophecy, and to anoint the Most Holy." None of these prophecies have been fulfilled, so there must be a provision for them to come to pass in 490 years.

First, the 49 years is a direct fulfillment of Ezra 9:9. Gabriel said the prophetic clock would start at the time that a decree was issued to rebuild Jerusalem. From the date of that decree to the time of the Messiah would be 483 years. We know from history that the command to "restore and rebuild

Jerusalem" was given by Ezra in 457 B.C. We must also dispel the notion that a Jewish year was based solely on the Moon cycle of just under 30 days.

The Jewish calendar is based on three astronomical phenomena: the rotation of the Earth about its axis (a day); the revolution of the moon about the Earth (a month); and the revolution of the Earth about the sun (a year). These three phenomena are independent of each other, so there is no direct correlation between them. On average, the moon revolves around the Earth in about 29½ days. The Earth revolves around the sun in about 365¼ days, that is, about 12.4 lunar months.

The civil calendar used by most of the world has abandoned any correlation between the moon cycles and the month, arbitrarily setting the length of months to 28, 30 or 31 days. The Jewish calendar, however, coordinates all three of these astronomical phenomena. Months are either 29 or 30 days, corresponding to the 29½-day lunar cycle. Years are either 12 or 13 months, corresponding to the 12.4-month solar cycle. Therefore, a Jewish year generally corresponds to the Gregorian calendar (named for Pope Gregory XIII, who introduced it in 1582). We do not have to calculate new time periods based on 30-day months to see exactly what event took place 483 years in Israel's future, we just go forward 483 years from Ezra's declaration or 457 B.C.

The first unit of 49 years (seven "sevens") covers the time that it took to rebuild Jerusalem, "with streets and a trench, but in times of trouble" (Daniel 9:25). The decree given to Zerubbabel authorized the rebuilding of only the Temple in 536 B.C. The decree issued to Nehemiah concerned only the rebuilding of the walls of Jerusalem. Ezra's decree was more general in nature, covering a variety of subjects. But we know from Scripture that he interpreted it to mean that the Jews were authorized to launch a general rebuilding campaign that included the temple, the city, and the walls. His interpretation is stated in Ezra 9:9 — "God has not forsaken us, but has extended loving kindness to us in the sight of the kings of Persia, to give us reviving to raise up the house of our God, to restore its ruins, and to give us a wall in Judah and Jerusalem" (Ezra 9:9).

Now, using Ezra's decree as the starting point (457 B.C.), if we count forward 483 years, we will arrive at 27 A.D. (There is only one year between 1 B.C. and 1 A.D. – no "0" year) According to the translator of Josephus, the Jewish new year that began in the fall of 27 A.D. marked the beginning of the last Jubilee Year that the Jews enjoyed in the land before their worldwide dispersal by the Romans in 70 A.D. and the very year of Jesus' triumphal entry into Jerusalem riding on a donkey colt and being proclaimed as blessed

73

as Messiah by the shouts of "Hosannah" which means "I beg you to save us, please!" (the "na" at the end of a Hebrew word means "please") We factor in the known fact that Herod the Great, the Herod that commanded that all Jewish boys under the age of two be killed in Bethlehem, died in 4 B.C. From this, we can assume from Jesus riding into Jerusalem happening in 27 A.D. that Jesus was born in approximately 6 B.C. by going back from 27 A.D. 33 and a half years. Herod's death in 4 B.C. plus the 483 years from Ezra's decree both lead to a confirmation that 27 A.D. was the year of Jesus' crucifixion.

Since the prophecies of Danial's 70 Weeks prophecy have still not happened, the final seven years of the prophecy for it to add up to 490 years must still be in the future since all of God's prophecies must come true. What is that seven-year time period? The Tribulation! So what, you say? Add 2,000 years to 27 A.D. and you arrive in 2027 A.D. Subtract the seven years remaining in Daniel's 70 weeks prophecy and you arrive at 2020. With errors in calendars and God's discretionary planning, the Rapture could be any day for sure! Makes you wonder, doesn't it?

Daniel Chapter 11 is probably the most detailed chapter of prophecy in the Bible with 135 prophecies in 35 verses that have all come true exactly! Alexander the Great and the Grecian Empire is detailed, the three kings in Persia, the splitting of Alexander's kingdom into four parts, the King of the North, one of Alexander's generals Seleucus I in Syria, the King of the South, another of Alexander's generals Ptolomy I in Egypt, Antiochus Epiphanes and his capture of Jerusalem as a type of Antichrist, then the parallel prophecy of Antichrist yet to be fulfilled in the Tribulation second half.

Daniel Chapter 12 describes Israel's going through the Great Tribulation lasting three and one-half years plus the very significant statement by a prominent angel that Daniel was to seal up these prophecies until the time of the end which is now. Also, the two time periods mentioned add 30 days and 45 more days to the last half of the Tribulation (3 ½ years equals 1260 days) which could refer to the completion of the final judgments plus the sheep and goat judgment plus preparation for the Millennial Kingdom which might include the actual dedication of the Millennial Temple from which Jesus will reign for a thousand years.

Additional About The 490 Years

Daniel says all these spiritual goals will be accomplished within a special period of 490 years. When did that period begin, and when did it end? It is when Daniel addresses these questions that he begins to give clues as to the timing of the First and Second Advents (Appearances in the flesh) of the

Messiah. The prophecy says that the starting point of the 70 weeks of years will be "the issuing of a decree to restore and rebuild Jerusalem" (Daniel 9:25). Keep in mind that this prophecy was given to Daniel by the angel Gabriel during the time of Israel's exile in Babylon. The approximate date was 538 B.C., shortly before the first remnant of Jews were allowed to return to Jerusalem in 536 B.C. under Zerubbabel. Jerusalem was in ruins at this time, having been destroyed by Nebuchadnezzar 50 years earlier in 586 B.C. (The captivity had begun in 606/605 B.C., exactly 70 years earlier, before the destruction of Jerusalem and the Temple in 586 B.C., when Nebuchadnezzar took Daniel and other "youths" to Babylon as hostages - Daniel 1:1-4.)

Daniel's prophecy next states that the 490 years will be divided into three periods as follows: seven weeks (49 years) plus sixty-two weeks (434 years) plus one week (7 years). He states that at the end of the first two periods (49 + 62 = 69 weeks or 483 years), the Messiah will be "cut off" meaning Jesus will die for the sins of the world, a seemingly clear reference to the crucifixion. The end of the 69 weeks marks the end of the First Advent or appearance of the Messiah. He then states that both Jerusalem and the Temple will be destroyed. That leaves Daniel's 70th week yet to be fulfilled when the Messiah makes His Second Advent, His Second Coming at the end of the 70th week.

The prophecy concludes by focusing on the last week of years. It says that following the death of the Messiah and the destruction of Jerusalem, "the prince who is to come" will make a covenant with the Jewish people that will enable them to reinstitute their sacrificial system. Daniel did not know that there was a 2,000-year separation between the death of the Messiah and the rise of the "prince" known as the Antichrist. The real nature of the "peace treaty" or "covenant" that the Antichrist strikes with Israel is in dispute, but the result will be the Jews will be able to have their Temple – the Tribulation Temple. This prince will come from the same people who destroyed the Temple (the Romans). We know from 2 Thessalonians 2 that this "prince who is to come" is the Antichrist, the "man of lawlessness" who is "the son of destruction." The same passage makes it clear that his covenant will enable the Jews to rebuild their Temple. Both passages — Daniel 9 and 2 Thessalonians 2 — establish the fact that in the middle of this 70th week (3 1/2 years into it) this "prince who is to come" will double cross the Jewish people and nullify the Daniel 9:27 "Peace Treaty". He will march into the rebuilt Temple and declare himself to be God. He will stop the sacrifices and he will erect "an abomination of desolation," most likely an idol of himself. The book of Revelation specifies that the Messiah will return to Earth 3 1/2 years after this desolation of the Temple takes place, and exact timing of the Second Coming from that date.

We have the timing of the two advents of the Messiah. He will come the first time, the First Advent as a Suffering Savior, at the end of 483 years and will be "cut off" or crucified and resurrected before the Temple is destroyed. He will return the second time, His Second Advent as a Conquering King at the end of a seven-year period that will begin with a treaty that allows the Jews to rebuild their Temple and reinstitute the Mosaic system of sacrifices. Cyrus' decree to return to Jerusalem from Babylon to Zerubbabel and Joshua in 538 B.C. (2 Chronicles 36:22-23 and Ezra 1:1-4) was specifically concerning the Temple restoration thus NOT addressing Daniel 9:27 requirement to restore and build Jerusalem.

When Was Messiah "Cut Off"?

The first person in modern history to calculate the 483 years to the "cutting off" of the Messiah was Sir Robert Anderson in his book, The Coming Prince (1894). Using the decree to Nehemiah in Nehemiah 2:1-8 issued in 445 B.C. as his starting point and using what he called "the 360-day prophetic year," Anderson calculated that it was exactly 173,880 days or 483 lunar years from the day the edict was issued to the day Jesus made His triumphal entry into Jerusalem. His calculations placed the crucifixion in the spring of 32 A.D. These calculations have remained almost sacred in Christian thinking for the past one hundred years. But they need to be examined carefully because there are serious problems with Anderson's calculations.

Some have used this basis for calculating Jesus' entry into Jerusalem as King while others have used Zerubbabel and Jeshua's return to Jerusalem from Babylon to rebuild the temple in 536 B.C. I believe both of these dates to be incorrect. The best solution as to when this prophecy begins is to interpret Daniel's prophecy beginning with the decree issued to Ezra in 457 B.C. The decree given to Zerubbabel in 536 B.C. authorized the rebuilding of the Temple. The decree issued to Nehemiah in 445 B.C. concerned the rebuilding of the walls of Jerusalem and not Jerusalem in general. Ezra's decree in 457 B.C. was more general in nature, covering a variety of subjects. But we know from Scripture that he interpreted it to mean that the Jews were authorized to launch a general rebuilding campaign that included the temple, the city, and the walls. His interpretation is stated in Ezra 9:9, "God has not forsaken us, but has extended loving kindness to us in the sight of the kings of Persia, to give us reviving to raise up the house of our God, to restore its ruins, and to give us a wall in Judah and Jerusalem" (Ezra 9:9).

Now, using Ezra's decree (Ezra 9:9) as the starting point (457 B.C.), if we count forward 483 regular 365-day years we will arrive at 27 A.D. (There is only one year between 1 B.C. and 1 A.D.) According to the translator and historian Josephus, the Jewish new year that began in the fall of 27 A.D. marked the beginning of the last Jubilee Year that the Jews enjoyed in the land before their worldwide dispersal by the Romans in 70 A.D. The time span I am proposing from 457 B.C. to 27 A.D. is also supported by another amazing piece of evidence. Do you remember how Daniel divided the first 483 years into two periods of time, first 49 years and then 434 years? Why did he do that? Go back and re read Daniel 9:25 and notice that he makes specific reference to the rebuilding of the city of Jerusalem. Did he divide the period into two parts to indicate that the rebuilding of the city would occupy the first 49 years?

In a recent booklet entitled "The Daniel Papers," a publication of the Radio Bible Class, notes, "According to Barnes and several other trustworthy Bible commentators, the historian Prideaux declared Nehemiah's last action in rebuilding the city occurred in the 15th year of the Persian ruler Darius Nothus (423-404 B.C.). His 15th year was the 49th year from the 457 B.C. decree. Josephus seems to support this idea in his remarks about the death of Nehemiah." In other words, this documentation confirms that the rebuilding of Jerusalem indeed did take 49 years or seven weeks of years just as Daniel's prophecy stated.

But, the most convincing evidence that the 27 A.D. date is the probable entry date for Jesus' ride into Jerusalem and the year of His crucifixion is the historically accepted date of Herod the Great's death. Remember in Matthew Chapter 2 when the wise men arrived in Jerusalem approximately 15 months after the birth of Jesus looking for Him, King Herod pretended to be excited to meet Him also, but ordered that all baby boys born in Bethlehem 2 years old or younger be killed? (Matthew 2:16) Then, since Joseph had an angel earlier appear to him in a dream and told him to flee to Egypt with his little family, Jesus was saved from Herod's decree.

The interesting thing is that Herod the Great's death occurred in 4 B.C. according to historians making his decree to kill the babies in Bethlehem at the latest 4 B.C. This means Jesus' birth would be at the latest in 5 B.C. and probably in 6 B.C. Let's see how that stacks up against the 32 A.D. date from Anderson and the 27 A.D. date from my interpretation. Counting backwards from 32 A.D. 33 years (actually 33 ½ years for Jesus' lifespan) and considering there is no time between 1 A.D. and 1 B.C., we arrive at 1 B.C. for Jesus' birth which we have a problem with since Herod died in 4 B.C. But, if we use 27 A.D. for Jesus' crucifixion and resurrection, subtract 33 ½ years, we arrive at approximately 6 B.C. for Jesus' birth which fits amazingly well with Herod's death at 4 B.C. That date gives ample time for Jesus' birth in 6 B.C., allows for a 15 to 18 month span to allow for the wise men to arrive and leave, then allows Herod to live a while longer to 4 B.C. when he dies and then allowing Jesus and his family to move back to Nazareth in Galilee from Egypt (probably Alexandria since there was a large population of Jews living there at the time).

What we have seen here is compelling because it places real events in conjunction with historical facts thereby confirming the Bible's amazing accuracy. We have seen that Daniel's seventy weeks has all but been fulfilled. The 49 plus 62 weeks, or 69 weeks (483) years, for Israel to, essentially, be restored to their God, Yahweh have happened ending with Jesus' death on the cross. But, we are not finished with Daniel's 70-week prophecy because we have one week of years, seven years left for the Jews to endure.

What About the 70th Week?

One puzzle remains about Daniel's prophecy. What about the 70th week? Is it past or future? I believe there is no doubt whatsoever that it is future. The reason for that conclusion is simple. The prophecy begins by stating that the 490 years will produce six consequences among the Jewish people which we covered earlier from Daniel 9:24. All six are still unfulfilled. The Jews are still in rebellion against God, they are still caught up in their sins, they are still refusing to accept the atonement for their iniquity, everlasting righteousness has not come to the Earth, all prophecy concerning the Messiah has not yet been fulfilled, and "the most holy" has not been anointed.

There must, therefore, be a "gap" in the prophecy. This may seem strange to the casual reader. But students of prophecy are familiar with prophetic gaps. They are very common in prophetic literature because of the peculiar nature of the prophetic perspective. God would show His prophets great future events and the prophets would present them as if they were happening in rapid succession because that's the way they appeared to them from their perspective. The prophet was like a person looking down a mountain range seeing one mountain top after another, seemingly pressed up against each other, but, in reality, separated by great valleys which could not be seen. Jesus Himself recognized this characteristic of prophecy when He read a prophecy from Isaiah in the synagogue in Nazareth. If you will check what He read (Luke 4:18-19) against what Isaiah wrote (Isaiah 61:1-3), you will see that Jesus stopped reading in the middle of a sentence because the rest of the sentence had to do with His Second Coming.

For Christians, Daniel's prophecy should serve to underscore the supernatural origin of the Bible. It should also serve as confirmation that Jesus of Nazareth was the promised Messiah. For Jews, the prophecy should be deeply disturbing for two reasons. First, it clearly teaches that the Messiah had to come before the Temple was destroyed in 70 A.D. That means that either God failed to keep His promise by not sending the Messiah in His First Advent or else the Jews missed recognizing their Messiah. Second, the prophecy clearly teaches that a terrible time of tribulation for the Jews still lies ahead in order to complete the last 7 years of judgment decreed by Jeremiah that add up to 490 years.

Moses said it would be a time of "distress" that would occur in "the latter days" (Deuteronomy 4:30). Jeremiah called it "the time of Jacob's distress" (Jeremiah 30:7), or, as modern prophecy watchers call it, "The Time of Jacob's Trouble". Daniel characterized it as "a time of distress such as never occurred since there was a nation until that time" (Daniel 12:1). Zechariah says two-thirds of the Jews will "be cut off and perish" during that terrible time (Zechariah 13:8). The process will be horrible. But the result will be glorious, for the remaining remnant will at long last turn their hearts to God, accept their Messiah, and cry out, "Blessed is He who comes in the name of the Lord!"

Modern View of the Rapture and the Second Coming

Let us say, without complete knowledge since "no one knows the day" but we "will know the season", that the 27 A.D. date is quite interesting because of the Hosea 6:2 verse, "After two days will he revive us: in the third day he will raise us up, and we shall live in his sight." Jesus was raised on the third day after being in the tomb. Israel was revived after about two thousand years of obscurity and will be revived to go into a thousand-year Millennial Kingdom when they return to Messiah (the Millennium being a "third" day of 1,000 years). Jesus' Age of Grace is to last about two-thousand years since we are at the two-thousand-year mark today since His Resurrection. Based on 2 Peter 3:8, "But, beloved, be not ignorant of this one thing, that one day is with the Lord as a thousand years, and a thousand years as one day" and the Hosea 6:2, "After two days will he revive us: in the third day he will raise us up, and we shall live in his sight", these verses and history seem to suggest strongly that the Age of Grace is about to end (the two days or two thousand years) with the Millennium (the third day or the one thousand years) on the immediate horizon. But we know that Daniel's 70th Week must occur prior to the Millennium because Israel must be "persuaded" to return to Messiah through the Tribulation, Daniel's 70th Week, after the end of the Age of Grace and before the Millennium in order for the Jews to return to their God and His Messiah.

We also know that the Jews that accept Messiah during the Tribulation will do so during the first half of the Tribulation (3 ½ years) mainly due to the 144,000 Jewish evangelists and the Two Witnesses, then will be divinely protected (probably in Petra, but certainly "in the wilderness") from the Satan-possessed Antichrist during the last half of the Tribulation. Why are the Jews protected? Revelation says that Antichrist wants to destroy them all (Revelation 12:6, 13-17), but they flee to the wilderness (biblically Ammon, Moab, or Edom where Petra is located) where God nourishes them which could mean not only protects them from Antichrist/Satan, but also from the Bowl Judgments of God's Wrath during the Great Tribulation or the last 3 ½ years of the Tribulation. So, could the two-thousand years from 27 A.D. to 2027 be the Church Age or the Age of Grace, and the 2027 date plus three and one-half years (about 2031?) mark the middle of the Tribulation or the time the saved Jews are protected? Could the two-thousand years (read 2 days) of the Hosea 6:2 verse be the time between Jesus' Resurrection and the Rapture of the Church?

What does this mean to us? If true, it is quite remarkable. If 2031 is the middle of the Tribulation, then the end of the Tribulation is about 2034 by adding 3 ½ years to 2031. Subtract the 7 years of the Tribulation from 2031 yields 2024. If the "In-Between" times (that contain the Ezekiel 38 and 39 war plus the Psalm 83 war and other prophecies) are indeed three and one-half years (the Ezekiel 39:9 prophecy of Israel burning the weapons of the war for seven years and assuming the Jews cannot burn those weapons if they are hiding from the Antichrist), then the Rapture would occur somewhere near 2020 (2024 minus 3 ½ years). If the "In-Between Times" assumption is incorrect and all of those "In-Between" prophecies occur during the Tribulation, then 2027 minus the 7 years of the Tribulation is again near 2020. We are now in 2019. The dates are assumptions and there are many suppositions based on Scripture that could be inaccurate as to the dates but certainly are not inaccurate concerning the occurrences to come. I believe that because of these arguments and explanations, we can safely state that we are on the very edge of Christ appearing in the air for His Church otherwise known as the Rapture. Are you ready? It could happen today!

One point of clarification for those that might confuse the Rapture with the Second Coming (which does happen quite often really). First of all, the Rapture is exclusively for Christ's Church, the Bride of Christ since Jesus is the Groom. No unbeliever will be raptured, no Old Testament saint will be raptured, only believers in Jesus Christ from His Resurrection until the very second of the Shout to "Come up here!" In contrast, Jesus' Second Coming happens at least seven years AFTER the Rapture and probably more like ten years after. In addition, the Second Coming is seen by everyone on Earth, believer and unbeliever alike, all who are alive and remain until Jesus sets foot on the Mount of Olives in Jerusalem revealing to Israel that He is the long-awaited Messiah to the Jews.

The Church is experiencing the Bema Judgment Seat of Christ and the Marriage Supper of the Lamb in Heaven while the rest of humanity is on Earth suffering through the Tribulation, the Time of Jacob's Trouble, so that the Jews can fulfill Daniel's 70th week and come to belief in Jesus Christ as Messiah. It just takes a lot to convince some people, and this has to be the ultimate conviction! At the end of the Tribulation, Jesus returns with His Bride to the Earth to stop the Battle of Armageddon (a war of Satan-led rebels against Israel and God), then set foot on the Mount of Olives exactly where He arose after His Resurrection.

So, there are many differences in the Rapture and the Second Coming. The Rapture is the next event to happen and it is imminent meaning we do not know the precise timing of it occurring, just the approximate time which is any day. The imminent nature of the Rapture tells us that we need to be ready AT ANY TIME for it to happen. On the other hand, if someone still alive during the Tribulation and sees the Abomination of Desolation occur in the Tribulation Temple in Jerusalem where the Antichrist enters the Temple and declares himself to be God, that person will know that exactly three and one half years or forty-two months or one thousand two hundred and sixty days later, Jesus will set foot in Jerusalem – the Second Coming! Therefore, those who have professed their belief in Christ and have accepted Him as their Lord and Savior will miss the Wrath of God by being raptured with the rest of the Church of Jesus Christ, then returning with Jesus when He makes His triumphal entry back into the world of man to stop Armageddon and set up His Kingdom in Jerusalem for a thousand years.

Old Testament Passages Pointing to the Last Days

When most pastors or teachers cover the End Times, they usually start with the Olivet Discourse Matthew 24, Mark 13, and Luke 21 or the Book of Revelation. For years the focus on end times discussions has remained in the New Testament. Unfortunately, that results in our teachers only giving us part of the entire discovery available to us in the Bible or, really, the end of the story. When reading a story, it makes sense to start at the beginning, rather than at the end and try to figure out the story from there. Yet the study of the "last days" in most churches today has us doing this very thing. We need to decide to start at the beginning of the book.

There are literally dozens of Old Testament passages that are crucial to understanding the "last days" if you search for them and study them. They are all important to the overall picture of a complete understanding of Bible Prophecy and how it relate to our day – the true "End Times". The following are just a few of the many that are in the Old Testament.

Jacob's Prediction of the Last Days

The first mention of the "last days" is in Genesis 49:1! "And Jacob called his sons and said, "Gather together, that I may tell you what shall befall you in the last days." Ironically, the first passage in the Bible that speaks of the last days is in the first book of the Bible and not the last, Revelation. This passage speaks of the last days of the twelve tribes of Israel. We can conclude from this that going back to the days of Jacob about 2,000 years before Christ, God knew His people would want to know their future. Is there any reason God would change His ways when it comes to our desires?

Jeremiah's Prediction of the Last Days

The "time of Jacob's trouble" comes from Jeremiah 30:7 that says, "Alas! For that day is great, so that none is like it: it is even the time of Jacob's trouble, but he shall be saved out of it". Jacob's trouble or Jacob's distress refers to the difficulties the Jewish people will face during the seven-year tribulation period. During this time, the Jewish temple will be rebuilt, yet desecrated. The Antichrist will break a covenant and set himself up as ruler and expect to be worshiped. He will force all people to receive a mark to buy or sell goods. In addition, much war and famine will occur, with Jews fleeing Jerusalem to the wilderness, probably Petra in Edom although the Bible does not specify – it just says, "the wilderness".

Despite these troubles, the Lord will fulfill His promises. In addition to saving and protecting His people the Jews, He will return in victory (Revelation 19:11-21). Following His victory, the Messiah will rule from Jerusalem in peace for 1,000 years, the Millennial Kingdom (Revelation 20:1-6). Following one last attack led by Satan at the end of the Millennium, the Lord will defeat His enemies, complete His final judgment (the Great White Throne Judgment), and establish a new Heaven, a new Earth, and a New Jerusalem where He will dwell with His people forever (Revelation 21-22).

In addition, Israel has already been re-established as a nation in 1948 following 1,813 years (1948 – 135 A.D. or the time of the Bar Kochba Revolt)) without a nation for the Jewish people. This historic change offers evidence that God has not abandoned the Jewish people but has kept His promises to bring Israel back to its land in the last days and save them. Though Israel will continue to experience difficulties now and in the future, God promises He will ultimately restore His people and offer peace during a time when He rules over His people.

Jeremiah 30:24 says: "The fierce anger of the LORD will not turn back, until He has performed and until He has accomplished the intent of His heart; in the latter days you will understand this." If God wanted to let the Jews know in advance the coming end of the Old Covenant and the establishment of the New Covenant, then isn't it logical that He would want us to know the end of the New Covenant and the Second Coming of Christ to set up His Millennial Kingdom?

Micah's Prediction of the Last Days

Micah 4 shows that Jesus was born in the last days of the Old Covenant: "And it will come about in the last days, that the mountain of the house of the LORD will be established as the chief of the mountains. It will be raised above the hills, And the peoples will stream to it." In the same context, Micah 5:2 reads: "But as for you, Bethlehem Ephrathah, too little to be among the clans of Judah, from you One will go forth for Me to be ruler in Israel. His goings forth are from long ago, from the days of eternity."

This prophecy is fulfilled in the last days of the Old Covenant according to Matthew 2:1-6, "Now after Jesus was born in Bethlehem of Judea in the days of Herod the king, magi from the east arrived in Jerusalem, saying, "'Where is He who has been born King of the Jews? For we saw His star in the east and have come to worship Him.' When Herod the king heard this, he was troubled, and all Jerusalem with him. Gathering together all the chief priests and scribes of the people, he inquired of them where the Messiah was to be born. They said to him, 'In Bethlehem of Judea; for this is what has been written by the prophet, and you, Bethlehem, Land of Judah, are by no means least among the leaders of Judah; for out of you shall come forth a ruler who will shepherd My people Israel.'"

Isaiah's Prediction of Judgment on Old Covenant Israel in the Last Days

In Isaiah 2:1-2, we see almost verbatim the words from Micah 4:1, about the last days of the covenant, "The word which Isaiah the son of Amoz saw concerning Judah and Jerusalem. Now it will come about that in the last days the mountain of the house of the LORD will be established as the chief of the mountains, and will be raised above the hills; and all the nations will stream to it." This segment of Scripture is full of description of the last days that can be traced through the New Testament to the book of Revelation.

Joel's Prediction that the Holy Spirit Would be Poured Out in the Last Days

Joel 2:28-32 is quoted by the apostle Peter in his sermon on Pentecost in Acts 2:14-21, "But Peter, taking his stand with the eleven, raised his voice and declared to them: 'Men of Judea and all you who live in Jerusalem, let this be known to you and give heed to my words. For these men are not drunk, as you suppose, for it is only the third hour of the day; but this is what was spoken of through the prophet Joel, "And it shall be in the last days," God says, "that I will pour forth of My Spirit on all mankind, and your sons and your daughters shall prophesy, and your young men shall see visions, and your old men shall dream dreams; even on My bondslaves, both men and women, I will in those days pour forth of My Spirit." According to the Prophet Joel, the Holy Spirit would be poured out in "the last days." This prophecy was being fulfilled in Acts 2 according to the Apostle Peter. His audience in Acts 2 are Jews from "every nation under Heaven."

These prophets and others were writing to the Jews of coming judgment upon them for breaking the covenant of Deuteronomy 28-32. Last days events mentioned in the Old Testament included the birth of the Messiah, the New Covenant coming, the pouring out of the Holy Spirit, and pending judgment on the Old Covenant system. Jesus clearly states that this judgment is coming upon the generation He came to in the First Century (Matthew 23:36, Matthew 24:34, Mark 13:30, Luke 21:32).

So, what does all this mean? The Old Testament references provide the context for the New Testament passages concerning the "last days." Today in a culture that is more fascinated with signs from world events than Scripture, it is rare to get the full picture of prophesy from the entire Bible both Old and New Testaments. In real estate the golden rule is "location, location, location." In eschatology, it's "signs, signs, signs." How about we go back to "Scripture, Scripture, Scripture"? That's where we put signs and future events in context for understanding. The Old Testament provides the context for the New Testament passages on the Last Days.

Other Old Testament Prophetic Passages Concerning Israel

What is a prophetic sign? It is basically a prophecy concerning an historical event or technological development that will characterize a future time. Let's consider the First Advent of the Messiah as an example. The prophet Micah prophesied that the Messiah would be born in the town of Bethlehem (Micah 5:2). Daniel said the Messiah would be "cut off" 483 years after an edict was issued to rebuild Jerusalem (Daniel 9:25). He also stated that this would take place before the destruction of the Temple in Jerusalem. And David stated in Psalm 22:16 that the Messiah's hands and feet would be pierced.

The first of these signs is geographical - the birth site of the Messiah. The second is historical and refers to the edict issued by Ezra (Ezra 9.9) in 457 BC. Counting 483 years from that date brings us to 27 A.D. The Temple was destroyed in 70 AD. So, the Messiah had to be "cut off" (that is, killed) sometime between 27 A.D. and 70 A.D. The third sign is technological in nature. The method of execution at the time David wrote Psalm 22 was stoning. Crucifixion was not even invented by the Romans until 700 years later.

Jesus was born in Bethlehem. He was executed in 27 A.D. (less than a week after His triumphal entry into Jerusalem on a colt), during the "historical window" between 27 A.D. and 70 A.D. And he was executed by crucifixion. The fulfillment of these signs in the life of Jesus serves to validate that He was the prophesied Messiah.

The re-establishment of the nation of Israel is a classic example of an end time historical sign. Over and over again the Hebrew Scriptures prophesy that in the end times, right before the return of the Messiah, the nation of Israel will be re-established (Isaiah 11:10-12; Ezekiel 37:1-12; Amos 9:13-15; and Zechariah 12:1-3). Jesus emphasized this sign in Matthew 24 when He told us to watch for the re-budding of the fig tree (a symbol of Israel: Hosea 9:10; Jeremiah 24:5; Matthew 24:32)). When that happens, He said, the generation that sees it "will not pass away until all these things [the return of the Lord] take place" (Matthew 24:34).

We must always remember that the key to End Times Prophecy is Israel. Why? The Old Testament points to Israel's restoration of land, of its people, of its language, regaining control of Jerusalem, and the trouble that the entire world will give Israel — all of which are signs of the End Times. Here are some of the specific signs of Israel entering the time of Jacob's Trouble or the bringing of Israel back to their God Yahweh:

Israel Entering Its Final Jubilee?

In early April of year 2020 Jubilee year 120 will begin. Genesis 6:3 says, "Then the LORD said, "My Spirit will not contend with humans forever, for they are mortal; their days will be a hundred and twenty years." The context of this verse is when the fallen angels had children with human women with the result being giants or Nephilim that could not receive salvation for their souls. The reference to the 120 years occurs BEFORE Noah's Flood when man was living 900 years or more. So, why this 120-year age? Today, man does not live anywhere close to 120 years so, perhaps it does NOT refer to man's age but the age of Man? Could it be a reference to 120 Jubilees?

This number 120 is how long it has been since Adam counting by Jubilee years (every 49 years or seven Sabbatical cycles of seven years plus another year which is the 50th year or the Jubilee year). 50 times 120 equals 6,000 which is the number of years that the Earth has been in existence since Creation. Of course, these are estimates, but they are certainly interesting to consider. What these calculations suggest and reveal is that the End Times are here now at this present time since God's Plan for the Human Race to be reconciled to Him through Jesus Christ is about to be completed. Notably, it has been 70 Jubilees – another significant number - or 3,500 years (70 times 50 equals 3,500) since Moses led the Jews out at Passover from Egypt, about 1442 B.C., in the presence of the Lord. Also, there were 40 Jubilees from Adam to Abraham (2,000 years), 40 Jubilees from Abraham to Jesus (another 2,000 years), and it has been, or will be in 2020, 40 Jubilees from Christ until 2020 (the last 2,000 years) which all add up to 6,000 years since Creation until now suggesting that the third 2,000-year timespan marks the end of man's time on Earth save the Millennium. God's Creation was over 6 days and He rested on the 7th which established a pattern for the work week but also, possibly, the pattern for man's existence on the Earth until restoration to God. Could all this point to man's existence on the Earth totaling 6,000 years and Christ's Millennial Kingdom being the 7th thousand-year period? If so, are we at the end of God's plan for mankind, the period that God said that His Spirit would not contend with man but for 120 Jubilees? What should come next? The Rapture? Then the Tribulation? Then the Millennium?

World Political Signs

1. Re-establishment of Israel after 1,813 years of obscurity (Ezekiel 36:22-37:1-2; Zechariah 12:1-6; Matthew 24:32-34; Mark 13:28-30; and Luke 21:29-31)

2. Arab hostility toward Israel (Ezekiel 35:1-36:7)

3. Russia as a menacing power to Israel (Ezekiel 38:1-39:16)

Signs of Israel

1. Regathering of the people (Isaiah 11:10-12 and Ezekiel 37:1-12)

2. Re-establishment of the state (Isaiah 66:7-8; Zechariah 12:1-6; and Matthew 24:32-35)

3. Reclamation of the land (Isaiah 35:1-2,7 and Ezekiel 36:34-35)

4. Revival of the language (Zephaniah 3:9)

5. Resurgence of the military (Zechariah 12:6)

6. Refocusing of world politics on Israel (Zechariah 12:2-3)

7. Reoccupation of Jerusalem (Zechariah 12:2-6)

These are additional signs that Israel and the End Times are inseparably linked:

1. Disobedience would lead to the nation of Israel being scattered amongst all nations.
    Deuteronomy 28:64, 'Then the LORD will scatter you among all nations, from one end of the Earth to the other.' See also Leviticus 26:33, Jeremiah 9:16, Ezekiel 12:15. In all, 6 different books of the Bible predict the scattering of Israel amongst all the nations of the Earth. History records this being fulfilled in 70 A.D. when the Temple was destroyed and in 135 A.D. when Jerusalem was destroyed by the Roman Empire and the remaining Jews were scattered amongst the nations.

2. God himself would restore the Jews to the land of Israel from all the nations.

    Jeremiah 16:14-16, "However, the days are coming," declares the LORD, "when men will no longer say, 'As surely as the LORD lives, who brought the Israelites up out of Egypt,' but they will say, 'As surely as the LORD lives, who brought the Israelites up out of the land of the north and out of all the countries where he had banished them.' For I will restore them to the land I gave their forefathers." In all, 13 books of the Bible speak of the nation of Israel being restored in their land from the nations in which they were scattered. This prophecy became history in 1948 when the

United Nations granted a homeland to the Jewish people and the nation of Israel was reborn! See also Jeremiah 3:14, 31:8-9, Isaiah 60:8-9, Deuteronomy 30:3, Amos 9:15, Ezekiel 37.

3. The desolate land of Israel would again blossom and be fruitful in the last days.

   Zechariah 7:14, "I scattered them with a whirlwind among all the nations, where they were strangers." The land was left so desolate behind them that no one could come or go. This is how they made the pleasant land desolate. History records that while the Jewish people were exiled amongst many nations, the land of Israel was a barren desert. Mark Twain visited Israel in in 1867 and published his impressions in Innocents Abroad. He described a desolate country – devoid of both vegetation and human population: "… A desolate country whose soil is rich enough, but is given over wholly to weeds… a silent mournful expanse…. a desolation…. we never saw a human being on the whole route…. hardly a tree or shrub anywhere. Even the olive tree and the cactus, those fast friends of a worthless soil, had almost deserted the country." See also Leviticus 26:33, Ezekiel 15:8, Jeremiah 9:12-13, 23:10, 44:22, Isaiah 32:13.

   Isaiah 27:6, "In the days to come, Jacob will take root, Israel will bud and blossom and fill the world with fruit." This is exactly what we marvel at today! Not only has God bought the Jewish people back into their land like He said He would in the last days, but He has also blessed the land so that they now export flowers and fruit around the world! Satellite photos show the green pastures of the nation of Israel, in sharp contrast with the surrounding desert lands of the Arab nations. See also Isaiah 35:1, Ezekiel 36:35.

4. God Himself would defend Israel and cause Israel to be mighty in battle.

   Zechariah 12:8, "On that day the LORD will shield those who live in Jerusalem, so that the feeblest among them will be like David, and the house of David will be like God, like the Angel of the LORD going before them." Taken in context, this verse speaks about God defending Israel in a battle to come in the last days. We have seen this occur several times since Israel became a nation again in 1948, often miraculously! They have been greatly outnumbered in key Arab-Israeli wars in 1948, 1967, and 1973. But, the nation of

Israel has survived and prospered. Only God could accomplish so great a miracle.

5. In the last days, Jerusalem would be a burden to the entire world.

Zechariah 12:2-3, "Behold, I will make Jerusalem a cup of trembling unto all the people round about... And in that day will I make Jerusalem a burdensome stone for all people: all that burden themselves with it shall be cut in pieces." Today, Jerusalem is a burden that causes trembling for all the nations just as God foretold. What makes this prophecy even more remarkable is that when the prophet Zechariah spoke these words around 520 B.C., Jerusalem lay in ruins. But God said it would become the focus of the world's attention! Today, Israel has 0.01% of the world's population, yet 33% of the United Nations resolutions have been passed, all against and none in favor of Israel except the initial one granting them their country back in 1947!

6. In the end, all nations shall come against Israel.

Zechariah 14:2, "I will gather all the nations to Jerusalem to fight against it; the city will be captured, the houses ransacked, and the women raped." Apart from the USA, Israel has few allies. One day, the Bible predicts, she will have no allies, and all nations shall be gathered against her. The end of this opposition will be the Battle of Armageddon which will draw the Tribulation to a close with the Second Coming of Jesus Christ!

7. God Himself, Jesus Christ, will return and fight for Israel against the attacking nations.

Zechariah 14:3-4, "Then the LORD will go out and fight against those nations, as he fights in the day of battle. On that day his feet will stand on the Mount of Olives, east of Jerusalem, and the Mount of Olives will be split in two from east to west, forming a great valley, with half of the mountain moving north and half moving south." The Battle of Armageddon is the final rebellion of unsaved mankind against Israel and Israel's God headed up by the Antichrist indwelt by Satan himself! The book of Revelation puts it like this... Revelation 16:14-16, "They are spirits of demons performing miraculous signs, and they go out to the kings of the whole world, to gather them for the battle on the great day of God Almighty... Then they gathered the kings together to the place that in Hebrew is called Armageddon." The Valley of Megiddo is near Jerusalem on a plain 200 miles long surrounded by mountains. Jesus stops this so-called battle with one word, then He sets foot on the Earth exactly where He left after His Resurrection – on the Mount of Olives. Revelation also prophecies the return of Jesus Christ on this day saying... Revelation 19:11, "I saw Heaven standing open and there before me was a white horse, whose rider is called Faithful and True. With justice he judges and makes war." Zechariah 14:4 says, "And his feet shall stand in that day upon the mount of Olives, which is before Jerusalem on the east, and the mount of Olives shall cleave in the midst thereof toward the east and toward the west, and there shall be a very great valley; and half of the mountain shall remove toward the north, and half of it toward the south."

8. The nation of Israel will finally recognize that Jesus was their Messiah, whom they crucified!

Zechariah 12:9-10, "On that day I will set out to destroy all the nations that attack Jerusalem. And I will pour out on the house of David and the inhabitants of Jerusalem a spirit of grace and supplication. They will look on me, the one they have pierced, and they will mourn for him as one mourns for an only child and grieve bitterly for him as one grieves for a firstborn son." Even though the Bible predicted that the Messiah would die, and have His feet and hands pierced, the nation of Israel has, for the last 2000 years, hardened their heart and not believed that Jesus was their Messiah. At the time of the end, they will again look to the one whom they pierced and how great the mourning and sadness will be on that day for what they did! Yet Jesus will pour out His grace upon Israel!

9. God will judge the nations depending upon their treatment of the Jewish people.

Joel 1:1-2, "In those days and at that time, when I restore the fortunes of Judah and Jerusalem, I will gather all nations and bring them down to the Valley of Jehoshaphat. There I will enter into judgment against them concerning my inheritance, my people Israel, for they scattered my people among the nations and divided up my land." This Valley of Jehoshaphat is the same place as where the Battle of Armageddon takes place. The punishment of the nations opposed to Israel will be accomplished at this time of the Second Coming which will happen just prior to Jesus setting foot on the Mount of Olives.

10. An explosion in knowledge and travel.

> Daniel 12:4, "But you, Daniel, shut up the words, and seal the book until the time of the end; many shall run to and fro, and knowledge shall increase." This increase in knowledge is occurring now at an exponential rate. The internet has played a large role in this, and Israel is the greatest contributor to this expansion of knowledge with the presence of all the best performers of computer technology, cancer research, military weaponry, and many others. We now play God with the very genes and DNA that make us human. Jesus will have to return soon to halt the "progress" because those who do not know God are experimenting in areas that will lead to horrendous results in genetic monsters or, perhaps even death to millions due to errors made in high technology.

11. Additional signs:

> All Nations Gathered to War, Isaiah 13:4; 66:18; Zechariah 12:1-4; 14:2; Jewish Revival, Ezekiel 37:9-14; Zechariah 12:10-14; 13:1-9; Abomination of Desolation, Daniel 9:27; 12:11; Second Advent, Ezekiel 39:21; Daniel 2:44; 7:13,14; Zechariah 14:4; Malachi 2:1-3; The Beast, or Antichrist, Isaiah 14:12-15; Daniel 7:8, 24; 8:19, 26; 9:26, 27; 11:36; Zechariah 11:15-17; 10; Nations, Daniel 2:42,44; 7:24; Kings of East, Daniel 11:44; Kings of South, Ezekiel 38:5; Daniel 11:40; Kings of North, Ezekiel 38:15; 39:2; Daniel 11:40; Joel 2:20; Signs in Sky, Isaiah 13:10; 24:23; Joel 2:10,30; 3:15; Zechariah 14:6,7; Remnant Saved, Joel 2:12, 17; 3:32; Amos 9:8; Zechariah 13:8,9; 14:2,5.

There are many others. We could spend hours and many pages covering them all. And each and every one either has or will come to pass, you have God's Word on it! Taking time to read, study, and ponder why God has told us of all the significant occurrences of His intervention with His people Israel shows us just how important Israel is to Him, and how important Israel is to our understanding of what God has planned for our immediate future! Besides, God has directly told us that those who discriminate against Israel or Israel's land will be judged and judged severely while "And I will bless them that bless thee, and curse him that curseth thee: and in thee shall all families of the Earth be blessed." (Genesis 12:3) So, why not celebrate the wonderful nation of Israel and its contributions to the world?

Old Testament Minor Prophets

We do not have the time or the space to cover every single end time prophecy in the Minor Prophets. Suffice it to say that all Old Testament prophets, from Isaiah to Malachi hold pictures of the coming day of the Lord or the End Times. We will cover only the most prominent ones starting with Hosea. Hosea Chapter 3 tells of Israel's return to the fear of the Lord in the later days. Hosea Chapter 14 says that Israel will return to the Lord and receive healing from her apostasy.

Joel Chapter 2 and 3 sound as if they were written yesterday. Chapter 2 begins with, "For the day of the Lord is coming, for it is at hand…". It goes on to say in verse 28, "…I will pour out My Spirit on all flesh; your sons and your daughters shall prophesy, your old men shall dream dreams, your young men shall see visions." Joel prophesies, "And I (God) will show wonders in the heavens and in the Earth; blood and fire and pillars of smoke. The sun shall be turned into darkness, and the moon into blood, before the coming of the great and awesome day of the Lord. And it shall come to pass that whoever calls on the name of the Lord shall be saved." Joel Chapter 3, verses 1 and 2 speak directly to those nations that are clamoring for a two-state solution to Israel and Palestinian conflict, when the real goal is to utterly destroy Israel. "For behold, in those days and at that time, when I bring back the captives of Judah and Jerusalem, I will gather all nations, and bring them down to the Valley of Jehoshaphat; And I will enter into judgment with them there on account of My people, My heritage Israel, whom they have scattered among the nations; they have divided up My land." All efforts to divide Israel or Jerusalem should be opposed at every turn because God's judgment will come if it is divided!

The Book of Amos Chapter 5 relates the judgment of God on Israel for afflicting the just, taking bribes, and diverting the poor from justice. In an answer to the self-righteous Jews who believed that they were worshiping God and earning salvation through vain and evil works, God through Amos says, "Woe to you who desire the day of the Lord! For what good is the day of the Lord to you? It will be darkness and not light…Is not the day of the Lord darkness, and not light?" Without repentance, God's judgement is inescapable! Chapter 9, however, is God's promise to rebuild the Davidic Tabernacle Israel in the Millennial Kingdom will never leave the land God has given them (Amos 9:15).

Obadiah promises that, "The house of Jacob shall be a fire…and no survivor shall remain of the house of Esau." Knowing that Iranians are descendants of Esau places this prophecy directly in our future. Micah 4 describes the time when the Messiah will rule in peace from Jerusalem over all the nations after they have been "threshed" by the Lord. Micah 5 prophecies that the Messiah will be the birthplace of Jesus. Also, the nations will be ashamed of their military might and shall come before the Lord trembling in fear.

Zephaniah contains strong messages to the nations that are Israel's enemies as well as to Israel for disobedience. Zephaniah 1 refers to the day of the Lord, "The great day of the Lord is near, it is near and hastens quickly...a day of trouble and distress, a day of devastation and desolation, a day of darkness and gloominess...". Chapter 2 covers the judgment of many nations by name like the Philistines (read Palestinians), Moab (Syria), Ethiopia, and Assyria (Northern Iraq and Southern Turkey). Then, Chapter 3 speaks of a faithful remnant of Israel who will be saved by the Lord their God resulting in joy and singing when He brings them back to their land along with fame and praise. This does not happen until the Second Coming.

Zechariah is a Minor Prophet who had much to say about the End Times. All the way through Zechariah, God is assuring the Jews that he will restore Israel's prosperity, rebuild Jerusalem, give Israel prominence in the Millennium, make Israel a shining lamp in the End Times, purify Israel by removing evil in the End Times, deal with all of Israel's enemies, provide for Israel's safety, and fully restore Israel spiritually, agriculturally, physically, and financially. Zechariah 12 shows us that we are living in the End Times because Zechariah 12:2 and 3 says, "Behold, I will make Jerusalem a cup of trembling unto all the people round about, when they shall be in the siege both against Judah and against Jerusalem. And in that day will I make Jerusalem a burdensome stone for all people: all that burden themselves with it shall be cut in pieces, though all the people of the Earth be gathered together against it." Is that not true today?

We hear of the persecution of the Jews by all their surrounding neighbors, of the rocket attacks that occur weekly but are not reported, and of the so-called two-state solution to the forever conflict with the Palestinians (read Philistines dating back to Samuel around 1,000 B.C.). The end of Zechariah 12 tells of the pouring out on the house of David and on Jerusalem when the Jews will look on Whom they have pierced, mourn for Him, and feel the guilt for having crucified Him.

Zechariah Chapter 13 lets us know that only one-third of the Jews will live through the Tribulation and be allowed into Christ's Millennial Kingdom as completed Jews or those Jews who have accepted Jesus as their Messiah, their Lord, and their Savior. We now come to one of the most significant chapters in the Bible concerning the Day of the Lord – Zechariah Chapter 14. As all the nations gather together to fight against the Lord at the battle of Armageddon at the very end of the Tribulation, Jesus returns to the Earth in His Second Coming accompanied with all saints who were raptured seven to ten years earlier to fight for Israel. After Jesus defeats Satan's armies with a single word, Jesus returns to the very spot from which He ascended – the Mount of Olives just East of the Temple Mount in Jerusalem. When His feet touch ground, the Mount of Olives will split from North to South creating a valley from East to West clearing the way to the Temple and providing a pathway for living waters to flow East and West to the Mediterranean and to the Dead Sea making the Dead Sea alive once more. Jesus will then rule from Jerusalem for a thousand years – the Millennium.

The last book in the Old Testament is the book of Malachi. After this book, there was a four-hundred-year scriptural silence before Jesus' birth. Malachi foretells of another "dual mountain" prophecy preceded by the awesome words, "For, behold, the day cometh, that shall burn like an oven; and all the proud, yea, and all that do wickedly, shall be stubble." (Malachi 4:1) Malachi goes on to foretell of Elijah the prophet coming before the Lord comes. Of course, Jesus called John the Baptizer Elijah (actually Elias) to prepare the hearts of fathers to their children and the hearts of children to their fathers (vs. 6). But, the real fulfillment of this prophecy is that the real Elijah, who did not die, will be one of the Two Witnesses of Revelation Chapter 11, minister for the first half of the Tribulation at the Temple in Jerusalem alongside the second witness (perhaps Moses, but probably Enoch because Enoch did not die either), then be allowed to be killed by the Antichrist, lie in the street for three days, then be resurrected in front of the entire world. This satisfies the Hebrews 9:27 "appointed unto men once to die" for both Elijah and Enoch. Elijah thus fulfills the verse, "Behold, I will send you Elijah the prophet before the coming of the great and dreadful day of the Lord."

Conclusion

We have covered many of the Old Testament prophecies concerning the End Times and shown how they often have an initial, partial fulfillment, then a later and complete fulfillment mostly in our immediate future. To have the knowledge of what God has planned for all of us soon is a true blessing and a great comfort. Of course, it is also a call to all of us that time is very short, and we must share the Gospel of Jesus Christ to everyone we meet so that they will not be subject to God's Wrath and the coming Tribulation.

Next, we will investigate the New Testament prophecies of the End Times and their obvious relevance to our current day and time. We should all come away from this study with a growing awareness of just how close we are to eternity and the wondrous blessing of serving with Christ, learning of Christ, and worshipping the Risen Savior for all eternity in His Presence! God Bless! And, Maranatha! Come, Lord Jesus!

We have spent quite some time covering the Old Testament prophecies of the End Times. It should be quite evident through these examples that Israel and the Jewish people play a very important part in the End Times. In fact, the End Times are the time reserved by God to bring His people Israel back into fellowship with Him and reveal His Messiah to them at last. We are indeed experiencing those very days right now!

What we have to realize and come to know is that God's Word is alive and "sharper than any two-edged sword" in both the Old and the New Testaments from Genesis 1:1 to Revelation 22:21! When God speaks, we should listen and, especially and emphatically, read God's Word for what it says without adding to it some interpretation of man. God's Word speaks clearly, He does not confuse like the enemy does. Some areas of Bible study may take more time than others, cross referencing, and prayer, but through the Holy Spirit's leading, we can know and understand what we need to carry out the Will of God in our lives. We can also realize that we already have the confidence and assurance that only knowledge of God through Jesus Christ, our Lord and Savior, can give to us! And, we must and should let that knowledge remove all fear, destroy anxiety, and establish joy in all circumstances in our lives!

Let us end this chapter with this. Trust God trust His Word, and trust that He is always in control! Trust what God has to tell us about our immediate future, what is to come for the Church, the Jews, for Israel, and for all of unbelieving humanity. We must realize how secure we are in Jesus Christ! With God, what can man do to me? I am a citizen of Heaven, one with Christ! Even so, Come Lord Jesus!

CHAPTER FOUR

SEQUENCE OF EVENTS TO COME AND WHY -
NEW TESTAMENT REFERENCES TO THE END TIMES

Preliminary Discussion

We have stated before that the reading of God's Word on a regular basis, a daily basis, in its entirety, is essential and mandatory to know God, to discern true meaning from God's Word, and to understand Bible Prophecy. Listening to others teach and preach on or about God's Word is useful, enlightening, and certainly recommended as long as care is taken to be sure that the Word being taught and preached by others is the accurate and trustworthy Word of God and not someone's biased interpretation or opinion.

To be sure, we have all heard of those who say certain parts of the Bible are either old-fashioned, do not pertain to the "modern" world, are hard to understand, or contain errors in translation. Let me assure you that none of those things are correct and can lead us down a road that terminates in unbelief. God is God! Because that is true, He is outside time, space, and His Creation or us. God cannot lie, so His inspired Word, straight from the inspiration of the Holy Spirit through about 40 blessed writers over a time span of 2,000 years, is true and eternal just as He is.

Many make statements that they generally hear from others such as: (1) the Bible has errors in it due to misinterpretations or bad translations; (2) the Bible, especially the Old Testament, is not pertinent to our "modern" age; (3) God is different in the Old Testament than He appears to be in the New Testament; (4) the Bible, in general, is hard to understand and interpret; and, (5) Prophecy is vague and difficult to see how it affects Christians in this time of advanced communications, computer technology, artificial intelligence, and the internet. Let me be clear. All of these are incorrect, absurd, and dangerous. And the significant reason, and there is only one reason, for these fallacies is the simple fact that individual people do not read God's Word for themselves! The danger lies in accepting these falsehoods as truth and miss out on the blessings that God has promised those that read His Word. Revelation 1:3 promises such a blessing when Revelation is read, "Blessed is he that readeth, and they that hear the words of this prophecy, and keep those things which are written therein: for the time is at hand."

God is the same yesterday, today, and forever (Hebrews 13:8), so He is the same God in both Testaments. Also, faith in God is the theme of both

Testaments showing clearly that the times were different, the circumstances were different, but God is consistent, truthful, and trustworthy because He is God! When it comes to Bible Prophecy, the claim that Prophecy is difficult to understand is almost universal in modern Christianity. Not true! This false claim is, again, generally what people hear and just repeat. When an individual commits himself to reading God's Word regularly, daily, the Spirit of God opens up the Word of God to our understanding. A.W. Tozer said, "We shall not seek to understand in order to believe, but to believe in order that we may understand." Put another way, we should not seek proof that God is wise. The unbelieving mind would never be convinced regardless of the proof presented. But the believing heart, the worshipping heart, never needs proof.

The Christian Church today, in general, is ignoring the Old Testament, is ignoring Prophecy, has turned against Israel, is losing sight of the true nature of God, is reading less and less of God's Word as individuals much less as churches, and is concentrating on prosperity when the Bible basically tells us that we will have difficulties and trials throughout our lives even after we become Christians. For these reasons and many others, we should be driven to learn more and more from God's Word. We should let our reading of the Bible show us that proper interpretation of the Word is to let Scripture interpret Scripture and leave personal opinions out of consideration. All of God's Word is relevant to our lives today, and the sooner we realize that, the sooner we will be in God's Will and live more joyously in a world gone mad!

Introduction

When we look at Bible Prophecy, we tend to think that the Old Testament has prophecies pertaining to the time before Christ and the New Testament prophecies pertain to His Second Coming. Actually, that is a very unfortunate stance since the Old Testament has a multitude of prophecies yet to be fulfilled even in our day. Plus, many of the Old Testament prophecies are extremely detailed in their content which seem to be shouting at us from the headlines of today's news sites. And, there are many prophecies in the New Testament that have as their basis prophecies from the Old Testament, the most prominent of which is Daniel's third vision of the seventy weeks which was completely fulfilled in Old Testament times except for the 70th week which is the Tribulation and the Time of Jacob's Trouble.

Scholars have concluded that about one-third of the Bible was and is prophecy or a foretelling of events that did or will come to pass. The Bible is the only book in all the world that has dared to prophesy events that will occur hundreds or thousands of years in the future from the dates of their writing. The prophet Ezekiel was called to prophesy "of the times that are far off" (Ezek. 12:27).

Fulfilled prophecies of the Bible are proof beyond dispute of the Living God Who knows all things from the beginning to the end because He is outside of time, infinite, and transcendent. There are hundreds of prophecies in the Bible that have been fulfilled. Dr. Harold Willmington of Liberty University has listed 416 Bible prophecies that have been fulfilled in accordance with their projected time table. Every prophecy of the Bible that should have been fulfilled to this date has been fulfilled. To cite just one example, Moses prophesied that because of spiritual apostasy Israel would be scattered into all nations, not just Assyria or Babylon (Deuteronomy 28). Moses also prophesied that in the end of the age Israel would be regathered out of all nations (Deuteronomy 30). After Moses, prophet after prophet to Jesus Christ foretold the dispersion of Israel into all the world, and then their return. We know all of this to be true as we look at a thriving nation of Israel today revived after over 1800 years being totally abandoned and suffered loss of their sovereignty as a nation.

We read in Genesis 10:25 that at the time of the building of the Tower of Babel, in the days of Peleg, God divided the land mass of the Earth into continents and islands. The explanation for that would take a lot of time and space, but, suffice it to say, that the one-and-only Ice Age lasted at least a couple of hundred years after the Flood of Noah, then started melting thus filling the oceans and dividing the land masses into islands and continents and probably sinking cities on the seashore like Atlantis – yes, Atlantis was a real city, not myth, probably. According to Acts 17:24-27, God purposed to disperse mankind into islands and continents to establish nations. Nations grew into empires, but God said that empires would fall and be broken up again into separate nations until His own King of Kings would reign supreme. The prophetic course of empires and nations is given in the second chapter of Daniel from the image of King Nebuchadnezzar's dream. What is important is that this sequence of empires stretches from ancient Babylon over 500 years B.C. all the way to today, some 2500 years later thus spanning much of the Old Testament and all of the New Testament!

- Babylon, the head of gold, would fall to Medo-Persia. Fulfilled, 538 B.C.

- Medo-Persia would fall to Greece. Fulfilled, 333 B.C.

- Greece would be divided into four empires: Egypt, Syria, Mesopotamia, and Asia. Fulfilled, 320 B.C.

- The four-part division of Greece would be absorbed by Rome, the iron empire, and the last world empire. Fulfilled, approximately 165 B.C.

- The Roman Empire would split and turn into separate entities. Fulfilled, A.D. 500.

- The split areas, certain of them from the Roman Empire, would continue to rule the world until the end of the age: the Spanish, French, British, German, Portuguese, Belgium, and Italian empires, etc.

- The separate small empires would bruise, or war, between themselves (Daniel 2:40). English-Spanish War; French and English wars; Napoleonic wars; World War I and II, etc.

- In the extremity of the age, the small empires would be broken into many smaller pieces (Daniel 2:41). Franklin Roosevelt and Joseph Stalin forced Winston Churchill to agree to a break-up of the Roman colonial system. The number of nations in 1945 of 70 rose to approximately 200 by the year 2000.

- A combination of European nations within the original Roman Empire will form a revived Roman Empire to bring forth the Antichrist. This now seems to be coming true with the present European Union having great difficulties with their member nations wanting to withdraw possibly leading to a new coalition of nations resulting in the Revived Roman Empire of Revelation.

I expect the Rapture any day! The reason? Number one would be we get to be with Jesus our Lord! The second would be the Jews will get God's full attention on them accepting their Messiah as Lord and Savior! The third would be that the unrighteousness of this world, the evil of this world, will be addressed directly by God through the Wrath of God being brought! So, exactly why do I, and many others including most of you, think the Rapture is so near? This proof is found in the End Times prophecies of the New Testament when read in conjunction with the End Times prophecies in the Old Testament. Full understanding of End Times prophecy is impossible without this approach!

The Rapture requires nothing to occur before it can take place, unlike virtually every other End Time prophecy. We cannot know the day or the hour of the Rapture. Mark 13:28-32 says, "Now learn a parable of the fig tree; when her branch is yet tender, and putteth forth leaves, ye know that summer is near: so ye in like manner, when ye shall see these things come to pass, know that it is nigh, even at the doors. Verily I say unto you, that this generation shall not pass, till all these things be done. Heaven and Earth shall pass away: but My words shall not pass away. But of that day and that hour knoweth no man, no, not the angels which are in Heaven, neither the Son, but the Father." This set of verses echoed in Matthew and Luke clear up any notion that we can know the exact day or hour of the Rapture and what follows. But we CAN know the general time through a close examination of many of the New Testament prophecies, especially this one in Mark.

First of all, the fig tree (Mark 13:28) is symbolic of Israel. Hosea 9:10 says, "When I found Israel, it was like finding grapes in the desert; when I saw your ancestors, it was like seeing the early fruit on the fig tree." Later, the Bible tells us of the glorious time when "Judah and Israel lived in safety, every man under his vine and his fig tree, from Dan even to Beersheba, all the days of Solomon." (1 Kings 4:25) Israel is celebrating their 71st anniversary this year of becoming an independent, sovereign nation after 1,813 years without a country. This fruit of the fig tree and true events happening in today's world tell us that we are, indeed, in the End Times.

The "things come to pass" (Mark 13:29) are the various signs that Jesus told His disciples about when they asked Him when the Temple would be completely removed, every stone, and what sign would foretell of His Second Coming (Mark 13:4), signs such as wars and rumors of wars, many false Christs, nation rising against nation and separations within nations, earthquakes, and famines. Jesus said when you see these signs, then He is even "at the doors". Look for the Temple Institute in Jerusalem "suddenly" realize that the ancient destroyed Temple of Jesus' day had to be near the Gihon Spring which locates the Temple South of the "Temple Mount" known today as the location of the Dome of the Rock! Problem solved! It has been a mystery for many years just how the Jews would build the Tribulation Temple where the Dome of the Rock, one of the three most revered sites in all the Muslim World, is currently located. The Jews will come to the realization that they can erect a Tabernacle like the one Moses had in the wilderness South of the Temple Mount and fulfill their long desire to have a Temple once again.

Mark 13:30 reveals that the very generation that sees these signs (Israel becoming a nation, wars and rumors of wars, etc.) will not pass away (all die out) until the Rapture and the Tribulation begin. Then, Jesus says in Mark 13:32 that no man, not even the angels in Heaven, know the exact day. Of course, Jesus knows NOW when He is calling us upward and when He will return. He did not know the date and probably did not want to reveal the date when He was walking the Earth with His disciples. And, Hebrews 10:24 and 25 admonishes us to not forsake the assembling of ourselves together, as we have not done this evening, but to provoke and exhort one another to love and good works AS WE SEE THE DAY APPROACHING! So, we CAN know the general time of the Rapture after all!

Last chapter, we finished up looking at many of the End Times prophecies we find in the Old Testament. If anything, this should show us, since we had to take most of two chapters to cover what the Old Testament had to tell us concerning what the Lord has to say about His people Israel, His land Israel, and His Church, that the Old Testament is current and applicable to our lives just as the New Testament is current.

Our faith is enhanced in the knowledge that God's Word in its entirety, both Old and New Testaments, is a cohesive, complete book of history, a unified story of the redemption of mankind's reconciliation with God, a restoration volume enabling those who accept Christ's sacrificial death and resurrection to see clearly that God's Plan for our future is exciting, is eternal, is full of joy and wonder, and is also quite terrifying to the majority of men and women who do not accept Christ as Savior and Lord.

We now will look at many of the New Testament End Time prophecies and how they refer amazingly back to their Old Testament counterparts. Time and space will not allow us to consider all of the New Testament prophecies in detail, that must come through your personal studies. We will see that full understanding of what God wants us to know and share with our loved ones, our acquaintances, those we meet in our lives that God brings to us, depends upon our complete grasp of the entire Bible and what God has to say about the End Times. We will realize that God wants us, His Church, to know His Plan for our future so that we can experience the joy of His salvation NOW. So that we can appreciate fully what Jesus has done for us, what we have accepted from Jesus, and what that means in total, meaning what is in store for us in our future, but also what kind of a future those who reject Jesus Christ are facing, both Jew and Gentile alike.

New Testament End Time Prophecies

We start with Matthew, Mark, and Luke. These three books all present the "same sight", the synoptic view ("syn" is same and "optic" is sight) or the same approach to revealing what happened to Jesus while He was here on Earth. John's Gospel, on the other hand, focuses on the deity of Christ and many other aspects of His life that the synoptic Gospels do not. In all three of the synoptic Gospels, or those three books that contain much the same details of Jesus' life here on Earth, Jesus answers His disciples' questions found in Matthew 24, Mark 13, and Luke 21 by listing signs foretelling of His return. Those signs in Matthew are false christs, wars and rumors of wars, nations rising against nations, ethnic and philosophical differences (kingdom against kingdom), famines, pestilences, earthquakes, false prophets, love waxing cold or love for one another decreasing rapidly, and the spreading of the Gospel worldwide which could only happen in this time of satellites, cell phones, and the internet.

Mark adds that there will be persecution of Christians to a great degree, but, when that comes, believers are to not worry what to say because the Holy Spirit will give them what to do and say. Luke adds that fearful sights and great signs will come from Heaven. All three synoptic Gospels address the coming of the Tribulation, Matthew and Mark specifically warn of the Abomination of Desolation from Daniel 9:27 and referred to in 2 Thessalonians 2:3-10 when Antichrist comes into the restored Temple and declares himself to be God. Then, all three books relate the Second Coming of Jesus with great glory, and Matthew and Mark say if Jesus did not stop the Battle of Armageddon in Revelation 19, all flesh would perish because of the great rebellion against God.

Matthew Chapter 24 gives the overview of Jesus judging the nations in the sheep and goat judgment that immediately precedes the start of Christ's Millennial reign on the Earth. Matthew 24:40,41 says, "Then two men will be in the field; one will be taken and the other left; two women will be grinding at the mill; one will be taken and the other left. Luke 17:34-36 addresses the same subject, "I tell you, in that night there will be two (men) in one bed; the one will be taken and the other will be left. Two (women) will be grinding together the one will be taken and the other left. Two (men) will be in the field; the one will be taken and the other left."

This set of verses deeply resonates with many Evangelicals today as they look forward to the Rapture – the day (they say) that Christ comes near the Earth to take his people away to Heaven with him. But who will actually be taken and why? The assumption that Rapture-believers incorrectly impose upon these verses is that those who "are taken" are the faithful people of God, being taken away to safety by Christ so that the judgment of condemnation can be dealt out on the sinners who "are left behind" on the Earth. But, and extremely import and significant, context clears up this misreading very quickly. Back up and look at verse Matthew 24:37. "As it was in the days of Noah, so it will be at the coming of the Son of Man. For in the days before the flood, people were eating and drinking, marrying and giving in marriage, up to the day Noah entered the ark; and they knew nothing about what would happen until the flood came and took them all away." That is how it will be at the coming of the Son of Man. Two men will be in the field; one will be taken and the other left…

Our Lord is making a comparison between the Day of His Return, His Second Coming, and the Flood in Noah's time. Apart from the huge battle of Armageddon occurring in Israel with millions willing and confident to fight against the King of kings and Lord of lords, life will be going on as usual until, all of a sudden, the wicked or unredeemed are taken away. Where? To hell or hades. Why? Because Jesus is about to set up His Millennial Kingdom, and only believers can enter. Just as the flood swept away the sinners who rejected God in Noah's day, so too will the Judgment sweep away the sinners who reject God at the end of our present age.

It's the sinners who are being "taken away," unlike the Rapture! Several times throughout Jesus' teachings he compares the Kingdom of God to a house or a banquet: when people are faithful to him, they are allowed to stay with God there forever. When people reject him, he will return "at an hour they do not expect" and they are "cast out" where there is "weeping and gnashing of teeth" (Matthew 21:40-41, 22:13, 24:50-51, 25:10-13, 25:30, 25:46).

So, since we believe in the Rapture, we know that these verses do not describe the event of Jesus taking away his faithful people. Rather, this is a picture of the judgment of those who reject God, and their separation from the inheritance of eternal life at the end of this age.

I Corinthians Chapter 15 we learn of Christ's reign in the Millennium and Christ's complete victory over death. We also learn of the "twinkling of an eye" speed at which the Rapture will occur. The trumpet of God will sound, then we shall all be changed from corruption to incorruption, from sinners to non-sinners, from mortal to immortal. We also get the most comprehensive description of the new bodies we all will receive at the Rapture, both the dead physically in Christ and the living that are in Christ at that soon coming time. Our present bodies are made of the dust of the Earth, corruption from Adam's sin; but, at the Rapture, since we ae in Christ, our bodies will "put on" incorruption" and immortality. We will get a resurrection body like Jesus has had since the Resurrection so long ago. This solidifies Jesus' victory over sin and death since we will live and reign with Jesus forevermore.

II Corinthians 5:9 and 10 tell of the Bema Judgment Seat of Christ which is also mentioned in Romans 4:10 – 12. What is the Bema Seat? A bema seat is a throne of judgment used by kings throughout the ages. Jesus' Bema Seat is His evaluation of believers and what each has done for Him. First of all, we, as believers, will not see God's Wrath nor punishment of sins because we have accepted Jesus' death on the cross and resurrection from the dead as substitutionary payment for our sins. And, since we are children of light and not of darkness (1 John 1:7 and 1 Thessalonians 5:5), we are not to see God's Wrath (1 Thessalonians 5:9). This means we are raptured before the Tribulation, will not be punished for our sins because of Christ's sacrifice, but we will be judged for what we did for Christ after salvation. That is the Bema Seat of Christ that occurs just after the Rapture. Our works will be evaluated whether we have built upon the foundation of the Lord Jesus Christ with gold, silver, and precious stones, or on worldly things resulting in works built with wood, hay, and stubble. Obviously, and since we know all our sins are forgiven, this judgment is focused on what we have done in Jesus' Name and not our own. If gold, silver, precious stones, then reward is given; if wood, hay, stubble, then those things done were not for Jesus and will be burned up, we will suffer loss, but we will still be in Heaven!

1 Thessalonians 4:13-18 describes the Rapture of the Church or all believers in Jesus Christ from His resurrection until that very day. Some ask the question about the Old Testament believers before Christ like Abraham, Noah, Moses, Mary and Martha, and all the others. Do they get new bodies like ours at the same time? The answer is no, not until the Second Coming. At the end of the Tribulation, Jesus Christ will return with all of the Christians who died during the church age or who were alive at the time of the Rapture. This occurs prior to the tribulation period (Revelation 19:11-15). After Jesus defeats the armies of the Anti-Christ (Revelation 19:19-21), Jesus then resurrects all of the bodies of those Christians who died during the Tribulation and all of the Old Testament saints. Revelation 20:4 includes the Tribulation saints.

"And I saw thrones, and they sat upon them, and judgment was given to them. And I saw the souls of those who had been beheaded because of the testimony of Jesus and because of the word of God, and those who had not worshiped the beast or his image, and had not received the mark upon their forehead and upon their hand; and they came to life and reigned with Christ for a thousand years." (Revelation 20:4)

The prophet Daniel predicted that the Old Testament saints would be resurrected when he said, "And there will be a time of distress such as never occurred since there was a nation until that time; and at that time your people, everyone who is found written in the book, will be rescued. And many of those who sleep in the dust of the ground will awake, these to everlasting life, but the others to disgrace and everlasting contempt. (Daniel 12:1-2) See what I mean by the New Testament and the Old Testament correlating perfectly?

Today's disappointing and dramatic refusal and rejection of Christ is a sign of the End Times. 2 Thessalonians Chapter 1 reveals Jesus Second Coming to take vengeance on those who do not know God and do not know or obey the Gospel of our Lord Jesus Christ. Chapter 2 says that the Day of the Lord, "that" day, will not come before a great falling away from God as well as a removal of believers occurs. Then and only then will the man of sin, the son of perdition, the Antichrist, will be revealed and exalt himself as God. Much more on this later.

2 Timothy Chapter 3 is perhaps the best description of our world today, of its corruption, of its blatant sin against God, of its outright arrogance and evil. "But know this, that in the last days perilous times will come: for men will be lovers of themselves, lovers of money, boasters, proud, blasphemers, disobedient to parents, unthankful, unholy, unloving, unforgiving, slanderers, without self-control, brutal, despisers of good, traitors, headstrong, haughty, lovers of pleasure rather than lovers of God, having a form of godliness but denying its power. And from such people turn away." (2 Timothy 3:1-5)

2 Timothy Chapter 4 has Paul warning Timothy, "For the time will come when they will not endure sound doctrine, but according to their own desires, because that have itching ears, they will heap up for themselves teachers; and they will turn their ears away from the truth, and be turned aside to fables." Paul mentions the coming of Christ three times in Chapter 4 of 2 Timothy.

2 Peter Chapter 3 tells us of this world that was judged by water in Noah's Flood some 4400 years ago will one day be destroyed by fire along with all the heavens. Then, Jesus will create a new Heaven and a new Earth for us to live in forever (Revelation 21:1, Isaiah 65:17, and Isaiah 66:22)

1 and 2 John have references to the Antichrist, the only places in the Bible that actually use the name Antichrist. Elsewhere, he is called the beast or the son of perdition and others. 2 Peter 3 and Jude both speak about scoffers and apostates in the church and outside of the church about the End Times, the Second Coming, the Rapture, the Tribulation, all of End Times prophecy as already happened, could never happen, will not happen. Pretty much describes what we hear when we listen to the mainstream news, doesn't it?

Before we get to the book of Revelation, we need to address one of the elephants in the room, Israel. The book of Revelation covers what we call the Tribulation which is Daniel's 70th week (Daniel Chapter 9), and the Tribulation is primarily for Israel since Jeremiah 30:7 calls it the time of Jacob's trouble. There is a considerable amount of false teaching within the church today that Israel is no longer important, that the Church of Jesus Christ has replaced Israel (Replacement Theology or Supersessionism). Proper and thorough study of God's Word shows this to be not only false but ridiculous and, indeed, blasphemous. The Covenant made by God with the Patriarchs included the everlasting possession of the land of Israel. This promise was made to Abraham (Genesis 12:7, 13:15 & 17, 17:8) and was confirmed to Isaac (Genesis26:3), and then to Jacob (Genesis 28:13), the father of the twelve tribes of Israel. There is no indication that God "transmuted" the promise of ownership of the land to a "spiritual inheritance" by the Church. To do so is to ascribe changeableness to God, and this is contrary to the statement of Romans 11:29 about irrevocable promises of God (compare Malachi 3:6 that states God never changes) which affirms that God has not set aside his call of Israel as a nation and never would.

A study of the New Testament usage of the word "Israel" (occurs 70 times) shows that in every case it refers to the people or land of Israel and never to the Church. Thus, throughout the Church dispensation or Age of Grace, the Church and Israel exist side by side with separate and distinct callings. Since the land of Israel and the people of Israel are inseparable in God's promises and dealings, and because people in association with a land imply a national entity or state, the New Testament again implies that a Jewish nation has an ongoing place in the plan of God. That this Jewish nation-state will find its fulfilment in a Millennial Kingdom at the end of the Tribulation, over which the Messiah, the Son of David, reigns from Jerusalem, is nowhere denied, and is in fact implied in the New Testament (Luke 1:32-33 – "reign over the house of Jacob forever", 2:32 – "the Glory of Your people Israel").

We need to recognize that the book of Revelation was written by John the Apostle late in his life, about 95 A.D., over 60 years after Jesus' resurrection. The official title of this book is "The Revelation of Jesus Christ", not John's Revelation or the book of Revelations. The entire book is one vision that John the Apostle was given by the Holy Spirit when he was exiled on the island of Patmos by Roman emperor Domitian in punishment for not worshiping the emperor. Domitian was an evil emperor, but he was not stupid. He could have killed John, but that would have made John a martyr and even more influential. So, Domitian just exiled John, which also backfired since John wrote and distributed to seven churches in Asia Minor this revelation of unveiling of what is to come on the entire world, but specifically for the Jews to bring them to their Savior, their Messiah, Jesus Christ.

Revelation Chapter 1 introduces the vision that John received, a promised blessing on all those who hear, read, and keep the words of this prophecy, and the command to write the vision down and send it to the seven churches in Asia Minor: in Ephesus, Smyrna, Pergamos, Thyatira, Sardis, Philadelphia, and Laodicea. Revelation Chapters 2 and 3 give us the messages Jesus had for each of these churches which represent three things: one, the churches that existed in John's day representing the condition of Jesus' Church in the first century A.D.; two, each church represents the Church Age or Age of Grace and the many conditions that have accompanied the life of Jesus' Church from the Resurrection to today; and three, these churches also represent the churches that exist today showing us the difficulties that all churches face from the world and from the people that attend the churches.

Revelation 3:10 is especially pertinent to our time since it refers to the Rapture and our assurance that we, as true Christians, will NOT go through the Tribulation. "Because you have kept My command to persevere, I also will keep you from (Greek "ek" which means "out of") the hour of trial which shall come upon the whole world, to test those who dwell on the Earth." This is logically and clearly evident that those true believing and obedient Christians in the End Times will not go through the Tribulation (the hour of trial on the WHOLE Earth which has not happened since the Flood of Noah) but be taken "out of" or raptured.

To go along with this encouraging prophecy, Revelation 4:1 says, "After these things (the letters to the churches) I looked, and behold, a door standing open in Heaven. And the first voice which I heard was like a trumpet speaking with me, saying, 'Come up here, and I will show you things which must take place after this.'" The picture is of John being raptured into Heaven to see what will happen after his leaving Earth, which is exactly what Paul told the Thessalonians and the Corinthians, that the Rapture happens with the Trump of God, and all true believers in Jesus Christ, living and dead, will join Him and be removed from the Wrath of God to come on ALL the Earth.

Now we get an explanation of what the Tribulation has in store for those "left behind", events mostly sequential with a few asides that are not sequential but necessary for understanding what God wants to accomplish during this very trying time. Chapter 4 gives us a glimpse, a pretty good glimpse, of God's Glory and the need to please such a Magnificent God. This leads into Chapter 5 and the scroll containing all three sets of God's Judgments (Seals, Trumpets, and Bowls) that the only One Worthy to open the scroll can open it, Jesus Christ.

Then follows a series of judgments, all grouped in sevens. The first group of judgments is the seven seal judgments (6:1–8:1). We see first, the Antichrist is given permission to reveal himself as the rider on the white horse. Then, war is enhanced and worse than ever before with the rider on the red horse. The third seal is famine and starvation symbolized by the rider on the black horse. Then, fourth, death, disease, massive drug abuse, and the release of animals as destructive are released with the rider on the pale green, sickening-colored horse. We see all of these conditions on a smaller scale today but isolated to certain areas of the globe. During the Tribulation, these will cover the entire Earth. The fifth seal represents the many, many martyrs slain during the very first months of the Tribulation calling out to God to avenge their deaths for being His witnesses. The sixth seal brings on the Earth the greatest earthquake, worldwide, that has ever happened even causing the sun to turn black and the moon red. The heavens seem to be falling as well, but the Greek word here translated "stars" can mean meteors, so a great meteor storm could what John saw.

In Chapter 7, there are 144,000 Israelites (7:1-8), 12,000 from each of the twelve tribes of Israel, that are sealed by God for protection from the Antichrist, and they travel the world as super Billy Grahams evangelizing everyone and being divinely protected at the same time. Also, worship by an innumerable number of (presumably Gentile) converts, tribulation martyrs (7:9-17), is revealed. In the midst of the outpouring of God's wrath in the form of seven seals, this vision of hope and salvation emerges. Once again, God's holiness (7:15-16) and Christ's redemption (7:17) are emphasized. Immediately after this glorious sight, in Chapter 8, the seventh seal is poured out (8:1) which is the seven trumpet judgments. But these judgments are so much worse than the seal judgments that a half-hour of silence occurs, even Heaven itself remains quiet for that half-hour.

The next series of judgments is the seven trumpets (8:2–11:19), which are designed largely after the plagues on Egypt. These trumpet judgments are more drastic, definite, and final than the seal judgments, but not as universal as the bowl judgments to follow. These trumpet judgments come hot and heavy, sequentially with nothing in-between. One third of all trees are burned up, all the green grass is burned up, a disaster in the sea poisons the sea killing one third of life in the sea as well as one third of all ships on the sea. Then, a meteor (Wormwood) falls into the rivers and streams causing one third of them to be poison. A third of the sun's light is lost which renders the moon to lose a third of its light. So, also, with the stars. As an introduction into the ninth chapter and the last three Trumpet Judgments, the last verse in Chapter

8 mentions an angel flying around the world proclaiming the last three Trumpet Judgments as "Woes" signifying the great destruction that was about to take place.

The fifth Trumpet Judgment or first woe is the release of the most hideous fallen angels of all that were imprisoned in the bottomless pit to come and torment unbelievers for five months each. The torment is so bad that all will seek death, but God prevents them from attaining death. The sixth Trumpet releases 200 million, perhaps the combined armies of the East (China, Korea, Indonesia, and maybe Japan) that is given permission by God to slay one third of all men alive. Today, that would be approximately two and one-half BILLION people!

Chapter 11 tells us about the two witnesses who arrive early in the Tribulation to prophesy in Jerusalem, at the new Temple, telling the world of Jesus' soon return and of the terrible nature of the Antichrist. They will be protected by God for three and a half years as well as being able to breathe fire on those who try to hurt them. It has always been speculation as to these two godly men are, but I believe that since Enoch and Elijah never died but were both translated to Heaven, it will be these two men since they are killed by the Antichrist at the mid-Tribulation point. Hebrews 11:5 gives a little more detail: "By faith Enoch was taken from this life, so that he did not experience death: 'He could not be found, because God had taken him away.' For before he was taken, he was commended as one who pleased God." This being "taken away" is what Enoch is most famous for. Only two people in the Bible are said to have been chosen by God to escape death, Enoch and Elijah. Another point to consider is that Enoch would represent the Gentiles of the Earth who believe and Elijah the Jews who believe. Enoch appears to have been given this privilege due to being a man who walked faithfully with God (Genesis 5:24) and pleased God (Hebrews 11:5). The most common assumption for Enoch's rapture is so that he could serve as one of the two witnesses, alongside Elijah, in the end times ("As they were walking along and talking together, suddenly a chariot of fire and horses of fire appeared and separated the two of them, and Elijah went up to Heaven in a whirlwind." (2 Kings 2:11)) They lay in the streets of Jerusalem for three and a half days with a great deal of celebration and gift-giving until God calls out to them from Heaven, "Come up here!", just as He did at the Rapture. This call to the two dead witnesses means that all men have now died or been raptured that placed their faith in God either in the Old Testament or in Jesus Christ. They stand to their feet in front of the world as all see this happen through our modern-day technologies, and then they ascend into Heaven in a cloud. A great earthquake happens at this time and 7,000 died in Jerusalem. The seventh trumpet follows (11:15-19), which is the seven bowl judgments.

We now learn of the woman and the war (12:1-18). The dragon who wages war on the woman is Satan; his hostility against the woman, Israel, and her child, the Messiah, are pictured quite vividly. After Satan's plans to consume the woman and her child had failed, he now contemplates his next move. Chapter 13 is the result of meditation. Now the beasts go after the saints (13:7), as well as the rest of the world (13:8). This parallels the Matthew 24:15-21 ("When ye therefore shall see the abomination of desolation, spoken of by Daniel the prophet, stand in the holy place, (whoever reads, let him understand) then let them which be in Judaea flee into the mountains: let him which is on the housetop not come down to take any thing out of his house: neither let him which is in the field return back to take his clothes. And woe unto them that are with child, and to them that give suck in those days! But pray ye that your flight be not in the winter, neither on the sabbath day: for then shall be great tribulation [last half of the Tribulation period], such as was not since the beginning of the world to this time, no, nor ever shall be.") and Mark 13:14-19 ("But when ye shall see the abomination of desolation, spoken of by Daniel the prophet, standing where it ought not, (let him that reads understand,) then let them that be in Judaea flee to the mountains: and let him that is on the housetop not go down into the house, neither enter therein, to take any thing out of his house: and let him that is in the field not turn back again for to take up his garment. But woe to them that are with child, and to them that give suck in those days! And pray ye that your flight be not in the winter. For in those days shall be affliction, such as was not from the beginning of the creation which God created unto this time, neither shall be."), scriptures that call for the Jews to flee to protection from God and not to even go back to pack because Satan is after them!

As a result of the outrage the Antichrist now possessed by Satan himself has for the Jews, he turns his anger toward the redeemed. Chapter 13 sees the rise of the beast who comes from the sea of nations making him a Gentile possessed by Satan declaring himself to be worshiped for the last half of the Tribulation known as the Great Tribulation which lasts three and one-half years. This is the Abomination of Desolation spoken of in Daniel 9:27 when the Jews are to flee from the Antichrist and to the safety of God. A second beast, the False Prophet, rises from the Earth making him a Jew, and he promotes the worship of the Antichrist as well as setting up the mark of the beast that everyone must have to buy and sell or eat.

The final series of judgments is the seven bowl judgments (15:1–18:24). Six out of seven of them are the same as the plagues on Egypt, only these are more climactic and universal. These bowls of God's Wrath are the most terrible, the most destructive, the most devastating of all the judgments because God is telling the unrepentant that this is the very last chance they have to accept Him and reject their personal sin. The first bowl creates sores on everyone with the mark of the beast. The second bowl turns all the Earth's seas to blood thereby killing all sea life. The third bowl is poured out on the rivers and springs turning them to blood and cutting off almost all drinking water. The fourth bowl of God's Wrath is poured out on the sun so that it scorches all men who then blaspheme God rather than seeking redemption. The fifth bowl creates darkness in the Antichrist's kingdom, a darkness so very dark that men feel pain and blaspheme God. The sixth bowl dries up the Euphrates River allowing the kings of the east to travel to Armageddon to fight against God. Then, the seventh bowl was poured out. A mighty voice from Heaven says, "It is done!" This bowl sends an earthquake that splits Jerusalem into three parts, every island disappears, every mountain falls flat, and one hundred-pound hailstones fall from Heaven also causing all men to blaspheme God, at least the ones left alive.

Chapter 17 deals with the spiritual Babylon, and chapter 18 with economic Babylon of the Tribulation. Care is taken to completely record the history of the rise of this "great harlot" (the rise of the ecumenical church that is led by a 'pope-like' figure) so that spiritual Babylon's destruction can be seen though God's eyes and justification for spiritual Babylon's destruction is understood. Her name is called "Mystery, Babylon" (17:5), thus indicating that this is not the literal city, as can be seen in the interpretation given (17:18). The spirit of Babylon lives on in the secular city: in John's day, it was Rome; in our day, Washington or New York. The economic fall of the great city is then described in 18:1-24. But rather than being a political and religious entity as in chapter 17, this city is commercial, as can be seen by those who lament over her demise (18:9-19). Though merchants and sea captains lament her fall, there is rejoicing by the godly (18:20).

Then, in rapid succession, come the seven last things (19:11–22:5), the first six of which are in chronological sequence covering the millennial kingdom. First, the glorious Second Coming of Christ is disclosed which includes us verse 14 (19:11-16). Second, the result of the battle at the end of the age (Armageddon) is planned for by summoning to a feast for birds (19:17-21). Third, Satan is bound for one thousand years while the Antichrist and the False Prophet are cast into the Lake of Fire, the first to be placed there for eternity (20:1-3). Fourth, the millennial kingdom is described, and the Old Testament saints get their resurrection bodies (20:4-6). Fifth, at the end of the one thousand years, Satan is again unleashed, a great rebellion ensues leading to another great battle of Satan against God, and, this time, all are destroyed, and Satan is cast into the Lake of Fire to join the Antichrist and the False Prophet (20:7-10). Sixth, the Great White Throne judgment takes place at the end of the millennium is recorded where all the unbelieving multitudes are judged by Jesus, face to face, found lacking, and each cast into the Lake of Fire for eternity (20:11-15).

The seventh last thing (21:1–22:5) is the eternal state. God, Jesus, creates a new Heaven and new Earth (21:3-8) which corresponds to Isaiah 66:22. John then tells us of the New Jerusalem (21:9–22:5). It is a dazzling city (21:9-21), in which there is no temple because God and the Lamb are its temple (21:22-27). Out of its midst is flowing the river of life (22:1-3a), and God and the Lamb provide its light (22:3b-5). It is 1500 miles in height, 1500 miles wide, and 1500 miles deep and probably shaped like a cube rather than a pyramid. I think it is a cube because the Holy of Holies in the ancient Temple was a perfect cube, 30 feet in each direction. This is enough room to provide one cubic acre to over 64 trillion people. Obviously, there will be a lot of room in the New Jerusalem for many other things besides people.

After this splendid finale to a vision of the future, John concludes his book with an appeal to the readers (22:6-21) which includes a dire warning not to add or take away from this book of prophecy lest the wrath of the Tribulation be added to them. Three give their testimony of the veracity of this book: an angel (22:6-11), Jesus himself (22:12-17), and John (22:18-21).

Conclusion

We have a much clearer picture of the End Times after looking at most of the End Times prophecies found in both the Old Testament and the New Testament. Hopefully, you now can see that studying the End Times, the Rapture, The Tribulation, and God's Plan for the ages can be more fully understood and appreciated.

The clear message to each of us is that our God loves us, died for us, and wants us to know what is in store for us in eternity. He also wants us to fulfill the Great Commission of Matthew 28 which is sharing the Gospel which also includes discussing eternal life. If you know biblical prophecy about the End Times, discussing the subject of eternal destiny and all associated questions and inquiries can be so much better answered with a clearer knowledge of the End Times prophecies in the entire Bible. And we all can see the necessity to get the message out because time is short. To miss the Rapture is to experience the horror of the Tribulation. Darkness is descending on all of us, but we are children of light. The world is facing great trouble and judgment, but we have hope in Jesus Christ.

Transitioning from the Old Testament Prophecies to the New Testament Prophecies

When we look at the New Testament prophecies concerning the End Times, it is not an easy thing to just change from Old Testament prophecy about the End Times to New Testament prophecy about the End Times because they are inseparably linked! There are many prophecies in the Old Testament that have parallels in the New Testament. Some have been fulfilled, some have not - yet. There are many of those prophecies in the Old Testament that have been amazingly fulfilled in Jesus Christ, yet some remain to be fulfilled. Some scholars have listed over 100 prophecies in the Old Testament just relating to the birth, earthly mission, death, burial, and resurrection of Jesus and not considering His Second Coming. To list just a few of these prophecies:

- He would be born of a virgin (Isa. 7:14).
- He would be an Israelite from the tribe of Judah (Gen, 49:10).
- He would be from the lineage of David (2 Sam. 7:12-13).
- He would be called Emmanuel, God with us (Isa. 7:14).
- He would be born in Bethlehem (Micah 5:2).
- Wise men would worship Him with gifts (Ps. 72:10; Isa. 60:3-9).
- He would be in Egypt for a season (Num. 24:8; Hos. 11:1).
- His birth would result in a massacre of infants (Jer. 31:15).
- He would be called a Nazarene (Isa. 11:1).
- He would make the blind to see, the deaf to hear, the lame to walk (Isa. 53:4-5).
- He would be rejected by His own nation (Ps. 69:8; Isa.53:3).
- He would ride into Jerusalem on a donkey (Zech. 9:9).
- A friend would betray Him for 30 pieces of silver (Ps. 41:9; 55:12-14; Zech. 11:12-13).
- He would be a man of sorrows (Isa. 53:3).
- He would be forsaken by His followers (Zech. 13:7).
- He would be scourged and spat upon (Isa. 50:6).
- He would be crucified between two thieves (Isa. 53:12).
- He would be given vinegar to drink (Ps. 69:21).
- His feet and hands would be pierced (Ps. 22:16; Zech. 12:10).
- His garments would be gambled for at His death (Ps. 22:18).
- He would commend His spirit to the Father (Ps. 31:5).
- Although crucified, no bones would be broken (Exod. 12:46; Ps. 34:20).
- He would be buried with the rich (Isa. 53:9).
- He would be raised from the dead (Ps. 16:10).
- He would ascend to Heaven (Ps. 24:7-10).

Are These Days the End Times?

- He would be seated at God's right hand to intercede for us (Ps. 110:1).

There are many other prophecies in the Old Testament relating to the triumphant return of Jesus Christ, His millennial reign, and His eternal Kingdom. Therefore, we can be sure that if all the prophecies concerning Jesus Christ at His first coming were fulfilled to the letter, then all the prophecies relating to His Second Coming will be fulfilled to the letter. The prophecies in the Old Testament concerning our Lord Jesus Christ will all be completely fulfilled as will all the prophecies in the New Testament surrounding the times we live in today, the times that will see His imminent return, the so-called End Times in which we live!

Shortly before His crucifixion and resurrection, Jesus Christ delivered a major prophecy of end-time events, recorded in Matthew 24, Mark 13 and Luke 21. He was asked by His disciples: "When will these things be? And what will be the sign of your coming, and of the end of the age?" (Matthew 24:3). Jesus responded with a description of conditions and events that would lead up to His second coming. Moreover, He said that when these signs became evident, His return would occur within one generation (Matthew 24:34). Could this be that generation? And what is a generation? Psalm 90:10 says, "The days of our years are threescore years and ten; and if by reason of strength they be fourscore years, yet is their strength labor and sorrow; for it is soon cut off, and we fly away." So, a generation is 70 years at least, maybe 80 years, and if we look at the fulfillment of specific Bible prophecies that we see occurring around us today, I believe that we can see, without question, that we, indeed, are that generation that will see the total fulfillment of all the End Times prophecies!

Throughout the nearly 2,000 years since Christ gave His prophecy, many have thought that theirs was the time of His return and turned out to be wrong, of course. But interestingly, there are a number of prophecies in the Bible that could not be fulfilled until our modern era, the post–World War II period and, more significantly, post-Israel becoming a nation on May 14, 1948! It is important to see that there is a sequence, a timing to all of the New Testament fulfillment of the End Times prophecies. It is also important to see that those prophecies come from unfulfilled Old Testament prophecies as well as those from the New Testament. It is also very important to see that God Almighty wants us to learn from our mistakes, to grasp His Truths, to see that we are completely unable to be sinless and righteous on our own which are the very requirements He has set to be able to be with Him in Heaven when we die.

114

Dispensations

Before we dig deeply into the sequential New Testament prophecies of the End Times, and in light of our complete understanding of how prophecy works, how prophecy makes logical and reasonable sense, we have to look **again** at what the Bible calls dispensations. The need to clearly see just how dispensations fit into prophecy becomes evident when we examine the timeline of the End Times. There is a chart attached to further explain this very important concept of dispensations and how we fit into God's Plan of Salvation of all mankind. How does the Age of Grace and the Tribulation fit together? Isn't the Tribulation God's Wrath and the Age of Grace all about the removal of God's punishment for sin? It seems that the Age of Grace and the Tribulation are different in message and action, and, in fact, they are of different dispensations entirely. The age of Grace is all about Jesus Christ and redemption and the Tribulation relates to the Dispensation of the Law and the Jews. How do these relate to each other in the sense that they seem to be out of order? When we examine deeply what the dispensations are, we see the connections and the sequencing clearly.

How do dispensations fit into Bible Prophecy? There are several ways why we need to know and understand dispensations. First, dispensations show us that God is a caring God who gives mankind every opportunity to discover that only through Him can we gain salvation. Second, dispensations give us a timeline of human existence both in the past, in the present, and in the future. Third, dispensations clear up questions that we have as humans concerning God and His plan for us not to mention our complete depravity and need for Him. Fourth, dispensations give us glimpses into the past, the struggles our forefathers went through so that we can possibly learn from past mistakes and not repeat them. Fifth, and last, dispensations show the way of the future, what is in store for the Earth, for mankind, and for us as saved people.

Often, when one is asked about the Dispensations of God, the response is, "What is a dispensation?" We have briefly covered this subject before, but multiple exposures to a subject solidifies the meaning into our minds and dispensations relate significantly to understanding Bible Prophecy. The easiest answer is that a definition of dispensation is an age or a length of time that God has used to teach mankind a lesson. What lesson in particular? That we, as humans, cannot live and succeed without God, cannot please God, cannot attain salvation and the reward of Heaven without God regardless of what we think or do.

Formally, the dictionary refers to dispensation in a number of ways from a special permission or release from a rule or a law to an act of providing something to people, dispensing something. It can mean a general state or ordering of things; specifically, a system of revealed commands and promises regulating human affairs or a particular arrangement or provision especially of Providence (God). The best way to look at a Biblical dispensation is that it is a scheme over a period of time according to which God carries out his purposes towards men. Systematic Theology, whose author was the founder of Dallas Theological Seminary Lewis Sperry Chafer, views Scripture as an unfolding revelation and doctrine or as a process of on-going "dispensing" of God's message to man.

Hebrews 1:1-2 says, "In many separate revelations (dispensations) – each of which set forth a portion of the truth – and in different ways God spoke of old to our forefathers in and by the prophets. But in the last of these days He has spoken to us in the person of a Son…"

The Greek word "oikonomia" signifies a disposition of affairs entrusted to someone. Thus 1 Corinthians 9:16, 17, the King James Version says, "For though I preach the gospel, I have nothing to glory of: for necessity is laid upon me; yea, woe is unto me, if I preach not the gospel! For if I do this thing willingly, I have a reward: but if against my will, a dispensation of the gospel is committed unto me," the Revised Version (British and American) "I have stewardship entrusted to me." In Ephesians 1:10, God's own working is spoken of as dispensation. "Having made known unto us the mystery of his will, according to his good pleasure which he hath purposed in himself: that in the dispensation of the fullness of times he might gather together in one all things in Christ, both which are in Heaven, and which are on Earth; even in him."

Later in Ephesians, Paul emphasizes the complete fulfillment of His will in Ephesians 3:1, 2, "For this cause I Paul, the prisoner of Jesus Christ for you Gentiles, if ye have heard of the dispensation of the grace of God which is given me to you-ward". Finally, Paul refers to his ministry as administration of God passed to him and intended to be given to a lost humanity in Colossians 1:25, "Whereof I am made a minister, according to the dispensation of God which is given to me for you, to fulfill the word of God".

Is Dispensationalism (the acceptance of dispensations throughout the Bible) necessary for salvation? Of course not! So, why is Dispensationalism important?

- Dispensationalism is a theological approach that teaches Biblical history as a number of successive administrations of God dealing with man

- Dispensationalism maintains fundamental distinctions of the way God deals with different tests for man to consider concerning sin and man's responsibility for sin

- At each stage of Dispensationalism, man has failed to be obedient to the responsibilities set forth by God mainly because of man's selfishness

- The method of salvation (justification by faith alone) never changes through all of the dispensations

- However, the responsibilities God gives to man, the questions God places into man's conscious as to whether man can survive and exist outside of God, does change

Is this concept of the Dispensations anything new? Certainly not! Early church fathers Justin Martyr (2nd century), Iranaeus (2nd century), Clement of Alexandria (late 1st and early 2nd century), and Augustine (late 3rd and early 4th century) all wrote of Dispensationalism. More current and respected church leaders and pastors also wrote extensively on Dispensationalism, men such as Jonathan Edwards (1700s), Isaac Watts (1700s), C.I. Scofield (1800s and early 1900s), Lewis Sperry Chafer (early 1900s), Charles Ryrie (late 1900s and died 2016), Dwight Pentecost (1900s and died 2014), and John Walvoord (1900s and died 2002).

The very foundations of Dispensationalism stem from the Bible and are also the foundations of Christianity:

- A literal interpretation of the Bible in its entirety

- God works in different ways with man in distinct periods of history – example, the Old and New Testaments

- Israel is made up from descendants of Abraham literally not spiritually

- Israel is heir to the promises made to Abraham

- There are two distinct groups in the Bible and in God's heart – Israel and the Church

- The Church began at Pentecost

- Salvation is by faith in accordance to the revelation given in a particular dispensation

- The Holy Spirit did not indwell permanently in all dispensations – only in the Dispensation of Grace

- Christ will reign in the future 1,000-year period known as the Millennial Kingdom (the last dispensation) which occurs after the Rapture and the Tribulation

Selfish In Nature

Mankind fell from Grace in the Garden of Eden. As a result of Adam and Eve's disobedience, sin and death entered the world. Sin can be thought of as an acronym. Selfish In Nature – SIN. Selfishness characterizes what each of us is born into, the very essence of our infancy is concentrating on what WE want to the exclusion of everyone else. What many refer to as the "age of accountability" is that particular age, and that age can differ from one individual to another, when we as one person standing in the presence of God are held accountable by God for our actions, emotions, spirituality, and behavior. And, as we all know all too well, we search for excuses for our sin if, that is, we are truly aware of hurt to others.

When it comes to God, our excuses do not stop. We still think again selfishly that we can make it on our own. After all, we are good, basically, or the good we do outweighs the bad, right? So, when God says that there is only one way to Him and that way is through His Son, Jesus Christ, we sort of look for other ways that we think are better or more doable, then test them out on God. But, He is way ahead of us. God has from the very beginning been allowing us as a human race, made in His image, to test out all the excuses that we could possibly come up with to avoid doing things God's way.

Those tests that God saw beforehand that we would ask to go through to prove our worth to Him (which we could never do because He is Holy and we are NOT) is what we call the dispensations. For instance, wouldn't we think that if we knew EXACTLY what God thought was sin, we could avoid it and be pleasing in His sight? Sorry, He already did that when He gave the Ten Commandments to Moses on Mt. Sinai in Midian (which, by the way, is not in the Sinai Peninsula but in Saudi Arabia in a place the Bible calls Midian). Or, how about this one, if Jesus Himself ruled on Earth and was visible to everyone, we would never do anything to displease Him. Sorry, again, because Revelation 20:7-9 says when Satan is loosed on the Earth after having been bound for a thousand years (while Jesus was ruling IN PERSON on the Earth), literally millions who have witnessed Jesus all their lives during the Millennium will rebel against Jesus and join in with the devil against Him. Of course, their outcome is eternity in the Lake of Fire.

Simplistically, we can easily see three dispensations or time periods that God has shown us in the Bible. All three ages or dispensations are centered on faith, the faith of the Grace of God to grant salvation to believers in Him. The first age or dispensation is Old Testament times before Christ where getting the approval of God was attained by faith such as that of Abraham. His faith was counted unto him as righteousness (Genesis 15:6, "Abram believed the LORD, and it was credited to him as righteousness.") The second age or dispensation is New Testament times after the resurrection of Christ where faith in Jesus Christ as Lord and Savior guarantees righteousness (Romans 4:5, "But to him that worketh not, but believeth on him that justifieth the ungodly, his faith is counted for righteousness.") Then the third age or dispensation is the Millennial Kingdom of Christ where Jesus Christ reigns on the Earth for a thousand years. But, even then, there will be those that can possibly live the entire thousand years but have their life cut short at 100 years because of the sin of rejection of Christ's sovereignty (Isaiah 65:20, "There shall be no more there an infant of days, nor an old man that has not filled his days: for the child shall die an hundred years old; but the sinner being an hundred years old shall be accursed.")

Dispensations Explained

There are actually seven dispensations that each answer a different situation or question or excuse that prove beyond a shadow of a doubt that we cannot please God on our own. Why? Because we are sinners, and Jesus was not a sinner. He lived a perfect life, sin-free as a human, so He could sacrifice His perfect human life for us thereby fulfilling the Law and then covering our many sins with His shed blood, for the Bible says in Hebrews 9:22 that there is no forgiveness of sins without the shedding of blood. And, since Jesus' blood was sin-free, His sacrifice covered all sin, past, present, and future for all men, for all time. The only act on our part is the act of the humility of repentance and acceptance of Jesus' sacrifice for our sins. Then we know that Jesus was raised from the dead and sits on the right of the Father in Heaven until He comes back for us in the Rapture (1 Thessalonians 4:13-18). The seven dispensations are the dispensations of Innocence, Conscience, Human or Civil Government, Promise, Law, Grace, and the

Millennial Kingdom.

For each of the dispensations, God is providing a time for mankind to live under specific circumstances that will answer precise questions dealing with our ability to function according to God's Will on our own without Him. The first dispensation of Innocence was in the Garden of Eden when all Adam and Eve had to refrain from was just one thing – not to eat from the Tree of the Knowledge of Good and Evil. God asked, "Can I trust you?" and they failed resulting in death, which was not known before, and changes to plants and animals and the Earth.

The second dispensation was of Conscience where mankind knew that disobeying God had severe consequences. God said, "Now that you know I expect obedience, can I trust you?" and they failed resulting in the Great Flood of Noah which destroyed all breathing life save for those on Noah's Ark. The third dispensation was Human Government which allowed mankind to have a ruler, Nimrod, to control Human nature. This failed because of the hubris of the people to build a tower to reach the Heavens and consult with fallen angels, the Tower of Babel. The result was a confusion of languages and dispersion over the entire planet.

The fourth dispensation was of Promise where God went to a specific man, Abram, and promised that if he would trust in God, God would bless him with a mighty nation. Over time, this nation was enslaved in Egypt because of their disobedience, but saved by their deliverer Moses. The fifth dispensation was called the Law which was given to the Jewish people at Mt Sinai in Midian, Arabia. God said He would define sin for the Jews so that they could obey but they had to be perfect in their obedience and not break even one of the 613 laws. Again, failure. They failed over many years and this dispensation ended with Jesus dying on the cross.

The sixth and current dispensation is the Age of Grace starting with the Resurrection and ending with the soon to come Rapture of the Church. This is also called the Church Age because God has provided a Savior for all to believe in and be subject to His Lordship. Unfortunately, only a small percentage of mankind has or is repenting of sin and accepting Christ's sacrifice on their behalf. One day, Jesus will call for His Church to rise and be with Him to avoid the Wrath of God to come on a sinful and rebellious world thus ending the Age of Grace.

The seventh and last dispensation is the Millennial Kingdom where Jesus Himself will reign in Person on Earth for a thousand years thus showing himself as God and King of kings and Lord of lords. Of course, many will reject Him because Revelation 20:7,8 tells us the number of the final rebellion is as the sand on the seashore. That's hard to grasp, but it is true. Even with Jesus visible, humans will still be so arrogant and rebellious to want their own way, they will rebel against Almighty God Himself.

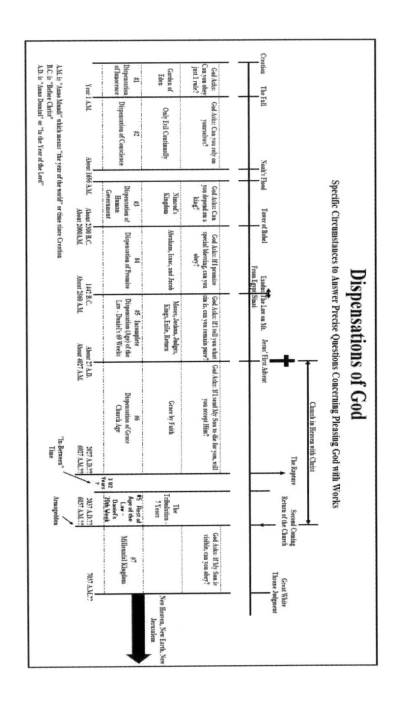

The Dispensation of Grace versus the Tribulation

The dispensation of Grace begins about the time of the Resurrection since Pentecost occurred soon after. That was in approximately 27 A.D. Subtracting 33 years from 27 A.D. we arrive at about 6 B.C. Since we know that Herod the Great died in 4 B.C. (remember, there is no year zero), that gives us about 2 years for Jesus to grow into a toddler before the wise men arrived with their gifts according to Matthew 2:11.

Counting from the Creation, the date of Jesus' resurrection (27 A.D.) would correspond to about 4027 A.M. or 4,027 years from Creation. The ending date for the dispensation of Grace can be assumed to be 2,000 years after the Resurrection because from Adam to Abraham was 2,000 years; from Abraham to Jesus was 2,000 years; and from Jesus to the Rapture should be 2,000 years as well. The date for the Rapture is approximate, of course, since the Rapture has not happened yet and it is supposed to be imminent. So, let's assume 2027 A.D. or 6027 A.M. (A.M. = After Creation or Anno Mundi or the Year of the World). That would make the duration of the dispensation of Grace to be about 2,000 years. Hosea 6:2 that says, "After two days will he revive us: in the third day he will raise us up, and we shall live in his sight". And, since we know that 2 Peter 3:8 says, "...that one day is with the Lord as a thousand years, and a thousand years as one day", then we are at the end of the second day – the second thousand years since Christ pointing to the "third day" or the Millennial Reign of Christ that lasts a thousand years.

The end of the Age of Grace marks the transition into the Tribulation or the Time of Jacob's Trouble, a return to the end of the Dispensation of the Law where God restores His people, the Jews, from their lost position and brings them to the belief and the saving Grace of their Messiah, Jesus Christ! It is very important to see that the Age of Grace is for the Church and the Tribulation is Daniel's 70th Week which is the very end of the Age of the Law for the Jews. The believing Jews of that time will be transformed into their new immortal Jesus-like bodies (just as the Church received after the Rapture) after the Battle of Armageddon, after the Sheep and Goat Judgment, and just before the Millennial Kingdom starts – the last or seventh dispensation. The people who are "raised up" from Hosea's prophecy are Israel and Judah, the Jews. The third day is the Millennium when Jesus does indeed "raise up" the living Jews and all living Christians that believe in Him from the Great Tribulation and allow them to enter His Millennial reign on the Earth as well as the Old Testament saints and those that perished in the Tribulation that became believers within the Tribulation, both Jew and

Gentile.

Since we are at present only about seven or so years from 2,000 years since Christ's Resurrection, the "second day" is just about over. That means the third "day" of 1,000 years, the Millennium, will come very soon. Christ's Second Coming is not that far away which means that the Rapture is even closer since it must come seven years before, and more probably ten years before, to allow for the seven years of Tribulation. Jesus is at the door! Even so, Come Lord Jesus!

End Times Prerequisites

Now, getting back to the end of the Age of Grace in which we exist at present, there are many New Testament End Times events that are occurring which Jesus told us about in Matthew 24 that have to occur before He calls His Church up to be with Him. Since we see all of these End Times events today occurring simultaneously and in increasing intensity in what is called "Convergence", we need to examine the most important of them. (refer to christinprophecy.org and Dr. David Reagan) Let's look at some of these events but certainly not all of them:

1. The human race would have the ability to exterminate itself

   In Matthew 24:22, describing world conditions prior to His second coming, Jesus said that "if that time of troubles were not cut short, no living thing could survive; but for the sake of God's chosen it will be cut short". Matthew 24:22 shows us that if Jesus Christ does not intervene in world affairs, the human race will be faced with extinction. It's crucial to note that humanity has had the capability for self-annihilation for only about 60 years, since both the United States and the Soviet Union developed and stockpiled hydrogen bombs and the world had to learn to live with MAD or "mutually assured destruction."

   At that time there were only three nuclear powers, the U.S., the Soviet Union, and Great Britain. By the middle of the 1960s France and China had joined the nuclear club. Today at least nine nations have nuclear warheads and the number looks set to increase with a nuclear arms race in the Middle East, Iran, and other rogue nations. Of course, the more nuclear powers we have in the world, the more likely it is that someone will use this deadly force for evil. Although international attention has been focused on the nuclear programs of North Korea and Iran during the last few years, little attention has been given to the possibility of some or all of Pakistan's nuclear arsenal falling into the hands of radical Islamists. China seems to be very interested in space weapons which include the possibility of launching nuclear devices from space to any point on the globe.

During the ongoing crisis in Pakistan, the Taliban and al-Qaeda and their sympathizers have steadily gained more power, territory and influence, making nuclear terrorism more likely. Consider the consequences for the rest of the world if Osama bin Laden (or others like him) had access to nuclear weapons! Our biased media today does not report on these kind of things, so that may answer some questions as to why we have not heard much from these terrorist organizations lately. Meanwhile, Russia and China are determinedly flexing their military muscles, raising fears of a return to Cold War era tensions.

The good news in all this is that Christians have an assurance that Jesus Christ will intervene to save mankind from annihilation. This prophecy could not be fulfilled until man had the potential for self-extinction through weapons of mass destruction. Again, only in the last 60 years has this become possible.

2. A Jewish homeland had to be reestablished in the Middle East

Luke 21 is a parallel chapter to Matthew 24. Notice Luke's account of Christ's long prophecy that answered the disciples' questions: "Teacher, . . . when will these things be? And what sign will there be when these things are about to take place?" (Luke 21:7). In response, Jesus showed that Jerusalem would be the central focus of the political and military upheavals that would immediately precede His return: "But when you see Jerusalem surrounded by armies, then know that its desolation is near . . . For these are the days of vengeance, that all things which are written may be fulfilled" (Luke 21:20-22).

Anyone living even a century ago would have found these words implausible, even impossible since Israel and Jerusalem were immaterial to world politics. Jerusalem in ancient times had been fought over countless times, but for four centuries from 1517 the city had been at peace under control of the Ottoman Empire. Some Jews lived there as a minority under Turkish rule. Events in the 20th century made Bible Prophecy very relevant to world politics because Israel became a nation once again, and Jerusalem came under Jewish control after almost two millennia.

The Old Testament prophet Zechariah was used by God to reveal a great deal about end-time events and the second coming of the Messiah. Zechariah lived and prophesied more than 500 years before Christ's first coming, yet his prophetic book tells us a great deal about our world of today. In Zechariah 12:2-3 God says: "Behold, I will make Jerusalem a cup of drunkenness to all the surrounding peoples, when they lay siege against Judah [the Jews inhabiting the land of Israel] and Jerusalem. And it shall happen in that day that I will make Jerusalem a very heavy stone for all peoples; all who would heave it away will surely be cut in pieces, though all nations of the Earth are gathered against it." In Zechariah 12:9 He adds, "It shall be in that day that I will seek to destroy all the nations that come against Jerusalem."

Reading these verses, it is possible to think that they apply to ancient events, as Jerusalem has been fought over repeatedly down through the ages. However, chapter 14 makes clear that this is talking about future, not past, events. The time setting is immediately before Jesus Christ's return. "Behold, the day of the Lord is coming . . . For I will gather all the nations to battle against Jerusalem; the city shall be taken, the houses rifled, and the women ravished. Half of the city shall go into captivity . . . Then the Lord will go forth and fight against those nations, as He fights in the day of battle. And in that day His feet will stand on the Mount of Olives, which faces Jerusalem on the east. And the Mount of Olives shall be split in two, from east to west, making a very large valley; half of the mountain shall move toward the north and half of it toward the south" (Zechariah 14:1-4). Note how obvious that the last part of this prophecy remains to be fulfilled.

Shortly before Zechariah, another Jewish prophet named Daniel lived during the time of the captivity of the Jews in Babylon. His book speaks of the Jews' daily sacrifices being cut off by the Antichrist in the end time (Daniel 12:1-13), an event that had a forerunner in the temple defilement under Syrian ruler Antiochus Epiphanes IV in 165 B.C. However, Jesus Christ confirmed this as a future event to precede His return (Daniel 11:31; Matthew 24:15). This means that these sacrifices must first be reinstituted in Jerusalem requiring Jewish rule over the city which was re-established in 1967.

One hundred years ago such developments were hard to imagine for the simple reason that no independent Jewish political entity existed in the Middle East. After rebelling against the Romans in 70 A.D. and again in 135 A.D., Judea was leveled and the ground salted by Hadrian and most of the remaining Jews were dispersed throughout the Roman Empire and beyond. It was at that time that Hadrian destroyed Jerusalem and renamed the land Palestina with Jerusalem renamed Aulina Capitolina. No Jewish homeland existed again until 1948, after 1,813 years, when the modern nation of Israel was established. It is important to know that during biblical times there was NEVER a country called Palestine! It was Israel!

An independent Jewish homeland was merely a dream for a small group of zealots a century ago. It moved a step nearer during World War I, when forces of the British Commonwealth took control of Jerusalem from the Turks in December 1916. A few months later in 1917, the British government pledged itself to the establishment of an independent Jewish homeland in the ancient lands the Jews had inhabited for centuries.

It was to be another 30 years before the dream was realized starting in 1947 with a League of Nations (forerunner to the U.N.) proclamation, then fulfilled in 1948. Yet since then, Israel has had to fight wars for survival in 1948, 1967 and 1973 and has suffered countless terrorist attacks and threats of annihilation from hostile neighbors determined even today to eliminate the Jewish state. Once again, this prophecy can now be fulfilled in our time as never before.

3.   The end-time king of the North and king of the South

In Daniel 11 we find an amazing prophecy about two leaders, the kings of the North and South, the heads of regions that were geographically north and south of the Holy Land. To understand this prophecy, we have to go to the time of Alexander the Great, who lived 200 years after Daniel. Alexander figures prominently throughout the book of Daniel, even though Daniel did not know his name and never knew him personally since he died almost two centuries before Alexander. God revealed to Daniel that after Babylon, Persia would arise as the greatest power of the region, to be followed by Greece. Not surprisingly, the prophecies regarding the rise of Greece are centered on Alexander the Great, one of the greatest conquerors in history.

Chapter 8 of Daniel tells of the coming war between Persia and Greece. A horn symbolizes royal power and authority. Persia had "two horns and the two horns were high; but one was higher than the other, and the higher one came up last." This refers to the Medo-Persian Empire, the coming together of two nations or peoples. As foretold here in Daniel 8:3, the Persians rose to greatness after the Medes accounting for the higher horn "coming up".

In Daniel 8:5 we read of Persia's later defeat by Alexander the Great: "And as I was considering, suddenly a male goat came from the west, across the surface of the whole Earth, without touching the ground; and the goat had a notable horn between his eyes" (Daniel 8:5). The "notable horn" or royal leader was Alexander the Great. The prophecy about his army not even touching the ground is a reference to the incredible speed with which he conquered the known world. All this was achieved in a very short time. Alexander died in 323 B.C. when he was only about 33 years old reportedly either by poisoning or a depraved lifestyle.

Even his sudden, unexpected death was prophesied: "The male goat grew very great; but when he became strong, the large horn was broken, and in place of it four notable ones came up toward the four winds of Heaven" (Daniel 8:8). When Alexander died, his empire was eventually divided between four of his generals, the four "notable horns". Two of these established dynasties would have a profound effect on the Jewish people, caught in the middle between them. These two dynasties were the descendants of Seleucus who ruled a vast empire from Antioch in Syria North of Jerusalem, and Ptolemy who ruled Egypt from Alexandria South of Jerusalem.

Daniel 11 is a long and detailed prophecy about the conflicts between these two powers, their respective leaders being referred to as "the king of the North" and "the king of the South." It is interesting to note that the first 35 verses in Daniel Chapter 11 contain 135 prophecies that were written long before they came to pass, yet every one of them happened exactly as Daniel wrote. This amazing accuracy led critics to believe that Daniel could not have written them because of their accuracy. Critics claim even today that that chapter in Daniel was written after Antiochus nearer the 165 B.C. date rather than the 536 B.C. date of Daniel. Of great significance is that whenever those two kings went to battle against each other, the Jews, being in the middle, suffered. This was to continue from the time of Alexander until the middle of the second century B.C., a period of almost two centuries. Then, suddenly, the prophecy jumps to the time of the end, the Tribulation.

In Daniel 11:40 we read: "At the time of the end the king of the South shall attack him; and the king of the North shall come against him like a whirlwind, with chariots, horsemen, and with many ships; and he shall enter the countries, overwhelm them and pass through. He shall also enter the Glorious Land [the Holy Land], and many countries shall be overthrown" (Daniel 11:40-41). The latter part of Daniel's prophecy of the North-South conflict describes a war between the leader who is the successor to the Ptolemaic rule of the ancient Egyptian Empire and part of the Psalm 83 war to come which is now part of the Islamic world, and a leader of a soon-coming European superpower, a revived Roman Empire which will rise to be the Antichrist himself of Revelation!

4.   An end-time union of European nations

In Daniel 2 and 7 we see prophecies about four great gentile empires that would arise in the period between the time of Daniel and the coming establishment of the Kingdom of God (Daniel 2:44). Daniel was himself living in the first of these great empires (Daniel 7:4) as a Jewish exile in ancient Babylon. Following the fall of Babylon in 538 B.C., the Medo-Persian Empire would become the greatest power, to be followed by Greece (Daniel 7:5-6). After Greece came the Roman Empire, "dreadful and terrible, exceedingly strong." This empire was to have "ten horns" and would continue in some form until the establishment of God's Kingdom at Christ's return (Daniel 7:7-9). As we saw in the previous section, horns represent leaders or governments.

We find more details in Revelation 17 where we read of a revived Roman Empire which consists of "ten kings who have received no kingdom as yet, but they receive authority for one hour as kings with the beast. These are of one mind, and they will give their power and authority to the beast" (Revelation 17:12-13). They will also "make war with the Lamb [Jesus Christ], and the Lamb will overcome them, for He is Lord of lords and King of kings" (Revelation 17:14). Again, it is clear that this prophecy is still future since nothing like this has ever happened in recorded history to the present, although signs of it coming true are also becoming evident.

Previous attempts to forge a united European empire, from Justinian in the sixth century through Charlemagne, Napoleon, Mussolini and Hitler, all involved force. The final resurrection of the Roman Empire will not be attempted in the same way. Revelation 17 suggests this will be a voluntary union. When these 10 leaders receive power, they will then give their authority to a single leader. Scripture refers to both this individual and the new superpower he leads as "the beast", acknowledging it as the continuation of the four gentile empires prophesied in Daniel, each one depicted as a beast or wild animal. Only now is it possible for this to be fulfilled.

In 1957, the Treaty of Rome was signed by six European nations that formed the European Economic Community. Today the EEC has grown into the European Union (EU) with 27 member-nations, soon to be 26 or less because of the "Brexit" movements. Out of these will likely come the 10 nations or 10 leaders that form the final resurrection of the Roman Empire.

Some have speculated that the 10 kings referred to in this prophecy will be leaders of 10 regions of the EU that will redraw the boundaries of Europe, ending the present nation-states. The Bible is not clear on exactly which 10 regions or nations will configure the final revival of the militaristic Roman superpower, only that this new superpower will indeed emerge just before Christ's return. An ominous development has come from the U.N. where the leaders of the world have envisioned dividing up the entire planet into regions that each have a king or leader. The U.S., Canada, and Mexico become one of the ten re-named "North America". Not surprisingly, the number of regions that are envisioned in this plan for the globe's future one-world organization? Ten!

5. The gospel will be preached in all the world

In His major end-time prophecy, Jesus answers the question posed by the disciples: "When will these things be? And what will be the sign of your coming, and of the end of the age?" (Matthew 24:3). After listing a number of signs of the nearness of His coming, He reveals that "this gospel of the kingdom will be preached in all the world as a witness to all the nations, and then the end will come" (Matthew 24:14). Also, in Mark 13:10, "And the gospel must first be published among all nations." The gospel is the good news of the coming Kingdom of God. This message could not be preached around the world without the Bible and freedom of religion. Both came gradually with the ascendancy of the English-speaking peoples from the 16th century until the present day.

It was only when the technological advances of television and radio and other means of mass communication after World War II and their widespread acceptance that it became possible to reach hundreds of millions of human beings with the message of the Bible. The gospel of the Kingdom of God continues to be preached to all nations through the internet and its use of global satellites. During the last 50 years it still has not been possible to reach all countries. China, with one quarter of the world's people, still does not allow evangelism because it opposes tyrannical rule. Other nations also try to suppress the publication of biblical truth and even the Bible itself. Many Islamic nations do not allow religious freedom. In some countries people risk the death penalty for changing religion. But none of this opposition will halt the spread of the Gospel since God is in control and He can always and does utilize dreams and visions to stir peoples' hearts.

6. Instant worldwide communications and God's final witnesses

In His major end-time prophecy of Matthew 24, Mark 13 and Luke 21, Jesus gave an outline of disasters that would occur on the world scene with increasing frequency and magnitude to the point where people would be shaken with fear (Luke 21:26). Discerning an increase in the scale of these events and reacting to them requires knowing about them. At the time this prophecy was given, it could be many months or years before people heard about various disasters, and many they would never hear about at all much less be able to put together the fact that catastrophes were on some kind of global increase.

Only with the proliferation of newspapers and other forms of mass communications did this become remotely possible. Yet the level of awareness and fear that Christ speaks of implies an even greater availability of information. This availability of information has only been since the development of rapid electronic communications. Only with the technological advances of the last few years has it become possible for the events in Revelation 11 to occur, specifically for people around the world to see the fate of God's final two Witnesses. These two witnesses, reminiscent of other biblical prophets like Elijah and Elisha, will carry God's final warning to the world in the first 3 ½ years of the Tribulation. In fact, one of the two Witnesses could very well be Elijah since he did not see death because he was "taken", and the other Enoch since God took him also.

"And I will give power to my two witnesses, and they will prophesy one thousand two hundred and sixty days . . . When they finish their testimony, the beast that ascends out of the bottomless pit will make war against them, overcome them and kill them. And their dead bodies will lie in the street of the great city which spiritually is called Sodom and Egypt, where also our Lord was crucified. Then those from the peoples, tribes, tongues and nations will see their dead bodies three-and-a-half days, and not allow their dead bodies to be put into graves. And those who dwell on the Earth will rejoice over them, make merry, and send gifts to one another, because these two prophets tormented those who dwell on the Earth" (Revelation 11:3, Revelation 11:7-10).

Note that people the world over will be able to see their dead bodies during the 3 1/2 days that they lie on display in Jerusalem. This was not possible before satellite television, portable communications devices, and the Internet. Again, only in the last few years has it become possible for this prophecy to be fulfilled. It still lies in the future, of course, but only now it is clearly possible for this to take place.

7. Will this generation see God's Kingdom established on Earth?

The establishment of the state of Israel in 1948 was the key to the fulfillment of Bible prophecy. This means that our generation will live to see Jesus Christ return and establish the Kingdom of God on Earth. After all, Jesus Himself said that once these things begin, the generation alive at that time "will by no means pass away till all these things take place" (Matthew 24:34). Since a generation according to Psalm 90:10 is 70 years, perhaps 80, and Israel is 70 years old (we are in the 70th year of Israel's existence until May 14, 2019), and we are the generation alive today that is seeing all of these signs converging at once, then we should be expecting the Rapture any day!

It's both sobering and encouraging to think that we appear to be living in the generation that will ultimately witness the most important event in the history of mankind. As Jesus Christ tells His followers in Luke 21:28, "Now when these things begin to happen, look up and lift up your heads, because your redemption draws near."

8. A Look at the Convergence of Coming End Times Human Events

To capture the meaning of the prophetic Word for today, here is a listing of human-oriented evil prophecies and technological advances in both testaments occurring all at once showing just how close we are to Christ's return. In the past ten years or so, these prophecies have started to occur, have converged (the "Convergence") so that all are happening at the same time, and now the intensity of them is impossible to miss. What we experience in our daily lives, what we seem to pay little attention to, what we need to grasp as highly unusual and overwhelmingly dangerous and disturbing is the recognition of just how close we are to the end of the age, the end of the Age of Grace, and the obvious fact that these are the very End Times that the Word of God speaks of. Note that the references to verses are from both the Old and New Testaments:

- Increase of wars and rumors of wars (Joel 3:9-10; Matt. 24:6-7)
- Extreme materialism (2 Tim. 3:1-2; Rev. 3:14-19)
- Lawlessness (Prov. 30:11-14; 2 Tim. 3:1-3)
- Population explosion (Gen. 6:1; Luke 17:26)
- Increasing speed and knowledge (Dan. 12:4)
- Departure from the Christian faith (2 Thess. 2:3; 1 Tim. 4:1, 3-4; 2 Tim. 3:5; 4:3-4; 2 Pet. 3:3-4)
- Unification of the world's religious, political, and economic systems (Rev. 13:4-8, 16-17; 17:1-18; 18:1-24)
- Universal drug usage ("sorceries" here can also refer to drugs) (Rev. 9:21)
- Abnormal sexual activity (Rom. 1:17-32; 2 Pet. 2:10, 14; 3:3; Jude 18)
- Intense demonic activity (Gen. 6:1-4; 1 Tim. 4:1-3)
- Mass slaughter of innocents by unconcerned mothers (abortion) (Rom. 1:31; 2 Tim. 3:3)
- Widespread violence (Gen. 6:11, 13; 2 Tim. 3:1; Rev. 9:21)
- Rejection of God's Word (2 Tim. 4:3-4; 2 Pet. 3:3-4, 16)
- Rejection of God Himself (Ps. 2:1-3)
- Blasphemy (2 Tim. 3:2; 2 Pet. 3:3; Jude 18)
- Self-seeking and pleasure-seeking (2 Tim. 3:2, 4)
- Men minus a conscience (1 Tim. 4:2)
- Religious hucksters (2 Pet. 2:3)
- Outright devil worshippers (Rev. 9:20; 13:11-14)
- Rise of false prophets and antichrists (Matt. 24:5, 11; 2 Pet. 2:1-2)
- False claims of peace (1 Thess. 5:1-3)
- Rapid advances in technology (Gen. 4:22; Luke 17:26)

- Great political and religious upheavals in the Holy Land (Matt. 24:32-34)

To these we could add the development of weapons of mass destruction; space travel; space weaponry; increase of deceivers and lying wonders; depreciation of nationalism and unimaginable rise of globalism mimicking the Tower of Babel times; wildly unstable financial markets and governments all over the world; and the difficult to grasp return to the socialism government movement. Now realize that ALL of these are occurring AT THE SAME TIME or converging simultaneously! This is unprecedented in history and most certainly a supreme sign that these are the END TIMES!

As we consider that over 90 percent of all the prophecies in the Bible have been fulfilled exactly as foretold, the less than 10 percent that apply to our immediate future will also be fulfilled exactly as foretold. Get ready! Are you prepared? Jesus will call His Church up very soon! Do you know Jesus as your Lord and Savior?

9. Obadiah and Similarities to Today

One of the Old Testament "Minor" Prophets was Obadiah who wrote a very small book, in fact, THE smallest in the Old Testament. In most Bibles, Obadiah takes only one page and a very short time to read. Obadiah's message was to Edom or the land of Esau, Jacob's twin brother. Even from the time of Jacob's return to the Promised Land from his wife's brother Laban's land, Esau and Edom had been unfriendly towards Jacob, read Israel, and had raised the attention of God.

Obadiah tells Edom, which is located South of Israel where Petra is located in a wilderness. Edomites apparently thought very highly of themselves, but God, because of past atrocities toward Israel, pronounces destruction, total destruction on Edom for their transgressions against Israel. All of this happened back in the time of the Babylonian Empire, and Edom was wiped out by Nebuchadnezzar. Arabs living in the land of Edom today will be removed from the Earth by the Psalm 83 and Ezekiel 38 & 39 wars thus enabling Israel to occupy the Edomite land.

But there is a parallel that I think God may be showing us. Israel is the "apple of God's eye" (Zechariah 2:8), and the Church belongs to Jesus Christ. Now Israel is Israel and the Church is the Church, make no mistake. But, since God is the same today and forever (Hebrews 13:8), and Jesus and God the Father are One (John 10:30), then it is reasonable to think that when God is upset at Edom for attacking and treating Israel wrongly, then Jesus must be upset when those alive today do the same to the Church. I know that Obadiah was written to Israel's enemy Edom, but consider how God may be seeing some today in the same light!

Obadiah 3 and 4 says, "The pride of thine heart hath deceived thee, thou that dwellest in the clefts of the rock, whose habitation is high; that saith in his heart, who shall bring me down to the ground? Though thou exalt thyself as the eagle, and though thou set thy nest among the stars, thence will I bring thee down, saith the LORD." The Edomites thought highly of themselves way back then, but consider the attitudes of many elites, many of the super-rich, many of the social media chiefs today. Sounds rather similar, right? It's just interesting to read Obadiah and know it's about Israel's enemy Edom, which, by the way came from Esau as did the Persians, or, as we call them today, Iranians. But if you substitute 21st Century socialists and liberals for Edom in Obadiah, the prophecy could be a prayer from our time to the Gracious Lord to take care of the opposition to Christianity and righteousness. Seems like a repeat of the similar attitudes Israel has experienced for centuries, and we are experiencing the same attitudes right alongside Israel today.

What's Next?

Here are the most significant New Testament Bible prophecies (and a few Old Testament prophecies) that remain in sequence to be fulfilled concerning the End Times and after, some are looming on the immediate horizon with many harbingers testifying to the truth of their soon appearance:

The Rapture

The actual word "Rapture" is not in the Bible, but in 1 Thessalonians 4:17 there is a translation "caught up" which is "harpazo" in Greek which is the actual disappearance of all dead and living Christians from everyday life and from cemeteries to be with Jesus "in the air". Rapture is an inclusive word used to describe the exclusive resurrection of Christians who have died in the past, along with the changing of Christians who are alive from mortal bodies to immortal bodies, all rising to meet Jesus Christ in the air. The aftermath of this event, which likely disrupts many countries especially the U.S., will be total chaos worldwide for a brief period of time. But soon those left behind will consider the Christian absence to be a good thing and the march toward a globalist one-world society will gain continual strength changing everyone's thinking to align with that of the soon-to-come Antichrist. The globalists will get their way and, at the same time, walk right into Satan's trap run by the Antichrist himself.

"In-Between" Wars

I believe that there will be a time that falls "in-between" the Rapture of the Church and the start of the Tribulation period of seven years thereby fulfilling Daniel's 70th week. Why? Primarily because of Ezekiel 39:9, "And they that dwell in the cities of Israel shall go forth, and shall set on fire and burn the weapons, both the shields and the bucklers, the bows and the arrows, and the hand staves, and the spears, and they shall burn them with fire seven years." This is the aftermath of what God does to the invaders of Israel by the enemies of Israel found beyond Israel's close-in borders. The enemies of Israel that are close-in neighbors are all destroyed in the Psalm 83 war, results in Israel having peace and safety (a requirement for the Gog Magog War to happen), which precedes the Ezekiel 38 and 39 war. If Israel is to burn the weapons of the Ezekiel war for seven years, they must do so before the middle of the Tribulation since at that precise time, Antichrist will be determined to kill all of the Jews, but the Jews will flee and be protected by God at the mid-Tribulation point, about 3 ½ years into the Tribulation. This means the Ezekiel war must occur sometime before the start of the Tribulation to allow for this burning of the weapons of war time period.

The sequence of Psalm 83 removing all close-in enemies of Israel results in peace in the nation of Israel – another prerequisite of the Ezekiel war (Ezekiel 38:11, "And you shall say, I will go up to the land of unwalled villages; I will go to them that are at rest, that dwell safely, all of them dwelling without walls, and having neither bars nor gates.") So, the Psalm 83 war precedes the Ezekiel 38 and 39 war, both occurring during the "In-between" time after the Rapture and before the Tribulation.

Other prophecies probably occur during this time as well such as the destruction of Damascus, Isaiah 17:1; the destruction of Elam (nuclear area of Iran), Jeremiah 49:34-39; and the complete removal of Islam as a hindrance to the Antichrist's rise to power, Ezekiel 39:2).

Psalm 83 War

The war referred to in Psalm 83 is a Psalm of Asaph wherein he asks God to intervene by shaming and destroying the countries, the nations that immediately border Israel on all sides – the nations that have hated Israel, they have spoken out against both Israel and God Almighty Himself. The Bible identifies those enemies of Israel today that have done just that. They are Edom, which is South of Israel and part of Jordan; Moab, which is Southeast in Southern Jordan; Gebal, which is Northwest of Israel and the old Phoenician land now Lebanon; Ammon, which is Jordan and to Israel's East; Amalek, which is to Israel's Northeast; the Philistines, which used to occupy Gaza (West) and today is Hamas; Tyre, which is old Lebanon (Northwest) and today Hezbollah; and Assur, which is Iraq today to Israel's East. Notice that these countries surround Israel and share borders with Israel.

Psalm 83 says God will put all these countries to shame so that all men will know that He is Jehovah, the Most High over all the Earth. The result of this war will be Israel living in peace without walls since all close-in enemies have been destroyed.

Gog Magog War

Ezekiel 38 and 39 tell of a major war consisting of Israel's enemies lying some distance away from Israel's borders. The war is a confederation of nations that almost all share in Islam as a religion, but all share in their hatred of Israel. The prime mover in the war is the land of Gog and Magog which we know to be Russia to Israel's direct North. Ezekiel tells us that their motivation is come and take a spoil from Israel at the direction of God Himself since only He knows the timing of the invasion. The rest of the confederation are Muslim countries: first Russia identified through the references to Meshech (Moscow) and Tubal (Tobolsk) both major cities in modern Russia; Persia, which is modern Iran to Israel's extreme East; Ethiopia, which is South of Egypt; Libya, West of Israel on Africa's Northern coast; Gomer, which is Eastern Europe and to Israel's Northwest; and Togarmah, which is Turkey today and to Israel's North.

The blood moons of 2014 and 2015 seemed to be of little consequence to the world and certainly to the U.S. But we must realize that signs in the heavens will almost always be directed to Israel. The blood moons of 2014 were when Russia moved against Crimea which basically moved their armies half the distance from Moscow to Israel in one move. Next, the blood moons of 2015 coincided with Russia moving to Syria to set up bases there ostensibly to assist in the ISIS invasion of Iraq, but in reality to assist Iran in its quest to destroy Israel. If you look at a map and trace the movement of Russian troops from Moscow to Crimea to Syria, you see that it takes the shape of a hook, exactly what God said He would do to them, "And I will turn thee back, and put hooks into thy jaws, and I will bring thee forth…to the mountains of Israel." (Ezekiel 38:4 & 8)

The Bible says that these nations will come against a land of unwalled villages, a people at rest dwelling in safety, to take a spoil. First of all, Israel is certainly not a land of unwalled villages. They have a 400-mile wall all around Judah and Samaria (the "occupied territories") to keep the violent Palestinians out of their country. And, Israel is certainly not at peace because of all the rockets falling on them as well as the Syrian activity North of them supported by Iran and Russia. But these situations will be reversed after the Psalm 83 war.

Next, Israel has found the world's most vast supply of natural gas off their shore in the Mediterranean Sea. There is also a prophecy in Deuteronomy 33:24 from Moses, "And of Asher he said, Let Asher be blessed with children; let him be acceptable to his brethren, and let him dip his foot in oil." Many believe this to be a prophecy that Israel will find very soon a storehouse of oil in the ancient land of Asher, one of Jacob's sons, which will entice Russia to come and try to steal it by conquest.

Ezekiel 38 says that God draws these rogue nations down to Israel. Then, Ezekiel 39 says that God will destroy five-sixths of the army to glorify His Name and show the world that He loves Israel and its people. This wipes out not only Russia but all of the contentious Muslims in the world because the prophecy includes all of the distant lands as well as on the mountains of Israel. The main impact of this is the freedom it gives to Israel but also to the Antichrist to rise to power since major opposition from Russia and Islam has just been destroyed.

Destruction of Damascus

Isaiah 17:1 describes an event that has never happened in human history – the total destruction of the eternal city of Damascus. When I say "eternal", that is from a human perspective since Damascus has existed from not long after Noah's Flood until today, some 4,500 years approximately. Damascus has seen many wars, many nations ruling it, and many despots governing it. It has remained. But the Bible tells us that in our immediate future, Damascus will become a "ruinous heap", without life, thoroughly destroyed. Some would say, "Have you seen Damascus today? It looks totally destroyed now!" True, but there are areas still with people living in Damascus, so the prophecy has not been completely fulfilled yet. Israel has threatened to destroy Damascus because of Syria's and Iran's constant attacks on Israel. But it has not happened yet. But it will soon and probably in the "In-Between" years.

Destruction of Elam

Jeremiah 49:34-39 contains a prophecy of the destruction of Elam. Where is Elam? Elam is an ancient land where Susa was located, the city of Ahasuerus (a Persian) and Esther. Elam also contains what we today call the Persian Gulf and the city of Bushehr. Bushehr is significant because much of the Iranian nuclear technology and installations are near there. Since Iran has been the world's most dangerous and prolific supporter of terror, plus the fact that Iran has been developing nuclear weapons and intercontinental ballistic missiles in that area and in Tehran as well as other areas, add to that Iran's stated main enemy in the world is Israel with the U.S. a close second, Israel likely has Bushehr targeted for a nuclear strike to eliminate Iranian threats of nuclear war. And that is exactly what the Jeremiah 49 prophecy describes. Jeremiah says God will break Elam's bow, a reference to their nuclear weaponry. He will scatter the remaining people from Elam to the four winds of Heaven which means that all will flee the nuclear fallout from the attack. Of course, God can do all of this without Israel. But it sounds like this could be what happens during the "In-Between" years.

Middle East Peace Treaty

We are instructed by Zechariah and other prophets that Jerusalem will be a matter of controversy to all nations in the last days. The only peace that Israel has ever known was in the days of Solomon, and since it became a nation in 1948 there has been no peace, even though there have been more than fifty peace treaties or agreements negotiated and signed. According to Daniel 9:27, the Antichrist will confirm or guarantee a peace agreement or treaty between Israel and its enemies. However, there will be no peace. In fact, this false peace treaty initiates the Great Tribulation period.

The Tribulation

In the chronological order of eschatology, the Tribulation is a seven-year period that completes the Dispensation of the Law, and is full of war, pandemic plagues, earthquakes, cosmological catastrophes, and other judgments that will kill approximately three-fourths of the population of the world. Daniel said of this period, ". . . and there shall be a time of trouble, such as never was since there was a nation even to that same time . . ." (Dan. 12:1). Jesus said, "For there shall be great tribulation, such as was not since the beginning of the world to this time, no, nor ever shall be" (Matt. 24:22). The Antichrist will lead the world during the first half of the Tribulation but transform into the possessed by Satan tyrant in the last half. The Tribulation period will end with the Second Coming of Jesus Christ at Armageddon who will send the Antichrist and the False prophet to the Lake of Fire.

Antichrist's Appearance

For the first half of the Tribulation, the Antichrist solidifies his leadership and advantage. He will be a great orator (Dan. 11:36); a political and commercial genius (Dan. 11:41; Rev. 13:16-17); he may be a homosexual (Dan. 11:37); and a clever liar and deceiver (2 Thess. 2:9-10). If you think about it, you might be able to picture in your mind a very good candidate for the Antichrist familiar to us all. At the middle of the Tribulation (after three and a half years), he gains political and economic control over all the world (Rev. 13:7, 16-17), and then demands on penalty of death that everyone worship him as God (Rev. 13:8; 2 Thess. 2:3-4). The last half of the Tribulation, the Antichrist will be the most cruel dictator the world has ever known. Literally millions will be killed for not worshipping him as God. Although Christians may never know exactly who the Antichrist is, he is in the world today.

Coming of Elijah; the Two Witnesses

Elijah and Enoch are the only two men who escaped physical death by being taken up to Heaven alive. According to the prophet Malachi, Elijah must come back to precede the Messiah when He comes in power and glory to bring in the Kingdom (Mal. 4:4-6). Malachi mentioned Moses also in conjunction with the coming of Elijah, and both Moses and Elijah were with Jesus on The Mount of Transfiguration when He revealed to James, John, and Peter His glory when He would come again. According to Revelation 11, God will send two witnesses to bring judgments against the Antichrist. There are two guesses as to the identity of these two witnesses since the Bible does not tell us directly. The first is that the two witnesses will be Moses and Elijah. This could be, but Moses actually died (Deuteronomy 34:5-7) and Enoch did not. The second guess is that the two witnesses will be Elijah and Enoch because neither died, Enoch represents the people before the Flood (and Gentiles in general) and Elijah the people after the Flood (and the Jews), and Hebrews 9:27 says, "And as it is appointed unto men once to die, but after this the judgment." But we will have to look down from Heaven to see who the two witnesses really are.

Abomination of Desolation

The Abomination of Desolation is referenced many places in scripture, four times in the book of Daniel alone. The "abomination" is when the Antichrist stands in the Temple Mount in Jerusalem on worldwide television and declares himself to be God. This will be ultimate abomination committed in the Temple (Dan. 12:11; Matt. 24:15; 2 Thess. 2:3-4). The "desolation" will be the actual desecration of the Tribulation Temple with a man claiming to be God all happening at the mid-point of the Tribulation when Satan possesses the Antichrist.

Israel's Hiding Place

Israel's hiding place is the flight of Israel at the middle of the Tribulation to a place of safety. Jesus foretold that after the Antichrist commits the Abomination of Desolation, he will make a final attempt to kill every Jew. To escape, the Jews in Jerusalem must immediately run for cover, specifically the wilderness (Revelation 12:6). Petra in History and Prophecy is a large cave city (Mt. Seir; Mt. Hor) and is one place that fits the biblical description of Israel's hiding place in the last half of the Tribulation. Petra is in ancient Edom, in the "wilderness", the ancient home of Esau. "Who will bring me into the strong city? who will lead me into Edom? Wilt not thou, 0 God ..." (Ps.60: 1,9-12; Ezek.35).

Mark of the Beast

After the Antichrist becomes the dictator of the world and is worshipped as God, he will demand that every person be assigned a number and a (code) mark. Only those who are assigned a number will be able to work, buy, or sell. Only those who acknowledge Antichrist as God will get the mark, and an attempt will be made to kill everyone who does not have the mark (Rev. 13:16-17). Only in our day does the technology exist to employ and enforce the mark of the beast.

Battle of Armageddon

The Battle of Armageddon (Rev. 16:16) will terminate the Tribulation period. This last battle will include armies from all nations. Millions of men will be involved, as we read in Revelation 9:13-21 that the nations of the East (probably centered around China) will send an army of 200 million men. There are scores of prophecies in both the Old and New Testaments that describe the coming conflict (Zech. 14:2-3; Zeph. 3:8; Isa. 65; Rev. 19, etc.). This battle will continue from Megiddo near modern Haifa to Bozrah (modern Beseira) in Jordan, a distance of 1,600 furlongs, or 176 miles. The evident purpose of this battle is to destroy Jerusalem and prevent the return of Jesus Christ. However, the entire army is destroyed by Jesus Christ and the armies from Heaven. The Antichrist and the False Prophet will be cast alive, without being judged, into the Lake of Fire, the first residents there to be followed by billions at a later date.

The Second Coming

Jesus said, "If I go away, I will come again." Angels on the Mt. of Olives at His ascension to Heaven said that He would come back to the Mt. of Olives (Acts 1:9-12). Zechariah said at that time the mountain would split (Zech. 14:1-5; Ez. 44:1-3), and the Eastern Gate that had been shut would open. At the Rapture, Jesus will not come to the Earth. At the Second Coming at the Battle of Armageddon, He will come down to Earth, and every eye of every person who survives the Tribulation, including the Jews, will see Him (Rev. 1:7; Mt. 24:27). During the Tribulation two thirds of the Jews in Israel will have been killed, but after the Battle of Armageddon, Jesus will go to Bozrah north of Petra, and lead the remnant back to Israel (Isa. 65). Then Jesus will establish His Throne upon Mt. Zion in Jerusalem and Judge (rule) the nations with a "rod of iron" (Rev. 2:27; 12:5; 19:15; Mt. 25:31,32).

The Millennium

Six times in Revelation 20 the thousand-year reign of Jesus Christ on Earth over the nations is mentioned. This will be the seventh millennium since Adam. During this thousand-year reign, all nations will destroy their armaments and there will be no war (Isa. 2:4). Leaders of the nations will be required to go to Jerusalem and worship the Lord and learn of His laws. If any go not up as commanded, that nation will be judged (Zech. 15:16-21); Matt. 25:31-32; Rev. 12:5). Solar changes in the Tribulation will revert Earth's ecology back to pre-flood conditions and people during the Millennium will live to be hundreds of years old because they live through all of the Millennium (Isa. 65:25). The Devil will be bound and God's curse upon the Earth for sin will be removed, and the ground will again yield everything that man will need {Ezek. 34:27; Isa. 65:25; Rom. 8:18-23). The law will be enforced and criminals swiftly executed (Isa. 65:20). The Millennium ends with another rebellion of the nations with countless millions rebelling against Jesus led by Satan himself, Jesus will stop the rebellion, and the Earth and everything in it will be burned up (II Pet. 3:10; Rev. 20:9,11).

The Great White Throne Judgment

The Great White Throne Judgment (Rev. 20:11) is the last judgment of the unsaved. The chronology of resurrection for those who inherit eternal life is given in 1 Corinthians 15:23: ". . . Christ the firstfruits; afterward they that are Christ's at his coming." However, Paul preceded this revelation with a qualifying phrase: "BUT EVERY MAN IN HIS OWN ORDER." The resurrection of the "saved" is Jesus Christ... all members of the church of the dispensation of grace . . . Old Testament saints ... martyrs of the Tribulation period. "This is the first resurrection" (Rev. 20:5). The saved of the Millennium will live to be almost 1,000 years old (no man has yet to live 1,000 years in the flesh), then they will go into the New Heaven and New Earth without experiencing death. All the unsaved dead of all ages will be raised to be judged according to their works. All of those raised at the Great White Throne Judgement without Jesus will go into the eternal Lake of Fire because their names are not written in the Lamb's Book of Life (Rev. 20:12-15; Mt. 25:41).

New Heaven and New Earth

The final, unfulfilled major prophecy of the Bible is a New Heaven and a New Earth (Rev. 21:1). Neither the heavens nor the Earth are clean in God's sight (Isa. 34:4; Job 15:15,16; Rev. 6:14). At the beginning of the eighth millennium, God who created the first heavens and the first Earth with the Words of His mouth will create new heavens and a new Earth where the redeemed, who had chosen Him because they wanted to, not because they had to, will love and worship Him forever.

John, in Revelation 21-22, describes in earthly language the New Heavens and the New Earth where the redeemed will live forever (see also Eph. 1:1-14). But no language is sufficient to describe, or our minds visualize, the unfathomable beauty and glory of God's new creation. "And the Spirit and the bride say, Come. And let him that heareth say. Come. And let him that is athirst come ...." (Rev. 22:17). Every person can come to the New Heaven and New Earth by receiving Jesus Christ as Savior and Lord. Jesus said, "... I go to prepare a place for you . . . that where I am, there ye may be also" (John 14:2-3).

Conclusion

The Bible describes events and conditions that would mark "the conclusion of the [current] system of things," or "the end of the world." (Matthew 24:3; King James Version) The Bible calls this time period "the last days" and the "time of the end," or "end times." (2 Timothy 3:1; Daniel 8:19; Easy-to-Read Version) These events are to be like birth pangs which we all know grow in frequency and intensity until the moment of birth. That is what all of these signs are doing at this very moment indicating convergence of the signs as a sure indication of the Rapture coming soon followed by all of the events of the End Times. The following are some outstanding features of last-days, or end-times, prophecies:

- War on a large scale, Matthew 24:7; Revelation 6:4
- Famine, Matthew 24:7; Revelation 6:5, 6
- Great earthquakes, Luke 21:11
- Pestilences, or epidemics of "terrible diseases", Luke 21:11
- Increase of crime, Matthew 24:12.
- Ruining of the Earth by mankind, Revelation 11:18
- Deterioration of people's attitudes, as shown by many who are "unthankful, disloyal, . . . not open to any agreement, slanderers, without self-control, fierce, without love of goodness, betrayers, headstrong, puffed up with pride", 2 Timothy 3:1-4
- Breakdown of the family, with people who have "no natural affection" and children who are "disobedient to parents", 2 Timothy 3:2, 3
- Love of God growing cold in most people, Matthew 24:12
- Noteworthy displays of religious hypocrisy, 2 Timothy 3
- Increased understanding of Bible prophecies, including those related to the last days, Daniel 12:4
- Global preaching of the good news of the Kingdom, Matthew 24:14
- Widespread apathy and even ridicule toward the evidence of the approaching end, Matthew 24:37-39; 2 Peter 3:3, 4
- The simultaneous fulfillment of all these prophecies, not just a few or even most of them, Matthew 24:33
- Increase in knowledge
- Daniel 12:4 ...'even to the time of the end: many shall run to and fro, and knowledge shall be increased.'
  - o   Up until recently in history, the fastest form of transport was a horse. Now man can travel at hundreds of miles per hour, and cross the globe in a day! Technology has developed at a rapid pace, which has led to great improvements in computer power, scientific discoveries and the medical profession. Just look at how much we have learned about the human body with things like DNA and Cellular Structures etc. And how about "running to and fro"? This is pointing specifically to our day with planes, trains, automobiles and the busyness of modern day life. We are definitely running to and fro and have knowledge like no time before us.
  - o   This Bible sign has a dual application. "running to and fro and knowledge increase" also applies to knowledge of Biblical truths (see Amos 8:12). During the "dark ages", for over 1000 years, knowledge of Biblical truths was suppressed by the Roman Catholic Church. But since the protestant reformation and

breakaway from Rome, God's people have been running to and fro in His Word FREELY and knowledge about great Bible truths have been revealed. God now has an end time remnant church with the FULL gospel truth to take to the world before the end comes, which was needed to fulfill the sign about taking the true gospel message to the whole world.

- • Ability to enforce the Mark
  - o Revelation 13:17 ...'And that no man might buy or sell, save he that had the mark, or the name of the beast, or the number of his name.'
  - o The powers of this world are now trying to make cash obsolete, and are actively pushing pure electronic forms of payment, like "PayPal" and "Google Wallet" for instance. We have the technology to do this now, which in times past wasn't possible. And look at the financial turmoil around the world today. This will help in bringing in a "unified" currency to help make it possible to enforce the mark of the beast. Technology isn't the mark, but technology is needed for proper enforcement of it.
- • Man of Sin revealed
  - o 2 Thessalonians 2:3 ...'Let no man deceive you by any means: for that day shall not come, except there come a falling away first, and that man of sin be revealed, the son of perdition.'
  - o "Apostasia" (falling away) means two things – a departure spiritually and a departure physically. I believe both meanings are found in this sentence from the Word. The spiritual falling away is the Church of Jesus Christ losing their first love, becoming the church of Laodicea, turning away from sound Biblical teaching and hermeneutics (interpretation). The physical departure is the Rapture itself meaning the Antichrist cannot appear before the Rapture takes place.
- • Violence and sexual immorality
  - o Matthew 24:37 ...'But as the days of Noah were, so shall also the coming of the Son of man be.'
  - o Luke 17:28-30 ...'Likewise also as it was in the days of Lot; they did eat, they drank, they bought, they sold, they planted, they builded; But the same day that Lot went out of Sodom it rained fire and brimstone from Heaven, and destroyed them all. Even thus shall it be in the day when the Son of man is revealed.'
  - o What was it like in Noah's day and Lot's day? We need to go to two other Bible verses to see what it was like. Genesis 6:13 tells us that in Noah's day the "Earth was filled with violence." And in Jude 1:7 it says that in Lot's day, Sodom and Gomorrah had given itself over to "fornication and strange flesh". Violence

prevailed in Noah's day and sexual immorality (including homosexuality) prevailed in Lot's day. And this would be a sign of the end times before Christ Jesus returns.

o   Since 2001, at least 14 countries have fully legalized homosexual marriage, Argentina, Belgium, Canada, Denmark, Iceland, Netherlands, Norway, Portugal, Spain, South Africa, Sweden, New Zealand, Uruguay, France, with some parts of Mexico and America doing the same. And there are more countries being added to this list all the time.

o   US Supreme Court Declares Gay Marriage LEGAL in Historic decision

o   There are currently 110 MILLION Cases of sexually transmitted diseases with 20 MILLION new cases every year in America alone!

- Rise in spiritualism

o   1 Timothy 4:1 ...'Now the Spirit speaketh expressly, that in the latter times some shall depart from the faith, giving heed to seducing spirits, and doctrines of devils.'

o   Many people don't realize that spiritualism has also invaded the majority of churches around the world, due to this false teaching of the immortality of the soul.

- Natural disasters

o   Luke 21:25-26 ...'and upon the Earth distress of nations, with perplexity; the sea and the waves roaring; Men's hearts failing them for fear, and for looking after those things which are coming on the Earth: for the powers of Heaven shall be shaken.'

- Earthquakes

o   Matthew 24:7 ...'and earthquakes in divers places.'

o   New Zealand felt a record 32,000 earthquakes in 2016 - link

o   As of April 2018, there were around 3,952 earthquakes happening a month.

- Unsealed prophecy

o   Daniel 12:4 ...'But thou, O Daniel, shut up the words, and seal the book, even to the time of the end.'

o   The prophecies of Daniel 2 and 7 have been unsealed

o   Daniel's 70-week prophecy has been unsealed

- False Christs and false prophets and false teachers

o   Matthew 24:4-5,11 ...'many shall come in My Name, saying, I am Christ ... and many false prophets shall arise and deceive many.'

o   Roman Catholicism, Islam, Hinduism, Buddhism, Sikhism, Folk Religions, Wicca, and many other 'new age' movements. With false prophets like the Pope, Muhammad, Krishna, Buddha, etc., leading these religions.

- o We also have many false prophets and leaders in "Christian" churches, like the prosperity gospel preachers and people like Oprah Winfrey leading these new age movements. People like Rick Warren who preach just enough truth and leave out any prophecy to lull the unlearned mind into following them into apostasy!
- World pushing for peace
  - o 1 Thessalonians 5:3 ...'For when they shall say, Peace and safety; then sudden destruction cometh upon them, as travail upon a woman with child; and they shall not escape.'
- War
  - o Matthew 24:6-7 ...'And ye shall hear of wars ... For nation shall rise against nation and kingdom against kingdom.'
- Famine
  - o Matthew 24:7 ...'and there shall be famine.'
  - o 2.4 BILLION people survive on less than 2 dollars per day!
- Christians being killed
  - o Matthew 24:9-10 ...'Then shall they deliver you up to be afflicted, and shall kill you: and ye shall be hated of all nations for my name's sake. And then shall many be offended, and shall betray one another, and shall hate one another.'
- Increase in sin
  - o Matthew 24:12 ...'And because iniquity shall abound, the love of many shall wax cold.'
  - o Idolatry, Adultery, Violence, Lust, Greed, Disrespect, Homosexuality, Theft, Lying, Aggression, Selfishness.
- Christians turning away from the Truth
  - o 2 Timothy 4:3-4 ...'For the time will come when they will not endure sound doctrine; but after their own lusts shall they heap to themselves teachers, having itching ears; And they shall turn away their ears from the truth, and shall be turned unto fables.'
- God destroys those who destroy the Earth
  - o Revelation 11:18 ...'And the nations were angry, and thy wrath is come, and the time of the dead, that they should be judged, and that thou shouldest give reward unto thy servants the prophets, and to the saints, and them that fear thy name, small and great; and shouldest destroy them which destroy the Earth.'
- Gospel preached to the world
  - o Matthew 24:14 ...'And this gospel of the kingdom shall be preached in all the world for a witness unto all nations; and then shall the end come.'

Let us all take these at face value as well as God's message to us all. First, repent, seek the Lord, accept Jesus as Lord and Savior, then we can observe from a perspective that is perfect as saved heirs of the riches of Heaven, outside of God's Wrath, witnesses of His Glory forevermore! Next, be observant of the signs of the End Times! They are right in front of our very eyes, but relying on the mainstream media will get you nowhere since they are not interested in anything Biblical. There are numerous internet sites that the Truth can be found. All it takes is a little effort and a strong, Spirit-led desire to know the truth. Last, rejoice in the indescribably blessing to be alive in these days when we will see our Savior face to face, witness His Bema Judgment Seat and Marriage Supper of the Lamb, and actually see Him descend to the Mount of Olives to set up His Millennial Kingdom where we will co-reign with Him for a thousand years. Even so, Come Lord Jesus!

CHAPTER FIVE

PRE-TRIBULATION RAPTURE EXPLANATION AND JUSTIFICATION

Introduction

The Rapture is a term most Christians and now even many non-Christians are familiar with. Some will say the word Rapture cannot be found in the Bible, and this is true. But, the important fact is that the concept of a Rapture, a "catching up" of all true Christians, both dead and alive, bodily to be with Jesus Christ "in the air" IS in the Bible.

The timing of just when this "catching up" takes place is also a subject of discussion and wonder among Christians as well as others. Again, the Bible is clear in its explanation as to when the Rapture takes place, but, in order to discern the truth, one must study many different Scriptures to arrive at the truth.

First of all, however, whenever anyone digs into the Scriptures for clarity, for instruction, for guidance, for anything at all, care must be taken to accomplish their study based on concrete, foundational principles without which Bible study is essentially a waste of time. Did I really say that? A waste of time? Yes! Emphatically! Let's look at those foundational principles by examining the Rapture of the Church from a Pre-Tribulation viewpoint.

What is the Tribulation you may ask? The Tribulation is Daniel's 70th Week from Daniel Chapter 9 where he explains that time is for the restoration of the Jews to their God. It is a time of God's Wrath, a time of terrible calamity, catastrophe, and death for not only people, but for animals, plant life, and the Earth. Will Christians see any of the Tribulation? The answer is a resounding "NO", as we will see.

My belief that there will be a Pre-Tribulation Rapture of the Church stands on the bedrock of the following foundational tenets:

A) The Bible is the Word of God

    The 66-book canon called the Bible is God's inerrant, infallible message to mankind, explaining His purposes and plans for the ages (2 Tim. 3:16-17; 2 Peter 1:20-21). No other document can be reliably trusted, nor remotely reach the requirements of authentication that we need to accept it as fact not myth. To suspect any word in the

Bible, any phrase, and statement, any concept, and precept, any doctrine is to destroy the entire Word of God and render it useless and meaningless.

B) The Bible is to be Interpreted Literally

God means what He says and says what He means. God wants His creations to know His will plainly. While God does indulge in picturesque descriptions and parables, an explanation is almost always provided, or context is provided for explanation. The Bible must be read in its simple sense because it means what it says. "If the plain sense makes sense, don't look for any other sense or you will end up with nonsense!" (Got this quote from Dr. David Reagan of ChristinProphecy.org)

C) The Church and Israel Are Separate Entities

Israel is not the Church and the Church is not Israel. A believer in Christ becomes a member of the Church, whether Jew or Gentile (Rom. 1:16), but a member of the Church does not become a form of spiritual Israel. God's promises to Israel as a people and nation are not the same as for the Bride of Christ, the Church. Israel is Jehovah's wife (Jeremiah 3:14, "Return, O backsliding children," says the Lord; "for I am married to you (Israel). I will take you, one from a city and two from a family, and I will bring you to Zion.") and the Church is the Bride of Christ (Revelation 21:9, "And there came unto me one of the seven angels which had the seven vials full of the seven last plagues, and talked with me, saying, Come hither, I will shew thee the bride, the Lamb's wife.")

D) A Literal 1000-Year Millennium

The Bible describes a future, literal 1000-year time period. The Greek word "chilias" for "one thousand" appears six times in Revelation 20, clearly marking the time period as having 1000 literal years. The purpose of this time period is for Jesus Christ to have an earthly kingdom from which to base His rule and to fulfill His promises (Gen. 13:14-17; 15:5,18-21; 2 Sam. 7:16-19; Isa. 10:21-22; 11:1-2; Jer. 23:5-8; 30:22; 31:31-34; Ezek. 11:18-20; 34:24; 36:24-28; Mic. 7:19-20; Hos. 3:5; Rom. 11:26-29).

E) A Literal 7-Year Tribulation

An upcoming time period has been set aside for God to pour out His wrath upon the evil of the world, to regather Israel back into its land, to force Israel to acknowledge Jesus as their Messiah, and for the Messiah to return and fight for His believing remnant (Deut. 4:26-31; Isa. 13:6-13; 17:4-11; Jer. 30:4-11; Ezek. 20:33-38; Dan. 9:27; 12:1; Zech. 14:1-4; Matt. 24:9-31). This time period begins with a covenant between Israel and the Antichrist (Dan. 9:27). The length of the Tribulation is seven years long, described in a variety of ways as "one seven" year block (Dan. 9:27), consisting of two "times, time and half a time" (two years + 1 year + half a year; Rev. 12:14), or two "1260 days" periods (Rev. 11:3), or two "42 month" periods (Rev. 11:2; 13:5).

F) Jesus Will Return Again to Earth

The Bible says Jesus will physically return and set His feet again on Earth on the Mount of Olives – the same location he arose from in Acts 1 (Zech. 14:1-21; Matt. 24:29-31; Mk. 13:24-27; Lk. 21:25-27; Rev. 19). Jesus returns is to defeat His enemies, set up His throne, restore Israel, rule with "a rod of iron" and share His authority with those who overcame in Him (Mat. 19:28; 25:31; Acts 1:3-6; Rev. 2:26-27; 3:21).

G) The Bible Teaches About a Rapture

1 Thessalonians 4:17 speaks of an event called "the Rapture", Latin "rapturo," Greek "harpazo," which means "to catch up, to snatch away, or to take out." "After that, we who are still alive and are left will be caught up together with them in the clouds to meet the Lord in the air. And so we will ever be with the Lord." Paul states that the concept of the Rapture is meant to encourage believers during this Age (1 Thessalonians. 4:18). Other New Testament references on the Rapture are John 14:1-4; I Corinthians 15:51-58; and 1 Thessalonians 4:13-18.

These bedrock statements about the Bible and its interpretation provide the foundation in which to analyze the following reasons for why I believe the Bible teaches a Pre-Tribulation Rapture of the Church.

The Age of Grace

The Abrahamic Covenant specifically states that ALL the families of the Earth will be blessed through Abraham's descendant. Later in Isaiah, God speaks to His Messiah, the Lord said, "It is too small a thing for you to be my servant to restore the tribes of Jacob and bring back those of Israel I have kept. I will also make you a light for the Gentiles, that you may bring my salvation to the ends of the Earth." (Isaiah 49:6) It is clear that God does not limit His salvation to just the Church or to just the Jews but to all. But, the killing of Jesus was the sign that the time for His Kingdom had not arrived. Therefore, the Age of Grace began at the resurrection of Jesus Christ, and it continues today. That era of Grace now 2,000 years in duration will end at the Rapture, and it is sometimes called the Great Pause (Dr. David Reagan and christinprophecy.org) because of the 2,000-year postponement of Daniel's 70th week.

"The Lord does not come to the world at the time of the Rapture, but only reveals himself to the members of His Body. At the time of his resurrection He was only seen by those who believed on Him. Pilate and the High Priest, and those who crucified Him, did not know that He was risen. So it will be at the time of the Rapture. The world will not know that He has been here, and will have no knowledge of Him until He comes with the members of His Body, at the close of the Tribulation." Billy Sunday (Billy Sunday (1862–1935) was a professional baseball player who later became a well-known evangelist. Throughout Sunday's evangelistic career, the kingdom of God was expanded by an estimated 300,000 souls. He preached more than 300 revivals with an estimated 100 million attendees. He was known for his arresting "fire and brimstone" preaching style.)

The purpose of the Great Pause is so the Lord can take from among the Gentiles a people for Himself. Of course, Jews that believe are included, but there will be but few Jews that accept Jesus as Savior because the need for the Tribulation still exists. A lot of Christians know about 1 Thessalonians 4 and 1 Corinthians 15 as referring to the Rapture of the Church, but did you know the Rapture is referred to in John 14, Isaiah 26:17-21, 1 Thessalonians 2:19, Philippians 3:20,21; 2 Thessalonians 2:1, 2 Thessalonians 2:3, Revelation 4:1, 1 John 3:2, Daniel 12:1,2? In Acts 15:14 it says, "Simeon (Peter) hath declared how God at the first did visit the Gentiles, to take out of them a people for his name." The Greek word translated "take" in this verse is "lambano". A look at the primary meanings of "lambano" reveals that the intent of the word is to describe one who takes something for the purpose of carrying it away. Once the church is complete, the Lord will carry us away before turning again to Israel. This is consistent with Paul's statement in Romans 11:25, "For I would not, brethren, that ye should be ignorant of this mystery, lest ye should be wise in your own conceits; that blindness in part is happened to Israel, until the fulness of the Gentiles be come in", that Israel has experienced a partial blindness until God is ready. The phrase "come in" means to arrive at one's destination, as when a ship has "come in". According to John 14:2-3, "In my Father's house are many mansions: if it were not so, I would have told you. I go to prepare a place for you. And if I go and prepare a place for you, I will come again, and receive you unto myself; that where I am, there ye may be also", our destination is Heaven. Once the church has been carried away to its destination in Heaven, taken by Christ from Earth and received by Him in Heaven, the blinders will fall from Israel's eyes, the Great Pause will come to an end, the "In-Between" times will occur, and then Israel will complete its final seven years of Daniel's 70 Weeks prophecy.

When Does the Rapture Happen?

The Rapture has to happen before Daniel's 70th Week can begin, because the 70th Week is all about Israel and not about the Church. After chapter 4 in the book of Revelation, the church is never referred to until Christ's Second Coming in chapter 19. This is a picture of the sequence of events in the End Times. First, the Rapture. Then, the Tribulation. Then, Jesus' Second Coming WITH His Church (that's us). In fact, Revelation 4:1 is a picture of the Rapture which is the kickoff of the Tribulation time. Daniel's 70th Week is the Jews final opportunity to be reconciled to God through the Messiah and prepare for the Kingdom He promised them so long ago. 2500 years before the fact, Zechariah prophesied that this would take place near the end of the 70th Week. Zech. 12:10 says, "And I will pour out on the house of David and the inhabitants of Jerusalem a spirit of grace and supplication. They will look on me, the one they have pierced, and they will mourn for him as one mourns for an only child, and grieve bitterly for him as one grieves for a firstborn son." Therefore, many Jews will accept Jesus as Lord and Savior, but, sadly, many will not.

As a result of the opening of the fulfillment of End Times prophecy, we come to what I consider the ULTIMATE PROOF of the immediacy of the Rapture and the ASSURANCE of it happening BEFORE any of God's Wrath otherwise known as the Tribulation. In fact, I believe that there are significant wars to come (the In-Between" time with Psalm 83, Gog Magog – Ezekiel 38,39, etc.) that will pre-date the Tribulation and involve nuclear war, but we as believers will not be here for those either. What is that "ultimate proof"? 1 Thessalonians 5:1-11!

"But concerning the times and seasons, brethren, you have no need that I should write to you. For you yourselves know perfectly that the Day of the Lord so comes as a thief in the night. For when they say, 'Peace and safety!' then sudden destruction comes upon them, as labor pains upon a pregnant woman. And they shall not escape. But you, brethren, are not in darkness, so that this Day should overcome you as a thief. You are all sons of light and sons of the day. We are not of the night nor of darkness. Therefore, let us not sleep, as others do, but let us watch and be sober. For those that sleep, sleep at night, and those who get drunk are drunk at night. But let us who are of the day be sober, putting on the breastplate of faith and love, and as a helmet the hope of salvation. For God did not appoint us to wrath, but to obtain salvation through our Lord Jesus Christ, who died for us, that whether we wake or sleep, we should live together with Him."

The "Day of the Lord" is, of course, in this case, referring to the Tribulation that is the Wrath of God on this sinful and evil world. A "thief in the night" is not what we usually think in our day. We usually think of a thief in the night as someone clandestinely breaking in, being very quiet and sneaky, stealing something, then leaving just as quietly. This is not how this was perceived in the time of Jesus on the Earth. A thief in the night was a strongarm break-in, loud and mean, with hostages, bodily harm, demands, possibly even death. The "sudden destruction" is what the thief does when he breaks in to get whatever he wants, and he comes without notice.

The reference to Christians NOT being in darkness is a direct message that we are different than the rest of the world. We are "all sons of light and sons of the day", not "of the night nor of darkness". Being "in the light" is a direct reference to Jesus Christ. John 1:1-5 says, "In the beginning was the Word, and the Word was with God, and the Word was God. He was in the beginning with God. All things were made through Him, and without Him nothing was made that was made. In Him was life, and the life was the light of men. And the light shines in the darkness, and the darkness did not comprehend it." This section at the very start of John's Gospel is the most powerful statement in the entire Bible because we learn that Jesus is the Creator God, He is the Light of men, and that those in the darkness cannot and will not understand any of this. This also means that the darkness, or those who do not know Jesus Christ as Savior and Lord, will be subject to God's Wrath. But those in God's Light, the Light of Jesus Christ, will NOT see or experience God's Wrath!

We go back to Thessalonians where it says, "For God did not appoint us to wrath, but to obtain salvation through our Lord Jesus Christ." We as believers are not to experience God's Wrath because we belong to Jesus and are in His Light, not in darkness. 1 Thessalonians 1:9,10 says, "For they themselves shew of us what manner of entering in we had unto you, and how ye turned to God from idols to serve the living and true God; And to wait for his Son from Heaven, whom he raised from the dead, even Jesus, which delivered us from the wrath to come." 1 Thessalonians 5:9 says, "For God hath not appointed us to wrath, but to obtain salvation by our Lord Jesus Christ," Romans 5:9 says, "Much more then, being now justified by his blood, we shall be saved from wrath through him." And Revelation 3:10 says, "Because thou hast kept the word of my patience, I also will keep thee from the hour of temptation, which shall come upon all the world, to try them that dwell upon the Earth." These verses conclusively show that God does not put His Wrath on believers in Jesus Christ. Therefore, Christians do not see any of the Tribulation, any of the "In-Between" time, just the sudden and unknown timing of the instantaneous "catching up" to be with Jesus in the air. Those in the dark, those who do not know Christ as Lord and Savior, WILL experience God's Wrath, the Tribulation, the Antichrist, the seals, the trumpets, the bowls of Revelation. How do we escape God's Wrath that comes on the entire world in the End Times? The Rapture!

We all know that the word "Rapture" technically does not appear anywhere in the Bible. But, being "caught up" ("harpazo" in the Greek) to meet the Lord in the air is precisely the same as the Rapture! 1 Thessalonians 4:14-18 assures us, "For if we believe that Jesus died and rose again, even so God will bring with Him those who sleep in Jesus. For this we say to you by the word of the Lord, that we who are alive and remain until the coming of the Lord will by no means precede those who are asleep. For the Lord Himself will descend from Heaven with a shout, and with the trumpet of God. And the dead in Christ will rise first. Then we who are alive and remain shall be caught up together with them in the clouds to meet the Lord in the air. And thus we shall always be with the Lord. Therefore comfort one another with these words."

The Rapture keeps us away from God's Wrath that comes on the entire world to wake up God's Chosen People, the Jews, to their Messiah, Jesus Christ. Throughout the Bible, we see how stubborn, how disobedient, how worldly the Jews have always been. But without the Jews, we would not have a Savior! God made covenants with the Jews to always love them, always protect them, and eventually save them. God knows it will take extreme measures to wake the Jews up to the saving knowledge of Jesus Christ, their Savior as well as ours. So, "Jacob's Trouble" (Jeremiah 30:7-11), what we know as the Tribulation and Daniel's 70th week (Daniel Chapter 9), is to get Israel's attention, turn them to Jesus, and to punish the world for its sin and disobedience to God. Then, Jesus can come and reign as King of kings and

Lord of lords for a thousand years, the Millennial Kingdom ("Thy Kingdom come, Thy Will be done, on Earth as it is in Heaven." Matthew 6:10).

The Confusing Interpretations of When the Rapture Happens

The most logical and provable point of view for the occurrence of the Rapture is Pre-Tribulation or the Rapture occurring BEFORE any of the Tribulation events or In-Between events. But some offer that the Rapture occurs "Pre-Wrath" meaning that the Rapture does not occur until God's Wrath begins during the Tribulation (and there are differing opinions as to just when God's Wrath starts – with the Seal Judgments, with the Trumpet Judgments, or with the Bowl Judgments), after the start of the Tribulation with Daniel 9:27's Peace Treaty. There are several problems with this view, and we will look at them.

Other views of the Rapture say it occurs at Mid-Tribulation, or at the middle of the Tribulation when Satan enters the Antichrist and the Abomination of Desolation occurs. The first half of the Tribulation contains all of the Seal Judgments and all of the Trumpet Judgments because the Book of Revelation tells us so. Since we as Christians do not see God's Wrath, the Mid-Tribulation view cannot be right because we would see a significant part of God's Wrath. The same can be said for the Post-Tribulation view placing the Rapture at the END of the Tribulation causing Christians to see ALL of God's Wrath! Let's look at the Pre-Wrath view which also explains the other views as well.

Objections to Alternatives to A Pre-Tribulation Rapture

1) The Name – The name "Pre-Wrath" is both confusing and vague. The Pre-Tribulation view argues that the entire 7 years of the Tribulation (Daniel's 70th Week of Years) constitutes a pouring out of the Wrath of God. The Mid-Tribulation view takes the position that only the second half of the Tribulation is the period of God's Wrath because, primarily, this view says that God's Bowl Judgments are His "Great" wrath when all the judgments (Seal, Trumpet, and Bowl) are God's Judgments. (refer to christinprophecy.org and Dr. David Reagan)

Some say that the Pre-Wrath designation refers to Satan's Wrath which comes after the Jews are protected by God and Satan releases his wrath on Christians and any available Jews during the last half of the Tribulation. Revelation 12 tells us when the wrath of Satan begins. It is AFTER the middle of the 7 years, which means after the Abomination of Desolation, (Dan 9:27; Matthew 24:15-16). "And the dragon was wroth with the woman and went to make war with the remnant of her seed, which keep the commandments of God, and have the testimony of Jesus Christ" (Rev 12:17). It is an error to say Satan's wrath happens in the first 3 ½ years of the Tribulation.

God's Wrath starts at the 1st Seal. His Wrath is already generally expressed from Heaven against all ungodly sinners, as Paul wrote in Romans, "For the wrath of God is revealed from Heaven against all ungodliness and unrighteousness of men, who hold the truth in unrighteousness" (Rom 1:18). During the seven years of the 70th Week, that general wrath is expressed in the judgments that start with the 1st Seal. It is Jesus, not Satan, breaking those Seals to begin pouring out judgments on a wicked world.

When the massacre of believers instigated by the Antichrist happens after the Abomination of Desolation, then the nature of the wrath of God changes. It is no longer a dispassionate dispensing of justice. The wrath expressed in the 6th Seal and beyond is a personal grudge against those who have wholesale murdered His believers. Paul wrote, "Dearly beloved, avenge not yourselves, but rather give place unto wrath: for it is written, Vengeance is mine; I will repay, saith the Lord" (Rom 12:19).

The timing of the Rapture is due to the closing out of the Dispensation of Grace, turning back to fulfilling promises made by God to Israel. The evidence we see for this is the nature of who is sharing the gospel with the world. The Church was given the Great Commission. We are to be Christ's witnesses. "But ye shall receive power, after that the Holy Ghost is come upon you: and ye shall be witnesses unto me both in Jerusalem, and in all Judaea, and in Samaria, and unto the uttermost part of the Earth" (Acts 1:8).

The Two Witnesses are also given a commission, "And I will give power unto my two witnesses, and they shall prophesy a thousand two hundred and threescore days, clothed in sackcloth" (Revelation 11:3). The Two Witnesses perform their ministry during the first 1,260 days of the 70th Week, the first half of the seven-year Tribulation, ending on the day the Antichrist commits the Abomination of Desolation. If the Church were still on Earth past the start of the 7 years, what need is there for two special witnesses? Christ already would have (if the Church were still here) MILLIONS of witnesses. After all, we have been given the commission to be Christ's witnesses, and that has never been revoked. There is no sensible or logical reason for God to introduce Two Witnesses when millions of witnesses are already here. When the Pre-Tribulation Rapture removes all those millions, there is then a need for Two Witnesses to preach Jesus Christ.

The entire seven years of the 70th Week (the Tribulation) is God's wrath, and as such, He will be pouring out judgment resulting in death and destruction on a rebellious world. It is for the reasons above, plus many others, that we know the Rapture of the Church happens before those final seven years of the Tribulation begin, the Pre-Tribulation Rapture.

2) The Chronology - The Pre-Wrath, Mid-Tribulation, and Post-Tribulation Rapture views violate the chronology of the book of Revelation. The sequence of events that is pictured in the book of Revelation clearly places both the Seal Judgments and the Trumpet Judgments in the first half of the 70th Week of Daniel. And the Bowl Judgments are clearly contained within Daniel's 70th Week, near its end. Any view other than the Pre-Tribulation view scrambles all this.

3) Imminence - A very strong objection to the Mid-Tribulation, Pre-Wrath, and Post-Tribulation views of the Rapture is the destruction of the imminence of the Lord's return. The Bible emphasizes that the Lord could return at any moment and that we should live looking for His return (Matthew 24:44, 1 Corinthians 1:7, Philippians 3:20, Philippians 4:5, Colossians 3: 4, 1 Thessalonians 1:10, 1 Thessalonians 5:6, Titus 2:13, and Revelation 16:15). The Mid-Tribulation, Pre-Wrath, and Post-Tribulation views say the Lord cannot return until after the Antichrist appears, the Jewish Temple has been rebuilt, and the world has suffered through years of the wrath of Man and Satan. Thus, according to any view other than the Pre-Tribulation view, we should be living looking for the Antichrist and not Jesus Christ.

4) The Wrath of God - Another strong objection to the Pre-Wrath Rapture view is its mistaken concept of the sovereignty of God. The view attempts to distinguish the wrath of Man and Satan from the Wrath of God. Both Man and Satan operate under the sovereignty of God. That's why Psalm 2 pictures God sitting in Heaven laughing at the evil plots of the world's political leaders. His laughing is not motivated by a lack of concern or some sort of derision. He laughs because He has the wisdom and power to orchestrate all the evil of

Man and Satan to the triumph of His Son.

There is an additional consideration that we should all see and accept. The Bible portrays God pouring out His wrath both directly (Sodom and Gomorrah) and indirectly (the destruction of both Israel and Judah). God poured out His wrath upon the rebellious northern nation of Israel by allowing the Assyrians to conquer it. God used the Assyrians as "the rod of My anger" (Isaiah 10:5) and "My war-club" (Jeremiah 51:20).

When the prophet Habakkuk complained about God doing nothing about the evil of the southern nation of Judah, the Lord revealed that He was going to pour out His wrath on that nation through Babylon (Habakkuk 1:6). And when the Lord was finished with Babylon, He raised up the Medes and Persians to conquer the Babylonian Empire, referring to the conquering army as "My consecrated ones" (Isaiah 13:3). During Daniel's 70 Weeks of Years, much of the wrath of God will be executed through the Antichrist, but it is still the Wrath of God.

5) The Tribulation - The Pre-Wrath and Mid-Tribulation Rapture views deny that the first half of Daniel's 70th Week is part of the Tribulation. Both halves of Daniel's 70th Week are referred to in the Scriptures as a time of tribulation. Matthew 24:9 refers to the first half as "Tribulation," and Matthew 24:21 classifies the second half as "Great Tribulation." Incidentally, Jesus' reference to the second half as the "Great Tribulation" does not mean it will be worse than the first half. Rather, Jesus called it that because He was speaking to a Jewish audience, and the second half of the Tribulation will be when the Antichrist will try to annihilate the Jews.

6) The Purpose of Daniel's 70th Week - The Mid-Tribulation, Pre-Wrath, and Post-Tribulation Rapture views distort the purpose of Daniel's 70th Week. Daniel 9:24-27 makes it clear that the purpose of Daniel's 70 Weeks of Years is to accomplish six things among the Jewish people:

- To finish transgression
- To make an end of sin
- To make atonement for iniquity
- To bring in everlasting righteousness
- To seal up vision and prophecy
- To anoint the most Holy Place

Just as the first 69 weeks of years (483 years) of the prophecy had nothing to do with the Church, neither does the final week of years. The last seven-year period of Daniel's prophecy is about the accomplishment of the purposes listed above among the Jewish people. Accordingly, the entire period of Daniel's 70th Week is referred to in Jeremiah 30:7 as "the time of Jacob's trouble." There is no purpose for the Church during Daniel's 70th Week.

7) The Church – The Mid-Tribulation, Pre-Wrath, and Post-Tribulation Rapture views say the Church must be present during the Tribulation. Incredibly, the argument has been proclaimed that the Church must suffer "for purging and purifying." The Bible says that the blood of Jesus is sufficient to cleanse us of all sin (1 John 1:7). The idea that the Church needs to be purified creates a Christian Purgatory, which is a blasphemy of the blood of Jesus.

8) The Seal Judgments - The Mid-Tribulation, Pre-Wrath, and Post-Tribulation Rapture views claim that the Seal Judgments do not constitute any portion of the Wrath of God. The judgments originate at the throne of God when Jesus begins to open each seal (Revelation 6:1) thus deliberately and sequentially doling out His Wrath on an unbelieving world. Further, they are referred to as "the wrath of the Lamb" (Revelation 6:16-17).

9) The Day of the Lord - The Mid-Tribulation, Pre-Wrath, and Post-Tribulation Rapture views of the Day of the Lord contend that they begin with the opening of the 7th Seal or with the blowing of the 7th Trumpet, or with the conclusion of the Bowl Judgments, and argue that the wrath of God does not begin until one or another of these points happens. The problem here is that the Day of the Lord is a term that is used in many different ways in the Bible, and it must always be interpreted in context. There are places when it refers to specific national judgments from God, as when Israel was destroyed by Assyria (Amos 5:18-20) and when Judah was destroyed by Babylon (Lamentations 2:21-22 and Ezekiel 13:5). In like manner the fall of Babylon is called the Day of the Lord (Isaiah 13:6- 13).

But there are also times when the term refers to end time events. In this regard, it sometimes refers to the return of Jesus at the end of Daniel's 70th Week (Isaiah 2:10-22, Joel 3:9-17 and Zechariah 14:1-9). In other end time contexts, the term is used in a broader sense. For example, in Zephaniah 1:14-18 it is used to refer to the entire period of the Tribulation when "all the Earth will be devoured in the fire of His jealousy..." In 1 Thessalonians 5:1-3 it says the Day of the Lord will come at a time when people are feeling safe and secure — which would be at the beginning of Daniel's 70th Week, after the Antichrist negotiates a treaty that guarantees peace for Israel. But the prophet Isaiah repeatedly uses a shorthand version of the term "in that day" to refer to the Millennium (Isaiah 4:2-6). In reference to the End Times, the broad use of the term refers to the period of time from the beginning of Daniel's 70th Week to the end of the Millennium.

Another problem is when the Day of the Lord is said to begin at the point where the Seal Judgments are followed immediately by the Trumpet Judgments. How could that be? The Bible says the Day of the Lord will begin with people celebrating peace and safety (1 Thessalonians 5:2-3). What feeling of peace and safety will exist when the world is experiencing the Trumpet Judgments? This must be a reference to the treaty of peace the Antichrist will negotiate at the beginning of Daniel's 70th Week and which will mark the beginning of the Tribulation (Daniel 9:27).

We are currently in the Day of the Spirit (Acts 2:17 and 2 Corinthians 3:8). Daniel's 70th Week plus the Millennium constitutes the Day of the Lord. The Eternal State will be the Day of God (2 Peter 3:12).

The Rapture and Why It Was So Huge to the Thessalonians

In order to fully understand the impact of the Rapture, we must place ourselves into that tiny first century church in Thessalonica, after the Resurrection, after Pentecost, about 50 A.D. when Paul had come and started this group of new Christians, left, then heard about some major concerns that they had because of the persecution they were receiving from Jews in the area. Refer to 1 Thessalonians 4:13-18. (This section is adapted from Dr. John MacArthur and GTY.org)

Verse 13: "But we do not want you to be uninformed," – or ignorant – "brethren, about those who are asleep, so that you will not grieve as do the rest who have no hope. For if we believe that Jesus died and rose again, even so God will bring with Him those who have fallen asleep in Jesus. For this we say to you by the word of the Lord, that we who are alive and remain until the coming of the Lord, will not precede those who have fallen asleep. For the Lord Himself will descend from Heaven with a shout, with the voice of the archangel and with the trumpet of God, and the dead in Christ will rise first. Then we who are alive and remain will be caught up together with them in the clouds to meet the Lord in the air, and so we shall always be with the Lord. Therefore comfort one another with these words."

The details of what happens to Christians after they die were elusive in the early church, and the Thessalonians were worried about that subject: "Where do Christians go after they die? What happens to their souls? And, in particular, what happens to their bodies?" This set of questions troubled young believers in the church at Thessalonica, as we might assume, because they didn't have the full revelation that we do in the New Testament. Their concern, however, was rather specific. Paul had been teaching them when he ministered to them about the fact that Jesus was going to return. And, in fact, he taught them as if it could happen in their lifetime.

They expected the coming of Christ. They also expected the judgment of God in an event called the Day of the Lord, a very familiar Old Testament term. But they were living in the expectation that this could happen in their lifetime. And nothing is said by Paul in any of his writings about this, either here or in 1 Corinthians 15, that would lead them to believe that it couldn't possibly happen in their lifetime.

There is then an imminent event, the return of Christ in some way that could happen in their lifetime. And the question they were asking is this, "What happens to Christians who die before His return?" They were so worried about what was going to happen to Christians that died that they would therefore miss the great event of the coming of the Lord, that they were burdened by it, if not actually grieved by the thought that some of the folks they loved would miss this event. And what made it seem more grievous was persecution. Many of them perhaps had died or would die under persecution.

Back in 1 Thessalonians Chapter 3 and verse 3, Paul talks about the fact that "they shouldn't be disturbed by afflictions. They should know that we have been destined for this. For indeed when we were with you, we kept telling you in advance that we were going to suffer affliction; and so it came to pass, and so you know." What's going to happen to those people who have been persecuted? They would be the noblest of the noble they would assume.

This Thessalonian Church was marked by love. In fact, this is the only church that Paul ever wrote to that he didn't drag out their sin and confront it. There isn't anything like that in his letters to them. They were marked by a profound love for one another, and even for those outside their local fellowship all throughout Macedonia. This added to the grief in their minds, if someone died and was to miss the second coming, were they going to be a disembodied spirit? Were they going to be a lesser saint? Were they going to miss the great event? Were they somehow not going to experience the presence of the Lord?

Paul answers the distress and the confusion and ignorance with a clear description of a single event that will be the next event on the prophetic calendar. We call it the Rapture, and that's because of verse 17. The verb "caught up," "harpazo" in Greek. It means to snatch up, to seize and carry off by force. It is the sudden swoop of an irresistible force that pulls you away. It is a violent snatching away. The term "Rapture" is simply a word to describe the snatching away, and that is exactly what verse 17 is saying. There will be a time when believers are snatched up by a sudden, divine, irresistible force. That's what this text is about, about that event.

This is not that event when He comes and His feet touch the Mount of Olives, and He turns the desert into a garden, destroys the nations, and establishes His Millennial reign. This is not Christ coming to Earth, because it clearly says He comes and meets them in the air. We know this is also not judgment, because there's no judgement here. This is strictly a snatching away of believers into the air to meet the Lord. That is the next event in the prophetic calendar for us.

There are at least four important things to see when studying the Rapture: the three **pillars** of the Rapture, the **participants** of the Rapture, the **plan** of the Rapture, and the **purpose** of the Rapture.

First, what are the pillars of the Rapture, the bases for our understand, expectation, and surety that the Rapture will happen? The resurrection of Christ is God's stamp of approval on what He did on the cross and the **first pillar**. It's more than that, it is our resurrection as well. So, if we believe that Jesus died and rose again, even so, from Christ's cross and resurrection, we are moved then to what happens to Christians at the Rapture. Even so, God will bring with Him those who have fallen asleep in Jesus. That's what the Thessalonians wanted to know.

What's going to happen to those who had died? Their spirits have gone obviously to be with the Lord. They didn't perhaps understand the fullness of that. But they would have understood that they would be with the Lord in some sense. They would understand that they would be in the possession of eternal life, and that's the **second pillar** of the Rapture.

But what about the bodies? And would they be always incomplete, separated spirit from body? And would they be somehow less than those who experience the Rapture? No, not at all. God will bring with Him those who have fallen asleep in Jesus. This is the promise of resurrection. God raised Jesus and He will raise all who are in Jesus, even those who have died.

How do you know this, Paul? How can you be sure? Here's the **third pillar**: This truth of the Rapture of the church (the gathering, the snatching) is based on the death of Christ and the resurrection of Christ in which we are involved. But it is also based on the revelation from Christ, verse 15: "For this we say to you by the word of the Lord. This we say to you by the word of the Lord." Where are you getting this information, Paul, "By the word of the Lord"? On the basis of divine revelation which is the **third pillar**. Paul received the word of the Rapture directly from God!

There is a reference to the Rapture in John 14:3, but John doesn't give us any kind of details or any kind of description for anything parallel to the detail of this text. What Paul means is that the Lord has personally revealed this to Him. The reason we know that is because 1 Corinthians 15:51 calls it a mystery. Up to now, nobody knew this. Jesus didn't give the details either in the Scripture or outside the Scripture, or it wouldn't have been a mystery. Mystery is something that has been hidden and is now revealed.

The Thessalonians did know about Jesus coming. They also knew about the Day of the Lord (the Tribulation). They knew that there was a time when Jesus would come and bring final judgment. They also knew that that final judgment was the culmination of a series of judgments in a cataclysmic event called the Day of the Lord. It's not a day in the sense of 24 hours, it's a day in the sense of an era or an epic, a very familiar term in the Old Testament. They knew that there was coming a final Day of the Lord, a time of judgment. But they didn't know about the Rapture.

The Day of the Lord is all over the Old Testament. Sometimes it's talking about a historical Day of the Lord when the Lord comes in judgment. Sometimes it's talking about that eschatological final Day of the Lord that we're talking about in 1 Thessalonians 5. But there's very little about the Rapture (except for, perhaps, Isaiah 26:17-21) in the Old Testament. It's built on the death, the resurrection of Christ, and revelation from Christ that up to this point was a mystery. This is a truth based on the reality of Christ's death, Christ's resurrection, and His own revelation to the apostles, a strong foundation. These are the three pillars of the Rapture.

Second, who are the **participants** in the Rapture, who is going to be involved? Paul says in verse 14, "God's going to bring with Him those who have fallen asleep." The dead are not going to miss this. Obviously, their spirits are already with the Lord. To be absent from the body is to be present with the Lord (2 Corinthians 5:8). Far better to depart and be with Christ. No middle ground, no purgatory, no soul sleep; but the body sleeps.

But the ones who have fallen asleep will not miss this event. It says in verse 15, "We who are alive and remain until the coming of the Lord." We? Does this mean Paul thought it could happen in his lifetime? It does. It didn't happen in his lifetime; it could have happened in his lifetime, because it is a signless event and imminent. It is a sudden cataclysmic snatching.

There are no indications in the Bible anywhere in the New Testament that there's any precursor to this. When you see in the Olivet Discourse in the gospels Jesus laying out all of the things that precede His coming, those are events that precede His coming in judgment to establish His kingdom, His Second Coming. This is not that, this is before that. "We who are alive and remain until the coming of the Lord will not precede those who have fallen asleep."

Again, there's no judgment here. Christ doesn't even come all the way to Earth. He doesn't split the Mount of Olives. He doesn't come to Armageddon. He doesn't defeat His enemies. He doesn't bring final judgment. He doesn't separate the sheep and the goats. He doesn't set up the Millennial Kingdom. All of that comes after the beginning of the Day of the Lord, and it is the culmination of the Day of the Lord which is a period of judgment. And by the way, the Rapture occurs at the end of chapter 4, and the Day of the Lord is described in chapter 5, and that's the sequence.

Paul not only didn't know when it was going to happen, but he also knew he couldn't know. Certainly, he had become familiar with the words of our Lord, Matthew 24:36, that no one knew the time, season, not even the Son knew that at that time. He also knew that it would be a while before Jesus came. If he followed the parables of Jesus in Matthew 24 and 25, in one of the parables we are reminded that our Lord says, "The Master is not coming for a long time." And in the parable of the virgins, the bridegroom is delaying. So he didn't know when. He was caught between the fact that it could happen in his lifetime, and it could be a very long time as well as it has turned out to be. What is the point of that kind of imminency? The point of that kind of imminency is preparedness. If we don't know, then we need to be prepared at all times; He's coming in an hour when you think not.

Now go back to the text and verse 15 again: "We who are alive and remain until the coming of the Lord, will not precede those who have fallen asleep." By just being alive, we are not going to have any advantage, that's the idea. It's to no advantage to be alive at the Rapture. All Christians alive or dead when Jesus comes to gather us and take us to the place that He's prepared for us in the Father's house, all of us will be gathered, no one will be left out. So, the pillars of the Rapture event, the death and resurrection of Christ, and the revelation of Christ, the participants – all believers dead or alive – all will be gathered up. No one will miss that event.

The third thing we need to see in verses 16 and 17 is the **plan** of the Rapture. There are some details here that we don't have in 1 Corinthians 15 or John 14. First, the Lord Himself will descend from Heaven. This is to fulfill the promise of John 14: "I will come. Don't let your heart be troubled. I'm going to prepare a place for you and I will come again and receive you to Myself."

The Lord will descend from Heaven. It's the Lord. It's not an angel, it's not a host of angels, it's the Lord Himself. This is not the Lord coming with 10,000 times 10,000 in judgment on the world and the establishment of His kingdom, this is the Lord coming personally, the Lord Himself. This is in contrast to Matthew 13 where in the coming of the Lord in judgment, the angels are the reapers. So that's why Jesus says in Acts 1:11 to the disciples who are looking as Jesus ascends into Heaven in the clouds, two angels in white clothing standing there, they said, "Men of Galilee, why do you stand looking into the sky? This Jesus, who has been taken up from you into Heaven, will come in just the same way as you have watched Him go." He's gone away.

How did He go away? In the clouds. That's exactly how He'll come back. "You have seen Him go; you will see Him return; you will meet Him. He will descend from Heaven." That's where He's been, John 14. He's coming down to take us there to be in Heaven with Him.

Then some indications of the grandeur of the event: "The Lord will descend from Heaven with a shout, "keleusma", a word of command, authority, urgency. It's actually kind of a military term. You would use it to suddenly and forcefully call the troops from being at ease to attention: "Back into your ranks. Get into position." Luther translated it in German "feldgeschrei" which means a call to stand up and get in line. That is the call: "Get ready."

In Psalm 47, which is a Millennial Psalm, we read, "God is gone up with a shout, the with the sound of a trumpet." Here He comes down. This is the call to the dead to rise, sort of like, "Lazarus, come out." Immediately all the souls in Heaven are joined to the bodies, some from the grave, some from the sea. They're all joined together. This is the power that Jesus claimed in

John 5 when he says He has the power of life, the resurrection of life. This is the resurrection of life.

There is also the voice of an archangel. This is without a parallel in Scripture. The only mention of an archangel is here and in Jude 9 where it's Michael. This is an archangel, it could be Michael, as he is identified with such a resurrection for Israel in Daniel 12, which comes later at the end of the Day of the Lord. Whoever this angel is, he adds his voice to the voice of the Lord Himself. And then comes the trumpet of God.

If you go back into the Old Testament you know that the trumpets were blown to assemble the people. There are many trumpets in the Old Testament. Whenever there was a festival, a celebration, a convocation; whenever there was some kind of triumph, some kind of judgment, a trumpet in Exodus 19 calls the people to meet with God, the trumpet of assembly would be called. In Zephaniah, in Zechariah, a trumpet is used as a signal of the Lord's coming to rescue His people from wicked oppression. It's a trumpet of deliverance.

And there are many trumpets associated with the end times, many; more of them with that period called the Day of the Lord. This trumpet is the last trumpet in the sense that it ends the Church Age, the Dispensation of Grace. It's not said to be a judgment trumpet, as the trumpets in Revelation 8 to 11 are, it's an assembly trumpet. And here we see the plan: the dead in Christ will rise first.

You might say, "Well, did the Jews in the Old Testament believe they were going to have a resurrection?" Absolutely, they believed they were going to be raised from the dead. You remember the book of Hebrews, chapter 6. The writer says, "Therefore leaving the elementary teaching about the Messiah, let us press on to maturity, not laying again a foundation of repentance from dead works and faith toward God." That's Old Testament theology of instruction about washings, laying on of hands, and the resurrection of the dead, and eternal judgment. Of course, the Old Testament saints believed in the resurrection of the dead. That was promised to them by God.

Job, chapter 19, verse 23, "Oh that my words were written! Oh that they were inscribed in a book! That with an iron stylus and lead they were engraved in the rock forever! As for me, I know that my Redeemer lives, and at the last He will take His stand on the Earth. Even after my skin is destroyed, yet in my flesh I shall see God; whom I myself shall behold, and whom my eyes will see and not another." Job believed in resurrection.

Psalm 16 talks about God not letting His holy one see corruption. And then Daniel, chapter 12, is the passage on resurrection, verse 1: "At that time (and this is looking at the end of the Day of the Lord) Michael, the great prince who stands guard over the sons of your people, will arise. There will be a time of distress such as never occurred since there was a nation until that time." That's the time of tribulation, the period of the Day of the Lord. It follows the Rapture and comes before the final judgment, "at that time your people, everyone who is found written in the book, will be rescued. Many of those who sleep in the dust of the ground will awake, these to everlasting life, the others to disgrace and everlasting contempt." There will be a resurrection of the unjust and the saints as well. The Old Testament teaches the resurrection of the body, and so does the New, as we have found.

I love this term, "The dead in Christ shall rise first." Even though they're dead they're still in Christ. Nothing can separate them from Christ, Romans 8. First Corinthians 15:23 identifies believers as "those that are Christ's, those that are in Christ." Death does not separate them from Christ. "So it is the dead in Christ who rise first, then" (verse 17) "we who are alive and remain" (still alive on Earth) "will be snatched up together with them in the clouds." You remember Acts 1? "You saw Him go in the clouds, you'll see Him come back in the clouds." And we're all snatched up in the clouds. The bodies meet, the spirits of saints already in glory. The rest on Earth who are alive are transformed on the way up. And we know how fast that is, as fast as it takes light to flash on the eye, in a minute portion of a nanosecond we're changed on the way up. This is the Rapture. We're all snatched up by this divine, irresistible force. This is an interesting word, this word harpazo. It's used in Matthew 11 of taking a kingdom by force. It's used in John 10 of a wolf snatching a sheep. It's used in John 10 where our Lord says that nothing can snatch us out of the Father's hand.

It's used in 2 Corinthians 12 where Paul was snatched up into the third Heaven. It's used in Acts 8 where Philip was caught up and disappeared, remember, when he was talking to the eunuch. Most importantly, it's used in 1 Corinthians 15:51 and 52, "In a moment, in the twinkling of an eye, at the last trump. The trumpet will sound, the dead in Christ will be raised imperishable, and we shall be changed," snatched up, transformed into our eternal condition like the risen resurrected Christ; and we will be joined together with the dead who receive their glorified bodies – and I love this – "and so we shall always be with the Lord." There will be a reunion.

Don't worry about those who've died. They're not going to be second-class saints, they're not going to be floating spirits while you have a glorified body. We're all going to be together. There is reunion, no one left out. We'll all be in that glorious final form. And, again, clouds are associated with this; we meet the Lord in the air. Again, this is not the Second Coming. He's not coming to Earth, we meet Him in the air.

Meeting the Lord is a common Old Testament idea, and here it's the experience of believers. And He gathers us and takes us to the rooms He's prepared for us in the Father's house, and we will always be with the Lord. Never after that will we be separated. At the end of the Day of the Lord, when He comes back in judgment, we come back with Him. When He sets up His kingdom on Earth, we reign with Him on Earth through the thousand years; and then in the new Heaven and the new Earth, we dwell with Him forever, never to be separated from the Lord.

We have looked at the pillars of this event, the participants of this event, the plan, and, finally, what is the **purpose** of telling us this? Verse 18: "Therefore, (what is all this there for?) comfort one another with these words." Nobody's going to be left out. God, who is the God of all comfort, comforts His people, not with some kind of emotional warm and fuzzy experience; He comforts His people with truth, the Truth, God's Truth, the only Truth!

2 Thessalonians 2:3 - Can the Rapture be found in this passage?

2 Thessalonians 2:3 says, "Let no one in any way deceive you, for it will not come unless the apostasy comes first, and the man of lawlessness is revealed, the son of destruction…"

The Bible never precisely states when the Rapture of the Church will take place. That's why there is so much disagreement over when it will occur. All positions are based on inferences in the Scriptures. Some believe the Rapture will occur in the middle of the Tribulation. Others place it near the end. And some combine it with the Second Coming. I happen to believe that the best inference of the Scriptures is that it will occur before the Tribulation begins.

I have many reasons for my belief, including Scripture verses, prophetic symbolism, and logic. With regard to Scripture verses, some of the more important ones that relate to the Rapture's timing are the following:

1. Luke 21:36, "…keep on the alert at all times, praying that you may have strength to escape all these things that are about to take place, and to stand before the Son of Man."

Jesus spoke these words in His Olivet Discourse which He delivered to His disciples the week He was crucified. They concluded a long speech in which He outlined the major signs of the end times that would signal the season of His return. Notice that He says that believers should live anticipating the Lord's appearance at any time, and that they are to pray for their escape from all the horrors of the end times which He had been talking about. To me, this passage strongly infers a Pre-Tribulation Rapture.

2. 1 Thessalonians 1:9-10, "…you turned to God from idols to serve a living and true God, and to wait for His Son from Heaven, whom He raised from the dead, that is Jesus, who **rescues** us **from** the wrath to come."

    I consider this passage to be one of the most convincing one that points to a Pre-Tribulation Rapture. After all, the Bible clearly teaches in both the Old and New Testaments that the Tribulation will be a period of the pouring out of God's wrath (Isaiah 24 and Revelation 6-19). This verse promises that Jesus will deliver believers "from the wrath that is to come." A similar promise can be found in 1 Thessalonians 5:9 which states: "For God has not destined us for wrath, but for obtaining salvation through our Lord Jesus Christ…"

3. Revelation 3:10, "Because you have kept the word of My perseverance, I also will keep you **from** the hour of testing, that hour which is about to come upon the whole world, to test those who dwell on the Earth."

    These are some of the words that Jesus addressed to the church at Philadelphia. They constitute a promise that true believers will be kept from the testing that will one day encompass the entire world. We know from many other scriptures, including Revelation 6-19, that the "hour of testing" will be the Tribulation period of seven years when the Wrath of God will be poured out on the Earth (Revelation 11:18 and 15:1).

These three passages are isolated because they give us clues as to the timing of the Rapture — namely, that it will take place before the Tribulation begins. There are many other verses that refer to the Rapture besides these. Some include for your personal study: John 14:1-3; Romans 8:19; 1 Corinthians 1:7-8; 15:51-53; 16:22; Philippians 3:20-21; 4:5; Colossians 3:4; 1

Thessalonians 2:19; 4:13-18; 5:9,23;2 Thessalonians 2:1; 1 Timothy 6:14; 2 Timothy 4:1,8; Titus 2:13; Hebrews 9:28; James 5:7-9; 1 Peter 1:7,13; 5:4; 1 John 2:28-3:2; Jude 21; Revelation 2:25.

An Old Testament passage, Isaiah 26:17-21, is also very strongly inferential to the Rapture which was a "mystery" at the time but is revealed to us now. "Like as a woman with child, that draweth near the time of her delivery, is in pain, and crieth out in her pangs; so have we been in thy sight, O Lord. We have been with child, we have been in pain, we have as it were brought forth wind; we have not wrought any deliverance in the Earth; neither have the inhabitants of the world fallen. Thy dead men shall live, together with my dead body shall they arise. Awake and sing, ye that dwell in dust: for thy dew is as the dew of herbs, and the Earth shall cast out the dead. Come, my people, enter thou into thy chambers, and shut thy doors about thee: hide thyself as it were for a little moment, until the indignation be overpast. For, behold, the Lord cometh out of his place to punish the inhabitants of the Earth for their iniquity: the Earth also shall disclose her blood, and shall no more cover her slain."

Note the reference to the dead living and arising, along with the living, after much travail and suffering. Of course, Isaiah is referring to the Jews, and eventually to the Abomination of Desolation when those Jews left during the Tribulation will have to flee to a place, we think Petra, where God will protect them from the Antichrist indwelt by Satan himself for the remainder of the Tribulation or three and one-half years. But Isaiah is looking forward to a time when he will be raised from the dead, referring to the time when that will happen, the Rapture for those in Christ, and the raising of the faithful dead before Christ before the Millennial Kingdom.

Notice what Jesus Christ said in Matthew 25:34 in reference to His earthly kingdom: "Then shall the King say unto them on his right hand, Come, ye blessed of my Father, inherit the kingdom prepared for you from the foundation of the world." The promise of God's earthly kingdom goes all the way back to Adam when God first placed man on the Earth (Acts 3:21) and it continues with Israel from Genesis 12 onward until we come to Paul, and everything after our dispensation of the Age of Grace. Everyone justified before God from Adam all the way up to those saved outside of Paul's ministry in the book of Acts have an earthly hope. The oldest Bible book, Job, makes it clear in Job 19:25-27 that these saints had a hope, not to die and go to Heaven [our hope], but a hope to be raised again and go into that earthly kingdom. Job 19:25-27: "For I know that my redeemer liveth, and that he shall stand at the latter day upon the Earth: And though after my skin worms destroy this body, yet in my flesh shall I see God whom I shall see for myself, and mine eyes shall behold, and not another; though my reins be consumed within me."

All who will be saved after our Dispensation of Grace, they too have an earthly hope - our Dispensation interrupts Israel's prophetic and earthly program for about 2,000 years. Thus, all people saved unto eternal life outside of our Dispensation of Grace, outside of Paul's ministry, they will all be resurrected together, for they all need go into the earthly kingdom that God promised them. They need to be resurrected after Jesus Christ comes back at His Second Coming, but before He initiates His kingdom on Earth. After the Rapture (when the Church the Body of Christ is taken into Heaven), and after the seven-year Tribulation, Jesus Christ will return to Earth (Revelation 19:11-21).

It is here on the Bible timeline that Revelation 20:4-6 will be fulfilled: "And I saw thrones, and they sat upon them, and judgment was given unto them: and I saw the souls of them that were beheaded for the witness of Jesus, and for the word of God, and which had not worshipped the beast, neither his image, neither had received his mark upon their foreheads, or in their hands; and they lived and reigned with Christ a thousand years. But the rest of the dead lived not again until the thousand years were finished. This is the first resurrection. Blessed and holy is he that hath part in the first resurrection: on such the second death hath no power, but they shall be priests of God and of Christ, and shall reign with him a thousand years." Note the believing Jews slain during the Tribulation, are clearly referenced in verse 4. This is the "Old Testament saints' resurrection" plus the resurrection of Israel's kingdom saints, both Jew and Gentile alike, and it will occur just after Jesus Christ returns to Earth at His Second Coming. Notice how verse 6 speaks of Israel's ministry as a kingdom of priests (Exodus 19:5-6; Isaiah 61:6; 1 Peter 2:8; Revelation 1:6; Revelation 5:10).

According to Jesus Christ, Israel's patriarchs Abraham, Isaac, and Jacob will be resurrected to enter and reign in their kingdom; obviously, their resurrection would be before the 1,000 years begin – at this same time as the Tribulation saints and the Old Testament saints. Matthew 8:11: "And I say unto you, That many shall come from the east and west, and shall sit down with Abraham, and Isaac, and Jacob, in the kingdom of Heaven."

Please understand that Israel's 12 apostles also need to be resurrected before the Millennial Kingdom can begin, for they will sit on 12 thrones judging Israel's 12 tribes in her kingdom: "Then answered Peter and said unto him, Behold, we have forsaken all, and followed thee; what shall we have therefore? And Jesus said unto them, Verily I say unto you, That ye which have followed me, in the regeneration when the Son of man shall sit in the throne of his glory, ye also shall sit upon twelve thrones, judging the twelve tribes of Israel. And every one that hath forsaken houses, or brethren, or sisters, or father, or mother, or wife, or children, or lands, for my name's sake, shall receive an hundredfold, and shall inherit everlasting life. But many that are first shall be last; and the last shall be first" (Matthew 19:27-30). Mark records similar statements in Mark 10:28-31.

Another Pre-Tribulation Passage?

There is another verse that is often cited as proof that the Rapture will occur before the Tribulation begins but contains a word that many do not know has two different interpretations that can both be true at the same time adding tremendous meaning to this verse. It is 2 Thessalonians 2:3, "Let no one in any way deceive you, for it will not come unless the apostasy comes first, and the man of lawlessness is revealed, the son of destruction..."

The reason it is often presented as evidence of a Pre-Tribulation Rapture is because it states that "the Day of the Lord" (The Tribulation) will not occur until "the apostasy comes first." How does this relate to the timing of the Rapture? (The bulk of this information is derived from Bill Salus and prophecydepotministries.net) Because the word, "apostasy" ("apostasia") means "departure", and a departure can be a spiritual departure from the faith and also a physical departure such as the Rapture. And thus, this verse is saying that the spiritual departure of the Church, mirroring the Laodicean Church of Revelation Chapter 3 being neither cold or hot causing Christ to spew them out of His mouth, happens before the Antichrist appears, and the physical departure of the Church in the Rapture must occur before "the man of lawlessness" (the Antichrist) is revealed and the Tribulation begins.

I am always suspicious of biblical doctrines that are based on alternative translations. People who are straining to prove a doctrinal point, will often look in a Greek or Hebrew lexicon for the definition of a word and then will choose whichever one fits their pre-conceived doctrine. The problem with this approach is that the true meaning of words must always be determined by their context, not by the possible alternative definitions. But, in tis case, let's look a little deeper.

The Greek noun, "apostasia", is used only twice in the New Testament. The other occurrence is in Acts 21:21 where it states that an accusation was made against Paul that he was "teaching all the Jews who are among the Gentiles to forsake ["apostasia"] Moses."

The word is used in verb form a total of 15 times in the New Testament, and only three of these have anything to do with a departure from the faith (Luke 8:13, 1 Timothy 4:1, and Hebrews 3:12). In other settings, the word is used for departing from inquity (2 Timothy 2:19), departing from ungodly men (1 Timothy 6:5), departing from the temple (Luke 2:27), departing from the body (2 Corinthians 12:8), and departing from persons (Acts 12:10 and Luke 4:13).

This insight about the use and meaning of the word is certainly compelling, but what is most convincing is that the first seven English translations of the Bible rendered the noun, "apostasia", as either "departure" or "departing." Those early Bibles were The Wycliffe Bible (1384), The Tyndale Bible (1526), The Coverdale Bible (1535), The Cranmer Bible (1539), The Great Bible (1540), The Beeches Bible (1576), and The Geneva Bible (1608).

The Bible used by the Western world from 400 A.D. to the 1500s, Jerome's Latin translation known as "The Vulgate", rendered "apostasia" with the Latin word, "discessio", which means "departure."

The first translation of the word to mean apostasy in an English Bible did not occur until 1611 when the King James Version was issued. So, why did the King James translators introduce a completely new rendering of the word as "falling away"? The best guess is that they were taking a stab at the false teachings of Catholicism.

Another interesting and significant point is that Paul used a definite article with the word "apostasia". The significance of this is emphasized by Daniel Davey in a thesis he wrote for the Detroit Baptist Theological Seminary: Since the Greek language does not need an article to make the noun definite, it becomes clear that with the usage of the article, reference is being made to something in particular. In 2 Thessalonians 2:3 the word "apostasia" is prefaced by the definite article which means that Paul is pointing to a particular type of departure clearly known to the Thessalonian church.

In light of this grammatical point, the use of the definite article would support the notion that Paul spoke of a clear, discernable notion. And that notion he had already identified in verse 1 of 2 Thessalonians when he stated that he was writing about "our gathering together to Him [Jesus]." This interpretation also corresponds to the point that Paul makes in verses 6 and 7 where he states that the man of lawlessness will not come until what "restrains" him "is taken out of the way." And what it is that restrains evil in the world today? The Holy Spirit working through the Church.

Conclusion

Is the pre-Tribulation doctrine true? The doctrine of the pre-Tribulation Rapture is not only valid, but it's really the only choice we as believers have. Otherwise, we're endorsing, knowingly or unknowingly, the un-biblical act of works salvation. That's right, if we hold to any other view, except a pre-Tribulation Rapture, we are by default, holding to a works-based salvation.

The Bible clearly teaches salvation is by faith alone. It also correspondingly teaches, a Rapture event will take place for all Christians, just prior to the Tribulation period. The timing of the Rapture is where most of the confusion or debate occurs.

The Bible, specifically the Book of Revelation, speaks about a unique group of people, who will come to faith in Jesus Christ during the Tribulation period. We commonly refer to this group as the Tribulation Saints. The distinction is no accident, a purposeful separation is made between the Bride or Church of Jesus Christ and the Tribulation Saints. It's during the Tribulation that we are told of a coming time of judgment and wrath upon the entire world, one that ultimately ushers in the second coming of Jesus Christ.

The pre-Tribulation Rapture is the event, which teaches, all Christians living just before the Tribulation, will be snatched out of this world and having their mortal bodies, translated into immortal bodies. We are promised to eternally live with the Lord Jesus Christ.

"Let not your hearts be troubled. Believe in God; believe also in me. In my Father's house are many rooms. If it were not so, would I have told you that I go to prepare a place for you? And if I go and prepare a place for you, I will come again and will take you to myself, that where I am you may be also. (John 14:1-3).

The Bible clearly says, the Antichrist will kill and overcome the Tribulation Saints. Also, we find no Rapture event depicted in the Book of Revelation for this group of people, the Tribulation Saints, which is very important. The Book of Revelation only speaks of two resurrections. The first resurrection being for the Tribulation Saints, who are martyred for Christ Jesus, and have not taken the mark of the beast. The first resurrection has no mention of the Church, the Bride of Christ, the marriage supper of the Lamb, nothing. Only those living during the Tribulation and coming to faith in Jesus Christ will take part in the first resurrection.

We can also see this group of Tribulation Saints in Revelation 6:9-11; 7:9-17:

"When the Lamb broke the fifth seal, I saw underneath the altar the souls of those who had been slain because of the word of God, and because of the testimony which they had maintained; and they cried out with a loud voice, saying, "How long, O Lord, holy and true, will You refrain from judging and avenging our blood on those who dwell on the Earth?" And there was given to each of them a white robe; and they were told that they should rest for a little while longer, until the number of their fellow servants and their brethren who were to be killed even as they had been, would be completed also." (Revelation 6:9-11).

"After these things I looked, and behold, a great multitude which no one could count, from every nation and all tribes and peoples and tongues, standing before the throne and before the Lamb, clothed in white robes, and palm branches were in their hands; and they cry out with a loud voice, saying, "Salvation to our God who sits on the throne, and to the Lamb." And all the angels were standing around the throne and around the elders and the four living creatures; and they fell on their faces before the throne and worshiped God, saying, "Amen, blessing and glory and wisdom and thanksgiving and honor and power and might, be to our God forever and ever. Amen." Then one of the elders answered, saying to me, "These who are clothed in the white robes, who are they, and where have they come from?" I said to him, "My lord, you know." And he said to me, "These are the ones who come out of the great tribulation, and they have washed their robes and made them white in the blood of the Lamb. For this reason, they are before the throne of God; and they serve Him day and night in His temple; and He who sits on the throne will spread His tabernacle over them. They will hunger no longer, nor thirst anymore; nor will the sun beat down on them, nor any heat; for the Lamb in the center of the throne will be their shepherd, and will guide them to springs of the water of life; and God will wipe every tear from their eyes." (Revelation 7:9-17).

The Tribulation Saints will be separated out for their sacrifice during the Tribulation period. These people alone will participate in the first resurrection according to Revelation 20:4-7, "Then I saw thrones, and they sat on them, and judgment was given to them. And I saw the souls of those who had been beheaded because of their testimony of Jesus and because of the word of God, and those who had not worshiped the beast or his image, and had not received the mark on their forehead and on their hand; and they came to life and reigned with Christ for a thousand years. The rest of the dead did not come to life until the thousand years were completed. This is the first resurrection. Blessed and holy is the one who has a part in the first resurrection; over these the second death has no power, but they will be priests of God and of Christ and will reign with Him for a thousand years."

Those that insist on the Church being IN the Tribulation have a serious problem. If only the Tribulation Saints are resurrected first, it means the entire non-Tribulation Church, everyone from Christ until the Tribulation, will have to be resurrected at the second resurrection. However, the second resurrection is called "The Great White Throne Judgment" (Revelation 20:11-15), the judgment of the unrighteous occurring at the END of Christ's Millennial Kingdom, and no one is looking forward to that one, not even those of us who just have to witness it. We will NOT be judged AT ALL for sin since we are covered by the blood of Jesus Christ. Obviously, the Church is not nor could never be suffering under God's Wrath for exactly what 1 Thessalonians 1:10, "And to wait for his Son from Heaven, whom he raised from the dead, even Jesus, which delivered us from the wrath to come", 1 Thessalonians 5:9, "For God hath not appointed us to wrath, but to obtain salvation by our Lord Jesus Christ", and Revelation 3:10, "Because thou hast kept the word of my patience, I also will keep thee from (Greek "ek" meaning "out of") the hour of temptation, which shall come upon all the world, to try them that dwell upon the Earth." Therefore, the Church is raptured BEFORE God's Wrath which begins with the first Seal Judgment just after the peace treaty the Antichrist signs with Israel found in Daniel 9:27 at the beginning of Daniel's 70th Week.

Besides the massive problem with the above, we also must accept another horrible reality of the Tribulation found in Revelation 13:7. Everyone IN the Tribulation who is a believer in Jesus Christ and therefore a saint must be overcome by Satan/Antichrist, which is clearly shown to occur, "And it was given unto him to make war with the saints, and to overcome them: and power was given him over all kindreds, and tongues, and nations". During this period, the Tribulation Saints, if they are IN the Tribulation, and the entire world are overcome by the Antichrist. Yet, Jesus said the Church would cannot be overcome by the very gates of hell in Matthew 16:18, "And I say also unto thee, that thou art Peter, and upon this rock I will build my church; and the gates of hell shall not prevail against it." Again, obviously, the Church is gone when this "overcoming" takes place inside the Tribulation.

The Bible is very clear on these points, we are **not** protected **through** the coming Tribulation, we are protected **from** the Tribulation, kept "out of" God's Wrath, all of which clearly demonstrates a removal before the

Tribulation period. This perfectly harmonizes with the most prominent and clear Rapture verses, 1 Corinthians 15:51-53 & 1 Thessalonians 4:13-18.

One additional fact, the Bride or Church, is situated in Heaven before the first resurrection! Let me repeat this, "the Church is in Heaven BEFORE the first resurrection!" Why would we need a resurrection if we're already in Heaven? The Tribulation Saints will still be waiting for the first resurrection to occur (Revelation 20:4-7), while the Bride or Church is in Heaven at the promised marriage supper of the Lamb. Revelation 19:7-9 says, "Let us rejoice and be glad and give the glory to Him, for the marriage of the Lamb has come and His bride has made herself ready. It was given to her to clothe herself in fine linen, bright and clean; for the fine linen is the righteous acts of the saints. Then he said to me, "Write, 'Blessed are those who are invited to the marriage supper of the Lamb.'" And he said to me, "These are true words of God.""'

Accordingly, if there is no Pre-Tribulation Rapture, the non-Tribulation Saints of the Church Age would have to wait for the second resurrection to occur over a thousand years in the future. We should all have a massive problem with this belief because it means the Church would miss the Millennial reign of Christ, which we are promised to be with Him, and even worse, we are to be judged according to our deeds or works along with the unrighteous dead! Revelation 20:11-15 says, "Then I saw a great white throne and Him who sat upon it, from whose presence Earth and Heaven fled away, and no place was found for them. And I saw the dead, the great and the small, standing before the throne, and books were opened; and another book was opened, which is the book of life; and the dead were judged from the things which were written in the books, according to their deeds. And the sea gave up the dead which were in it, and death and Hades gave up the dead which were in them; and they were judged, every one of them according to their deeds. Then death and Hades were thrown into the lake of fire. This is the second death, the lake of fire. And if anyone's name was not found written in the book of life, he was thrown into the lake of fire."

One can make little sense of End Times prophecies without a Pre-Tribulation Rapture, which makes the two resurrections major obstacles to reconcile, as does the empty promises of our redemption, and ultimately it would make Jesus' sacrifice upon the cross a needless act. The pre-Tribulation doctrine plays a significant role in the continuity and understanding of God's eternal plan for mankind, the Church, and the judgment of the spiritual forces of darkness.

We can see the faithful Bride, the Church age believers throughout the ages that have trusted in the Lord Jesus Christ, and the Lord's promised salvation by faith in Christ. We cannot add any personal good works to the perfect work of Christ upon the cross. It is through this perfect work of atonement by Jesus Christ, that we are justified before a Holy God. And we can trust His promised protection from the coming wrath, which will come upon the entire world. The timing is at His choosing, but in the Bible, He gives us many signs to be looking for, the greatest is the return of the Jews to Israel and restoration of Jerusalem which has already happened.

I do believe the time is extremely near, which means the Rapture could occur very soon. Repent of your sins and place your trust in Christ today because we are not promised a tomorrow. The time is quickly running out. Even so, come Lord Jesus!

CHAPTER SIX

RESURRECTIONS AND JUDGMENTS IN GOD'S WORD

Introduction to Resurrections and Judgments

God's Attributes are awesome and wonderful. He is the big three – Omnipresent (everywhere), Omniscient (all knowing), and Omnipotent (all powerful). He is also Merciful, Gracious, Loving, and Compassionate. He is Just and Holy, Righteous and Sovereign. We all must try to see that He is all of these all at once in infinite dimension. He cannot display one of His Attributes without all the rest at the same time. He uses all of His attributes with each decision, with each judgment, to determine His Will in our lives - His attributes cannot be separated to be used independently from other attributes. All His actions, His decisions, His Will incorporates every one of His Attributes in infinite quantity, undiminished in any way by use. So, when we consider His Justice, we must realize that He uses His infinite Love, Compassion, Mercy, and Grace at the same time. In other words, God performs judgment because He wills it, for specific reasons, perfectly timed, perfectly apportioned, and wholly called for or just.

God uses resurrections to display His Will. He resurrects the dead to show His Power and also to demonstrate His approaches to Mercy, Grace, and Justice. There are different kinds of Justice and different kinds of resurrections. The Bible reveals that there will be more than one resurrection and more than one judgment. We need to organize the information on resurrections and judgments in order to understand why there are multiple resurrections and multiple judgments. All of these judgments and resurrections play an important role in our complete understanding of End Times events and coming prophecies, some good and exciting, but most being fearful and concerning.

God's Judgments

A great deal of confusion exists with respect to the subject of God's judgments and particularly regarding the final judgment. We will cover all the major judgments (past, present, and future) that we find in Scripture to help resolve this confusion. For instance, many do not understand that instead of one final judgment, the Bible teaches that there are at least five future judgments that differ in respect to time, purpose, subjects, and circumstances. Understanding these various judgments will give insight into God's program, but the goal here is not just information. God wants Christians to understand the truth of the judgments to both comfort and motivate them to godly living. He wants those who have not trusted in Christ to understand the judgments that this might motivate them to trust in Christ as their personal Lord and Savior because He bore the judgment for their sin in their place. The Christian will not face the final judgment because Christ was judged for us, but all believers will face a judgment called the Bema Judgment Seat of Christ. All unbelievers will face God's final Great White Throne Judgment, but the nature of that judgment is severe yet completely deserved.

The Certainty of Judgment

Resurrection will be followed by judgment. Solomon wrote, "Fear God and keep His commandments... For God will bring every act to judgment, everything which is hidden, whether it is good or evil" (Ecclesiastes 12:13-14). The apostle Paul emphasized the certainty of judgment. In Romans 2:16 he wrote, "God will judge the secrets of men through Christ Jesus." And in Romans 14:10,12 he stated, "We shall all stand before the judgment seat of God... So then each one of us shall give account of himself to God." The writer to the Hebrews summed it up succinctly: "It is appointed for men to die once and after this comes judgment" (Hebrews 9:27).

We will look at past judgments that God has spoken to us about in the Scriptures, cover the present judgments that we face in our daily lives, believer or not, then the future judgments that are severe for the ungodly, yet merciful for the godly. We must remember, however, that God's judgments are His Will and are done with His Love and His Holiness, but also with His Justice and Mercy at the same time. (The following is a compilation from my many years of study, but some information comes from gty.org, prophecywatchers.com, and christinprophecy.org)

The Past Judgments

The Judgment of Satan and the Fallen Angels

God's judgment was used to cast Satan down from his position in Heaven as the anointed cherub, probably the "highest" angel God ever created, with all those angels who followed him to this Earth and its atmosphere as the primary abode of their operations (Ephesians 2:2, "the ruler of the kingdom of the air," ("air" is the Greek, "aer", the atmospheric Heavens). Evidently, immediately after Satan's fall which was caused by his arrogance, pride, and narcissism, God sentenced Satan and his angels, who fell for Satan's arguments about his being "like" the Most High God (Isaiah 14:14, "I will ascend above the heights of the clouds; I will be like the most High.")

condemning them to the Lake of Fire (Matthew 24:41). Though anticipated as certain and viewed as accomplished, this sentence against Satan and his evil host will not be carried out until after the Millennial reign of Christ (John 12:31 with Revelation 20:10). The basis of Satan's judgment and final disposal is the finished work of Christ on the cross first anticipated in the "protevangelium" or "First Gospel" of Genesis 3:15, "And I will put enmity between thee and the woman, and between thy seed and her seed; it shall bruise thy head, and thou shalt bruise his heel." Then in anticipation of His death on the cross, the Lord spoke of Satan's judgment and doom in John 12:31; 16:11, and Luke 10:18-19. Compare also Romans 16:20; Ephesians 1:20-21; Colossians 2:14-15; Hebrews 2:14-17.

The Edenic Judgments of Genesis 3

After the fall of Adam and Eve, and as a judgment for mankind's disobedience regarding the tree of the knowledge of good and evil (Genesis 2:17), certain curses or judgments were placed upon Satan (the promise of his final doom), upon Adam and Eve, and upon the Earth. Adam and Eve died spiritually and began to die physically. They were originally made perfect and would have lived forever, but physical death became a certainty for their future because they ate of the tree of the knowledge of good and evil against God's command. Therefore, as the Scripture says, "And inasmuch as it is appointed for men to die once and after this comes judgment" (Hebrews 9:27). The judgment of Genesis 3 included the loss of the perfect Edenic conditions and in its place, the curse of the Earth with its often extreme weather conditions, disease, thorns, and the warfare with Satan and his hosts (cf. Romans 8:18-22; Ephesians 6:10-12; 1 Peter 5:8).

The Judicial Judgment - All Are Under Sin

All of mankind without distinction are under the curse of sin and judged as sinful and separated from God apart from the saving grace of God in Christ. All fall short of the glory of God—the immoral, moral, and religious (Romans 1:18-3:9, 23). The only exception is the person of Jesus Christ who, through the virgin birth, escaped the sin problem that is normally passed down from generation to generation.

Galatians 3:22, "But the Scripture has shut up all men under sin, that the promise by faith in Jesus Christ might be given to those who believe."

Romans 3:19, "Now we know that whatever the Law says, it speaks to those who are under the Law, that every mouth may be closed, and all the world may become accountable to God."

Romans 5:12-15, "Therefore, just as through one man sin entered into the world, and death through sin, and so death spread to all men, because all sinned for until the Law sin was in the world; but sin is not imputed when there is no law. Nevertheless death reigned from Adam until Moses, even over those who had not sinned in the likeness of the offense of Adam, who is a type of Him who was to come. But the free gift is not like the transgression. For if by the transgression of the one the many died, much more did the grace of God and the gift by the grace of the one Man, Jesus Christ, abound to the many."

The Judgment to Moral Degradation

According to Romans 1:18-32, when men turn away from the knowledge of God revealed so vividly in Creation, God, as an expression of His holy wrath, turns men over to their own devices and foolish imaginations. This always results in moral degradation. Paul teaches us that the varied forms of the awful sinfulness of man have their beginnings in the rejection of the revelation of God in Creation. Ungodliness is always the source of unrighteousness; ungodliness (turning away from God) leads to idolatry (man worshipping the products of his own mind and hands), and idolatry leads to unchained sensuality and immorality.

As children of darkness refused to follow the light, they were brought to folly in their thoughts, "became vain in their [corrupt] reasonings, and their foolish [senseless] heart was darkened." The intellectual revolt against what they knew to be right was attended by a darkening of the whole understanding. The refusal to accept the truth destroys the power to discriminate between truth and error and is because God "gave them over" to a depraved mind.

But this happens as a judgment from God against man's arrogant independence. This condition is the expression of God's wrath (vs. 18) and twice we have the statement that this moral breakdown occurs because God "gave them over" (vs. 24 and 25). Compare also Ephesians 4:17-19, "This I say therefore, and affirm together with the Lord, that you walk no longer just as the Gentiles also walk, in the futility of their mind, being darkened in their understanding, excluded from the life of God, because of the ignorance that is in them, because of the hardness of their heart; and they, having become callous, have given themselves over to sensuality, for the practice of every kind of impurity with greediness."

The Judgment of Christ for the Sin of the World

The Judgment of Christ for the Sin of the World takes on two aspects:

(1) Christ's judgment for sin, dying in the place of the sinner, bearing his sin and judgment on the cross as the sinner's substitute. Isaiah 53:4-6, "Surely our griefs He Himself bore, and our sorrows He carried; Yet we ourselves esteemed Him stricken, Smitten of God, and afflicted. But He was pierced through for our transgressions, He was crushed for our iniquities; The chastening for our well-being fell upon Him, And by His scourging we are healed. All of us like sheep have gone astray, each of us has turned to his own way; But the LORD has caused the iniquity of us all to fall on Him."

2 Corinthians 5:21, "He made Him who knew no sin to be sin on our behalf, that we might become the righteousness of God in Him."

1 Peter 2:24, "...and He Himself bore our sins in His body on the cross, that we might die to sin and live to righteousness; for by His wounds you were healed."

Romans 3:24-26, "...being justified as a gift by His grace through the redemption which is in Christ Jesus; whom God displayed publicly as a propitiation in His blood through faith. This was to demonstrate His righteousness, because in the forbearance of God He passed over the sins previously committed; for the demonstration, I say, of His righteousness at the present time, that He might be just and the justifier of the one who has faith in Jesus."

Sin requires a penalty, the penalty of spiritual death as God's holy judgment on sin. Jesus Christ, the sinless and perfect Son of God, the only one who could qualify as our substitute, died to satisfy the demands of God's absolute holiness. Sin calls for judgment and the cross of Jesus Christ became that place of judgment. It was there Christ paid the penalty for the sin of the world (1 John 2:2).

(2) Christ's Judgment Unto Sin's Reign; the Judgment of the Believer's Sin Nature

Not only did Christ die for our sin as the Lamb of God (John 1:29), but He died to break the reign of sin in the lives of those who put their trust in Him as their Savior. This means that, through co-identification with Christ in His death on the cross, the believer's sin nature was also judged, crucified, with Christ in His death so that its power has been broken or neutralized. Though the death of Christ does not obliterate the presence of the sin nature and though it is still a powerful enemy (Romans 7:15-24), the believer's union with Christ in His death and His gift of the indwelling Holy Spirit provides for divine forgiveness for the fact of the sin nature and for victory over its reigning power through the guidance of the Holy Spirit.

Romans 6:4-11, "Therefore we have been buried with Him through baptism into death, in order that as Christ was raised from the dead through the glory of the Father, so we too might walk in newness of life. For if we have become united with Him in the likeness of His death, certainly we shall be also in the likeness of His resurrection, knowing this, that our old self was crucified with Him, that our body of sin might be done away with, that we should no longer be slaves to sin; for he who has died is freed from sin. Now if we have died with Christ, we believe that we shall also live with Him, knowing that Christ, having been raised from the dead, is never to die again; death no longer is master over Him. For the death that He died, He died to sin, once for all; but the life that He lives, He lives to God. Even so consider yourselves to be dead to sin, but alive to God in Christ Jesus." See also Colossians 2:10-13; Galatians 2:20; and Romans 8:1-2.

Present Day Judgments

Though believers are saved and justified by faith in Christ as the crucified Savior and making Him Lord of our lives, the Scriptures assume that Christians will battle with sin and will not always be victorious. First, when we observe Communion, we must take care not to heap judgment on our heads. Second, it is necessary for believers to judge their own sins in the light of Scripture. Third, if we are somehow disrespectful or not fully truthful with God, we can suffer the ultimate punishment. And fourth, we have to observe and determine if we and our closest neighbors, companions, friends, associates are behaving either worldly or biblically.

God has a sequence for His major judgments and resurrections, but we must always keep in mind that He judges our lives as we live them. The New Testament clearly teaches us that one of the ministries of our Heavenly Father is the ministry of loving discipline which is a "now" judgment. God's discipline is patterned after the principles of Proverbs 13:24 which reads, "He who spares his rod hates his son, but he who loves him disciplines him diligently." Discipline is an evidence of love.

So we read in Hebrews12:4-11, "You have not yet resisted to the point of shedding blood in your striving against sin; and you have forgotten the exhortation which is addressed to you as sons, 'My son, do not regard lightly the discipline of the Lord, Nor faint when you are reproved by Him; For those whom the Lord loves He disciplines, and He scourges every son whom He receives.' It is for discipline that you endure; God deals with you as with sons; for what son is there whom his father does not discipline? But if you are without discipline, of which all have become partakers, then you are illegitimate children and not sons. Furthermore, we had earthly fathers to discipline us, and we respected them; shall we not much rather be subject to the Father of spirits, and live? For they disciplined us for a short time as seemed best to them, but He disciplines us for our good, that we may share His holiness. All discipline for the moment seems not to be joyful, but sorrowful; yet to those who have been trained by it, afterwards it yields the peaceful fruit of righteousness."

From this passage in Hebrews and others like 1 Corinthians 11:27-32, God disciplines His children for the following reasons:

(1) To bring a wayward child who refuses to judge himself back into fellowship (1 Corinthians 11:31-32; Psalm 32:3-5).

(2) It is part of the training process by which God's children are brought into the experience of God's holiness (Hebrews 12:10).

(3) It is an expression and a proof of God's love (Hebrews 12:6, 8).

(4) It is designed to produce obedience and to protect them against untimely physical death (Hebrews 12:9; Romans 8:13; 1 Corinthians 11:30).

(5) It yields the peaceful fruit of righteousness (Hebrews 12:11).

Proper Observance of Communion

Communion a serious matter with consequences both for time and eternity since the failure to do so leads not only to the loss of rewards, but the judgment of God's discipline of His believing children as a loving Father and as the Vine Dresser who must prune the vine for production (Hebrews 12:4-11; John 15:1-7). A very interesting, enlightening, and important passage to this subject is 1 Corinthians 11:27-32 for in this passage we have a reference to both the self-judgment of the believer and the discipline judgment of God on believers.

1 Corinthians 11:27-32 says, "Therefore whoever eats the bread or drinks the cup of the Lord in an unworthy manner, shall be guilty of the body and the blood of the Lord. But let a man examine himself, and so let him eat of the bread and drink of the cup. For he who eats and drinks, eats and drinks judgment to himself, if he does not judge the body rightly. For this reason many among you are weak and sick, and a number sleep. But if we judged ourselves rightly, we should not be judged. But when we are judged, we are disciplined by the Lord in order that we may not be condemned along with the world."

Some of the Christians at Corinth were being externally religious. They were assembling themselves with other believers and partaking of the Lord's supper, but they were out of fellowship with the Lord and were controlled by the sinful nature, the flesh, rather than by the Holy Spirit. This is why earlier the Apostle called them "fleshly" (the Greek "sarkikos", "adapted to, controlled by the flesh") (3:3). Unfortunately, this condition had continued because some of these believers had failed to examine their hearts and judge their sin by honest confession followed by a commitment to deal with it in the power of the Spirit (11:28, 31). As a result, a number of things occurred: (1) they were making a mockery of the significance and meaning of the Lord's supper (11:27); (2) they were experiencing personal discipline by the Lord which existed in three conditions, evidently progressively so (11:30, 32); and though not mentioned here, (3) they were producing wood, hay, and stubble - they were losing rewards (1 Corinthians 3:14-15).

As to the immediate consequences, some were weak (feeble, a loss of energy), some were sick (probably chronic disease), and some were asleep (physical death, sin unto death) (11:30). But these were not the only consequences of failing to judge sin in their lives. There were also divisions and factions and the focus on personalities rather than the Savior. They were showing favoritism and hurting other believers rather than showing love and concern as it should be among believers in Christ. In other words, when we fail to honestly judge sin in our lives it spills over in one area after another. As the loving Father that He is, God must break out His discipline in His loving commitment to bring us back to Himself.

Christians need to examine their hearts and actions for sin according to the Scripture and then judge the sin they find as sin and confess it to the Lord. Our tendency is to rationalize and excuse our sins, but God says we are to judge them as sin to God. Confession of sin restores us to fellowship and to the Spirit's control. With the Spirit back in control and the believer in fellowship (in the state of abiding in the Vine) he or she can then produce fruit for which they will receive rewards at the Bema Judgment Seat of Christ.

Believers Need to Judge Their Own Sins

Paul describes in the Book of Romans a much deeper frustration, one with which only Christians can identify and one with which all Christians can identify. The Christian's agony comes from realizing that our sinful flesh refuses to respond to the requirements of God's Law. Those things which we as Christians despise, we find ourselves doing. Those things which we as Christians desire, we fail to accomplish. No matter how much we may wish to serve God in our minds, we find ourselves sinning in our bodies. As Paul describes his frustration in Romans 7, with his mind he desires to serve God. He agrees with the Law of God and rejoices in it. He wants to do what is right, but his body will not respond. He watches, almost as a third party, as sin sends a signal to his body, and as his body responds, "What would you like to do?" Paul finds, as we do, that while our fleshly bodies refuse to obey God and do that which we desire and which delights God, they quickly and eagerly respond to the impulses and desires aroused by sin.

Every Christian who reads Romans 7:14-25 should immediately identify with Paul's expression of frustration and agony due to the weakness of his fleshly body: "Wretched man that I am! Who will set me free from the body of this death?" (Romans 7:24). We are confronted with a dilemma as we try to live righteously. If there were no answer for this question, we would hardly dare to press on. But there is an answer! Those of us willing to honestly identify with the agony of Romans 7 will be ready for the joy of God's gracious provision for living righteously in Romans 8:1, "There is therefore now no condemnation to them which are in Christ Jesus, who walk not after the flesh, but after the Spirit."

God Disciplines His Children

Scripture has a lot to say about discipline, whether it is God's discipline, self-discipline, child discipline, etc. When we think of discipline we should always think about love because that is from where it derives. People who play sports discipline themselves for the sport that they love. God disciplines His children when they start straying. He will not let them stray because they are His. But, often, God has to get our attention in order to shape us or to turn us away from our sin. Deuteronomy 8:5-6 says, "So obey the commands of the LORD your God by walking in his ways and fearing him. Hebrews 12:5-7 says, "My son, do not make light of the Lord's discipline, and do not lose heart when he rebukes you, because the Lord disciplines the one he loves, and he chastens everyone he accepts as his son." Endure hardship as discipline; God is treating you as his children. For what children are not disciplined by their father?

But there is the possibility that sin can draw us away from God towards our own desires. We, of course, do not lose our salvation, but we could lose our lives just as Ananias and Saphira did in Acts Chapter 5. Both died as a result of not being fully truthful to their brothers, sisters, and to God. We must be obedient to God, fully disclose our inward thoughts, and hide nothing from Him. To do otherwise invites discipline, perhaps discipline we do not expect but may certainly deserve.

Our Judgment of Our Fellow Believers and Non-Believers

There is the judgment that we must make on our fellow believers, the world, and the non-believers as well. This is a commonly misunderstood verse whereby Christians and non-Christians alike think the meaning is not to make judgments or decisions based on our observations of others. Generally speaking, the principle is stated in Matthew 7:1-5, "Do not judge lest you be judged. For in the way you judge, you will be judged; and by your standard of measure, it will be measured to you. And why do you look at the speck that is in your brother's eye, but do not notice the log that is in your own eye? Or how can you say to your brother, 'Let me take the speck out of your eye,' and behold, the log is in your own eye? You hypocrite, first take the log out of your own eye, and then you will see clearly to take the speck out of your brother's eye."

What the verse is really saying is that we are not to judge others in the sense of condemning them or passing judgment on the opinions of others on doubtful matters as discussed in Romans 14:1-5, "Now accept the one who is weak in faith, but not for the purpose of passing judgment on his opinions. One man has faith that he may eat all things, but he who is weak eats vegetables only. Let not him who eats regard with contempt him who does not eat, and let not him who does not eat judge him who eats, for God has accepted him. Who are you to judge the servant of another? To his own master he stands or falls; and stand he will, for the Lord is able to make him stand. One man regards one day above another, another regards every day alike. Let each man be fully convinced in his own mind."

However, Scripture **does** call us to show what we might call critical discernment on certain matters, or, in other more familiar words, we MUST judge in our everyday lives. For instance, Matthew 7 which tells us not to judge, is immediately followed with the command, "Do not give what is holy to dogs, and do not throw your pearls before swine, lest they trample them under their feet, and turn and tear you to pieces" (Matthew 7:6). How do we know who falls into the category of swine, those incapable of appreciating the truth, if we do not make certain judgments? Furthermore, we are called upon to make judgments in the sense of evaluations when it comes to selecting elders and deacons, or in dealing with those who have fallen into sin (1 Timothy 3:1-13; Titus 1:9-16; Galatians 6:1-5; 2 Thessalonians 3:6-15). The message here is not to condemn others as if we were greater, less sinful, without need of judgment ourselves. Instead of misusing this critical verse, it is obvious that we all need to exercise discernment or judgment in our everyday lives, it goes without saying and is obvious. The Bible does not contradict itself! It is inerrant! So, when we see what we believe to be contradictory, we need to investigate to discern the true meaning of God's words to us so that we can easily comply.

The Future Judgments

The Judgment of the Bema (The Judgment Seat of Christ)

The next prophetic event in God's timetable will be the Rapture or the catching up of the body of Christ, the Church, as described in 1 Thessalonians 4:13-18. A number of things occur at this time. There is the glorification of living believers in glorified bodies, the resurrection of those believers who have died in the Lord also in glorified bodies, and the translation of both to meet the Lord in the air. This will be followed by their examination before the Judgment Seat of Christ. This is not the final judgment mentioned in Revelation 20:11-15 which is limited to only the unbelieving world. Rather, the Judgment Seat of Christ is for the body of Christ, the Church, and it occurs before the start of the Millennium. A similar judgment will occur for resurrected Old Testament and Tribulation saints, probably just before the start of the Millennium (Daniel 12:1-3 with Revelation 20:4).

The Judgment Seat of Christ is not a place and time when the Lord will mete out punishment for sins committed by the child of God. We are forgiven of all of our sins because of Christ's shed blood on the cross, and, if we confess our sins daily, then the Holy Spirit can lead us without fleshly interference. Christ Himself will not remember our forgiven sins when we are with Him after the Rapture. Rather, it is a place where rewards will be given or lost depending on how one has used his or her life for the Lord. Both Romans 14:10 and 2 Corinthians 5:9 speak of the "judgment seat." This is a translation of one Greek word, the word "bema". While bema is used in the Gospels and in Acts of the raised platform where a Roman magistrate or ruler sat to make decisions and pass sentence (Matthew 27:19; John 19:13), its use in the epistles by Paul, because of his many allusions to the Greek athletic contests, is more in keeping with its original use among the Greeks.

This word was taken from Isthmian games where the contestants would compete for the prize under the careful scrutiny of judges who would make sure that every rule of the contest was obeyed (2 Timothy 2:5). The victor of a given event, who had participated according to the rules, was led by the judge to the platform called the Bema. There the laurel wreath was placed on his head as a symbol of victory (1 Corinthians 9:24-25).

In all of these passages, Paul was picturing the believer as a competitor in a spiritual contest. As the victorious Grecian athlete appeared before the Bema to receive his perishable award, so the Christian will appear before Christ's Bema to receive his imperishable award. The judge at the Bema bestowed rewards to the victors. He did not whip the losers, either did he sentence them to hard labor. In other words, it was a reward seat and portrayed a time of rewards or loss of rewards following examination. So, the Bema Judgment Seat of Christ is a reward seat, not a time of punishment where believers are judged for their sins. Such would be inconsistent with the finished work of Christ on the cross because He totally paid the penalty for our sins.

Though believers are under no condemnation in respect to their sins, having been justified by faith (John 3:18; 5:24; Romans 8:1, 13-17), they are subject to judgment at the Judgment seat of Christ in relation to their works done after salvation. At the Judgment Seat of Christ believers' works will be evaluated (subjected to the judgment fire of the Lord) to demonstrate whether they are good (will last, and will be rewarded) or bad (will be burned up and, consequently will suffer loss), for Christ (gold, silver, precious stones) or for themselves (wood, hay, stubble), and rewards will be conferred (2 Corinthians 5:10; Romans 14:10-12; 1 Corinthians 3:9-14; 9:24-27). The goal of the Christian in his life is to be pleasing to God whether in time or eternity. The Judgment Seat of Christ is not related to salvation but to the bestowal of rewards, and every Christian is assured that he will receive some reward (1 Corinthians 4:5; Ephesians 6:8; 2 Timothy 4:8; Revelation 22:12).

The Judgments of the Tribulation

While the Bema is going on in Heaven (with the church in the Lord's presence), a series of terrible judgments will begin to unfold on the Earth for a period of seven years to be culminated by the return and manifestation of

Christ to Earth as the Great White Horse Rider of Revelation 19. With the beginning of the Tribulation period, Christ opens the scroll with its seven seals releasing the Antichrist to start his domination of the Earth. Six seals mark the start of God's Wrath on the Earth. The seventh seal announces the seven trumpet judgments that will finish out the first half of the Tribulation and cause massive amounts of death and destruction on the entire Earth. The seventh trumpet blasts the news of the coming seven vials or bowls of God's Wrath, the most terrible actions against the planet and its inhabitants, human and animal, that has ever been, and against the Earth to the point that there will not be any square inch of the Earth's surface that is not affected with ruin. The Earth's human population will see two-thirds of its people die in horrible ways because of their sin and rebellion against God. All of the bowl judgments occur in the last half of the Tribulation, called the Great Tribulation, with God's people, the Jews, divinely protected and the saved by Jesus Christ assured of their eternal life but not necessarily saved from physical death.

The main point to see here is that this entire period is the expression of God's Wrath in increasing degrees of judgment to be poured out on the world. The world seeks to find answers to its problems through the one world movement of the last days and apart from the true God as He has revealed Himself in Christ. So, much as we see in Romans 1, God turns the world over to the consequences of its choices. The result is the one world system of the Beast as described in Revelation meaning the One-Worlders will get their way, but the outcome will definitely not be Paradise as they expect. It will begin with an apparent time of prosperity and peace created by this one world government under the deceptions of the man of lawlessness. But even this will be God's judgment and the expression of His Wrath. While people are saying peace and safety, then sudden destruction will come as birth pains upon a woman in travail. The judgments of this time will grow in intensity and conclude with an awesome display of God's wrath against a Christ-rejecting world.

The Judgment and Reward of Resurrected Old Testament and Tribulation Saints

While many would place the resurrection and reward of Old Testament saints with that of the Church at the Rapture, a number of factors favor this at the conclusion of the Tribulation at the same time as the resurrection and reward of Tribulation saints mentioned in Revelation 20:4.

(1) Daniel, who wrote concerning the termination of God's program for Israel in chapter 9, places the resurrection of the righteous in Israel

as occurring after "a time of distress such as never occurred ..." Clearly this is the Tribulation, Daniel's Seventieth Week, or "the time of Jacob's Distress (Trouble)" mentioned by Jeremiah (Jeremiah 30:7; Daniel 9:27).

(2) Resurrection is viewed in Scripture as an event that terminates one program and initiates another, and one would not expect Israel's resurrection could come until God had finished the seventy years decreed for His people, the Jews, according to Daniel 9:24-27. Since the events mentioned in Daniel 9:26 (the cutting off of Messiah and the destruction of city and sanctuary) had to occur after the 69 weeks of years had run their course but before the seventieth week begins, there has to be a space of time, the parenthesis of the church age (the Dispensation of Grace or Church Age), between the conclusion of the sixty-ninth week and the beginning of the seventieth.

(3) The resurrection (Rapture) and Bema Judgment Seat of Christ for the raptured Church concludes this parenthesis, the Church Age, but Old Testament saints (the righteous dead) are not resurrected and rewarded until after the seventieth week when God concludes His program with Israel as far as the seventy weeks of Daniel are concerned. The Tribulation saints, both Jew and Gentile, are rewarded by being given their place as heirs in the Millennial Kingdom of Christ.

The order of God's resurrection program which includes the judgment of rewards would seem to be:

    a.   the resurrection of Christ as the beginning of the resurrection program (1 Corinthians 15:23);

    b.   the resurrection of the Church Age saints at the Rapture (1 Thessalonians 4:16);

    c.   the resurrection of tribulation period saints (Revelation 20:3-5), together with

    d.   the resurrection of Old Testament saints (Daniel 12:2; Isaiah 26:19).

The Judgment of Living Israel (Sheep and Goat Judgment)

The Scripture teaches that before Messiah can begin to reign, there must be a judgment to determine who will enter into Messiah's kingdom since "they are not all Israel (spiritually regenerated believers who put their trust in Jesus Christ as their Messiah) who are Israel (physical descendants only)"

(Romans 9:6). The rebels of unbelief must be removed so that only Messiah-believing Israel will enter into the kingdom (cf. Ezekiel 20:34-38; Matthew 25:1-30).

Part of this removal occurs through the Tribulation judgments themselves (Revelation 6-19; Zechariah 13:8-9). But those who are not killed by these judgments will be gathered, judged, and the rebels removed with only believers going into the millennial kingdom.

Matthew 24-25 set the chronology and thus the time. The order is:

1. The Tribulation judgments (Matthew 24:4-26)
2. The visible return of Jesus Christ (Matthew 24:27-30)
3. The regathering of those Israelites who were left after the tribulation judgments, both believing and unbelieving Jews (Matthew 24:31; Ezekiel 20:34-35a)
4. The judgment of the Nation of Israel (Sheep and Goat Judgment) (Matthew 25:1-30; Ezekiel 20:35b-38)

At the end of the Tribulation, the Lord Jesus will return personally to Earth (Zechariah 14:4), but Ezekiel 20:34-35 shows God brings Israel out from the nations where she has been scattered throughout the times of the Gentiles (gathers her to the last person, Ezekiel 39:28). But Israel is first gathered at the borders, outside the land of Israel, called in Ezekiel 20:35 "the wilderness of the peoples," for judgment, face to face, one by one as sheep pass under the shepherd's rod.

Revelation 7:14 shows us that salvation in the Tribulation (as in the church age) is through faith in the person and work of Jesus Christ as the Lamb of God. This is further confirmed by the message of the book of Romans where the Apostle shows Israel's problem to be one of seeking to establish her own righteousness by keeping the Law rather than accept God's righteousness by faith in Christ (Rom. 9-11). Matthew 25:1-30 shows that God will judge living Israel to separate the saved from the unsaved. In this passage and in Malachi 3:2-3, 5, and Ezekiel 20:37-38, the individual's works will be brought into judgment, but not because they are saved by their works, but because their works demonstrate they are rebels who have failed to trust in Jesus.

The Judgment of Living Gentiles (Sheep and Goat Judgment)

Just as Christ will judge the Jews still alive at the end of the Tribulation (Sheep and Goat Judgment) when Christ personally returns to Earth, so He will also judge those Gentiles who remain (Matthew 25:31-46). At the judgment of the Gentiles Christ will separate the sheep, representing the saved, from the goats, representing the lost (Matthew 24:31-46). Though salvation is by grace and through faith, the saved who come out of the Great Tribulation will be identified by their acceptance of Jesus Christ as Savior and Lord as today plus loving their Jewish brothers as we are to love one another.

The Final Judgment of Satan, the Fallen Angels, and Demons

Throughout the centuries as anticipated in the enmity mentioned in Genesis 3:15, there has been constant warfare between the holy angels who minister to God's people and Satan and his unholy fallen angels and the demonic spirits that are the spirits of the Nephilim that cannot be saved because their DNA was corrupted by fallen angels who fathered them (Genesis 6). Nevertheless, as mentioned earlier concerning the judgment of Satan, God has manifested His power by defeating Satan and his hordes. While, for God's own purposes, Satan has been allowed to continue his nefarious schemes, Scripture speaks of three sure events regarding the activity of Satan and his demonic forces: his binding during the Millennium which includes all fallen angels and demons, his short release along with his fallen angelic and demonic hordes, and his and all fallen angels and demons final incarceration in the Lake of Fire. Then all opposing powers against the Lord will be dealt with in judgment (Revelation 20:1-3, 7-10; 2 Peter 2:4; Jude 6; 1 Corinthians 15:24-26).

The Judgment of the Great White Throne

Revelation 20:11-15, "And I saw a great white throne and Him who sat upon it, from whose presence Earth and Heaven fled away, and no place was found for them. And I saw the dead, the great and the small, standing before the throne, and books were opened; and another book was opened, which is the book of life; and the dead were judged from the things which were written in the books, according to their deeds. And the sea gave up the dead which were in it, and death and Hades gave up the dead which were in them; and they were judged, every one of them according to their deeds. And death and Hades were thrown into the lake of fire. This is the second death, the lake of fire. And if anyone's name was not found written in the book of life, he was thrown into the lake of fire."

This vision of the Great White Throne describes the last and final judgment of history. It is an awesome and solemn scene and one which should cause everyone to stop and think about the eternal implications of this future event. For the non-Christian, the one who has never trusted in the person and work of Jesus Christ, it should cause him to want to search out the truth regarding Jesus Christ, to embrace Him in faith as the Savior from his sin and eternal doom, and rely on Him as Lord of his life. For the Christian, the future reality of this event should cause deep concern because of the many (including some of our friends and relatives) who will face this throne of judgment because they never received the Savior by faith.

All who have scoffed at God, denied His being, rebelled at His rule, or rejected His sovereignty, and in the process, also rejected His Son, the Lord Jesus Christ, must at this time stand before this throne to be condemned to eternal judgment. May the reality of this judgment cause us to carefully reflect on the serious consequences of this passage on a Christ-rejecting world.

Revelation 20:5 and 11-15 show this takes place after the conclusion of the Millennium following the doom of Satan and the destruction of Heaven and Earth, but before the eternal state of the new Heavens and Earth of Revelation 21:1.

Heaven and Earth are seen fleeing from the face of Him who sits on this throne (20:11). In other words, they are destroyed, dissolved (2 Peter 3:7, 10-12). Colossians 1:17 says that Jesus "holds all things together" implying that the unknown inter-atomic forces that hold atoms, electrons, proton, and neutrons together is Jesus Christ, the Creator Himself! When the time comes for Jesus to destroy the Heaven and the Earth, all Jesus has to do is simply "let go", and the destructive forces of nuclear fission will manifest itself to an infinite degree thus destroying everything in the universe except the spirits of the unbelieving dead and those of us in Jesus Christ in New Resurrection bodies. The point here is the Great White Throne Judgment does not occur on Earth or in Heaven as we know it, but somewhere beyond, perhaps in extreme outer space or utter nothingness. This indication is also clear that it does occur in the new Heavens and Earth which are not created until after this event (20:11 with 21:1).

In other words, God has removed Satan and his fallen angels and demons, the False Prophet and the Beast, and is about to judge the rest of the unbelieving dead. So, it is only fitting that He also judge the old Earth and Heavens that has been the arena of Satan's activity and man's sin and rebellion. This evidently takes place after the resurrection of the unbelieving dead from the grave and Hades. They are resurrected, gathered before the throne and actually behold the dissolution of Heaven and Earth as a foreboding preparation for their judgment. All their hopes and dreams had been placed in an Earth and system that was passing away (1 John 2:17), and now they see it dissolve before their very eyes along with any false hope they might have had. "And no place was found for them," i.e., for Heaven and Earth. In the eternal state there will be no place for that which reminds men of the rebellions of Satan and man with all its wickedness and sorrow (Revelation 22:3; 21:4; Isaiah 65:17).

This judgment by Christ is called "great" because of the awesome intensity and the degree of its importance. Here each unbeliever's eternal destiny is declared and determined with ample proof and reason. It is great because it is the final judgment and puts an end to all judgment for all time. It is great because all the unbelievers of all time, from Cain to the final revolt at the end of the Millennium, will be here assembled to face the bar of God's holy justice.

It is called "white" because it will be the supreme and undimmed display of the perfect righteousness and justice of God to all mankind. Throughout history God has revealed Himself in Creation (Romans 1:18-21), a revelation man has ignored. Through the Scriptures and the remnant of His people, He has taught man that he must have God's righteousness, that God is of purer eyes than to approve evil or to accept or look upon wickedness (Habakkuk 1:13), that all have sinned and come short of God's glory (Romans 3:23), and that the penalty of sin is eternal death, separation from God (Genesis 2:17; Romans 6:23; Ephesians 2:2). Now these facts will become evident to each individual and proven without question.

It is called a "throne" because here the Lord Jesus Christ will sit in absolute majesty and sovereign authority to judge and disperse a Christ-rejecting world to the eternal Lake of Fire. In Revelation 4:2 John beheld a throne set in Heaven from which the Tribulation judgments proceeded. The word throne is used more than 30 times in Revelation, but this throne, the great white one, is to be distinguished from all others as the most significant one of all.

The judge is the Lord Jesus Christ (John 5:22-23, 27). All judgment has been placed into His hands as the perfect Son of man, Son of God, the one qualified to judge by virtue of his sinless humanity and defeat of Satan and sin through the cross (Revelation 5:1-14).

Those judged are "the dead, great and small," those who had no part in the first resurrection (Revelation 20:5,6 - the righteous Tribulation dead and the Old Testament righteous dead). Specifically, this is the dead of the second resurrection, the resurrection of the unjust, the resurrection unto the second death mentioned in Revelation 20:5-6, 12-14, and John 5:29b. "The dead, great and small" emphasizes that no one is exempt. All who have died without faith in Jesus Christ, regardless of their status in human history, religiously, politically, economically, or morally, must stand before this throne of judgment.

Revelation 20:13a shows they come from:

(1) "The sea," a reference to all those who died at sea and were not buried in the Earth.

(2) "Death," a reference to all those who were buried in graves in the ground, cremated, or destroyed in any other way on Earth.

(3) "Hades," a reference to the place of torments, the compartment which contains the souls of all unbelievers (Luke 16:23). The sea and death (i.e., the ground) contain the bodies and Hades contains the souls. At this resurrection the soul and body are reunited, and the person is brought before the throne.

The basis of the judgment is what is found in the two sets of books, the books which are opened, and the other book, the Book of Life (Revelation 20:12b, 13b, 15a). Note that the text says, "and the books (plural) were opened, and another book (singular) was opened, which is the Book of Life." We have two sets, the books and the book which is mentioned again in verse 15a.

The Books: The identity of the books is not specifically revealed, and we can only speculate from a comparison of other passages of Scripture and from the nature of these verses:

(1) The first book opened will probably be the Scripture, the Word of God, which contains the revelation of God's holy character, the moral law, the declaration of man's sinfulness, and God's plan of salvation through faith in Christ. This book also reveals that even when men do not have the written Word, they have the law of God written in their hearts (Romans 2:14-16), and the revelation of God-consciousness in creation so that they are without excuse (Romans 1:18-21; 2:12). Undoubtedly, then, the Scripture will be used to demonstrate the clearness of the plan of God and that man is without excuse. John 12:48 is very pertinent here, "He who rejects Me, and does not receive My sayings, has one who judges him; the word I spoke is what will judge him at the last day."

(2) The second book will be the book of works or deeds. Verses 13 and

14 state that the unbelieving dead will be judged according to their deeds (works). Undoubtedly then, one book is the book of works which contains a record of every person's deeds as a witness of the true nature of their spiritual condition. "Deeds" is the Greek word, ergon, which refers to anything that is done, "a deed, action, or work." It is used of good deeds (Matthew 26:10; Mark 14:6; Romans 2:7), of evil deeds (Colossians 1:21; 2 John 11), of dead works (Hebrews 6:1; 9:14), of unfruitful deeds (Ephesians 5:11), of ungodly deeds (Jude 15), of deeds of darkness (Romans 13:12; Ephesians 5:11), and of works of the Law (Romans 2:15).

The principle here is that Jesus Christ died for their sins no matter how evil, that He might forgive them and give them a righteousness from God, that they may have a perfect standing before God. As Paul declares in Romans 5:1-2: "Therefore having been justified by faith, we have peace with God through our Lord Jesus Christ, through whom also we have obtained our introduction by faith into this grace in which we stand; and we exult in hope of the glory of God."

But when men reject the knowledge of God and His plan of salvation, they in essence determine to stand on their own merit, or in their own righteousness. So, the book of works will contain a record of all the unbeliever's deeds, good and bad, to demonstrate the truth of Romans 3:23, "for all have sinned and fall short of the glory of God." All fall short of God's perfect righteousness and have therefore no basis upon which to stand accepted (justified) before a holy and just God. This judgment proves them sinners and in need of the righteousness which God freely gives through faith in Jesus Christ.

(3) The Book of Life: This book contains the names of all believers, of all who have put their faith in Christ and God's plan of salvation or righteousness through the substitutionary death of Christ. Or, to put it another way, it is a record of those who have not rejected God's plan of salvation and have responded to Christ in faith; for these their faith is reckoned for righteousness and their sins have not been imputed to them (Romans 4:4-6, 22).

At the Great White Throne Judgment, the Book of Life is produced to show that the participant's name was not found written in the Book of Life because of their rejection of Jesus Christ. They, therefore, have no righteousness and cannot be accepted before

God, but must be cast into the eternal Lake of Fire. The Book of Life contains the names of believers, those justified by faith and who have a righteousness from God imputed to their account. These and only these are accepted by God and will spend eternity with Him (Romans 10:1-4; Philippians 3:9).

The Judgment or Punishment of the Second Death

Revelation 20:14 says, "And death and Hades were thrown into the lake of fire. This is the second death, the lake of fire." "Death" refers to the body now resurrected while "Hades" refers to the soul, the immaterial part of man. Both body and soul are eternally separated from God in the eternal Lake of Fire, a very real, literal, and eternal place according the Scripture.

It is so important to note the emphasis here. The real issue is whether one's name is in the Book of Life, not one's deeds. The deeds of the unbeliever are only examined to show that the person, no matter how much good they have done, falls short of God's holy demands. Paul shows us in Romans that all categories of people, the good, the bad, and the ugly, are really in the same boat and on their way to eternal separation from God.

Obviously, most see that the immoral person deserves the wrath of God, as the Apostle describes in Romans 1:18-32. But he also shows us that the same applies to the good person and moral person as well as the religious person (Romans 2:1-3:23). In the face of the awesome holiness of God, they are sinners and cannot stand in the presence of God on their own merit. The awesome fact is that salvation is through faith in Jesus Christ. The loss of salvation, and ultimately the one sin that separates a person from God and confines him to the eternal Lake of Fire, is because of failure to trust in the Lord Jesus Christ for forgiveness and a perfect righteous standing before God.

Separation of Resurrections and Judgments

Daniel said in Daniel 12:2, "...And many of them that sleep in the dust of the Earth shall awake (be resurrected), some to everlasting life, and some to shame and everlasting contempt." John 5: 28, 29 says, "Marvel not at this: for the hour is coming, in the which all that are in the graves shall hear his voice and shall come forth; they that have done good, unto the resurrection of life; and they that have done evil, unto the resurrection of damnation."

This does not mean that the resurrections and judgments of the saved and unsaved will take place at the same time and place. Those in the Old

Testament who have not believed in God through faith from Adam up to the time of Christ, the New Testament non-believers from Christ to the Rapture, the time of the Tribulation non-believers, and the non-believers during the Millennial Kingdom all have to be judged prior to their final destination of the Lake of Fire. All of these non-believers will face the Great White Throne Judgment just after their resurrection called the resurrection of the dead. The time of this judgment is just after the Millennium and just before the New Heaven and the New Earth.

The Old Testament believers, Abraham, Moses, Joshua, Daniel, Isaiah, etc., will be resurrected near the end of the Tribulation. Revelation 20:4 says:

1. The Judgment Seat of Christ (Revelation 4:4). It will take place in Revelation chapter 4 after the Rapture happens (Revelation 4:1). The resurrection will take place at the same time as the Rapture when the Christians receive their glorified bodies (Revelation 4:1-4). Paul, in his second book to Timothy tells us about a crown which all believers will receive at the appearing of Jesus Christ.

    Paul said, "...the time of my departure is at hand. I have fought a good fight, I have finished my course, I have kept the faith: Henceforth there is laid up for me a crown of righteousness, which the Lord, the righteous judge, shall give me at (on) that day (the day of His appearing at the Judgment Seat of Christ): and not to me only, but unto all them also who love His (Jesus') appearing." (II Timothy 4: 6-8)

    Shortly after entering Heaven the four and twenty elders (the Christians) will get their crowns. Remember, the New Testament Christians will all get their crowns (rewards) at the same time and event. They are wearing them on their heads in Revelation 4:4. Peter, in his first letter, wrote about the same event. "And when the chief Shepherd (that's Jesus) shall appear, ye shall receive a crown of glory that fadeth not away."

    The New Testament Saints are the Bride of Christ. This body of believers will receive their crowns of rewards immediately after the Rapture occurs. Right before we return to Earth with Jesus, we will be wedded to Christ Himself (Revelation 19: 7-9). He will marry the Church, the Body of Christ, in some mysterious way. If we are going to participate in those two events (the wedding and marriage supper), which take place in Heaven, we have to go there first. Those Scriptures (II Timothy 4:6-8 and II Peter 5:4) are not referring to the

Second Coming of Christ. They are referring to the Lord appearing in the Rapture.

2.   The Old Testament Saints. These Saints and Prophets will be resurrected, judged, and given rewards in Revelation 11:18. (Note: Jesus does not return to Earth in Revelation 11:15-18. The tribulation saints will be resurrected in Revelation 7:9-17, and will probably be judged in Revelation 11:18 when the Old Testament saints and prophets are judged.

(Note: The unsaved people of the Old Testament will be resurrected and judged in Revelation 20:11-15 along with the unsaved of the New Testament. The unsaved people who died during the tribulation period, those unsaved people who Matthew 25: 41-46 refer to, the lost of the millennial period, and those who died in Satan's and man's final rebellion, will be judged there as well.).

3.   The Judgment of the Nations. In Matthew 25: 31-46 we are told about another judgment. In this judgment the Lord is not judging the people for the things they did or did not do, nor is He judging them on the basis of the talents that God has given them and what they did with them.

This judgment will involve two groups: the saved people (the tribulation saints.), who are alive and enter the kingdom (Matthew 25: 31) and the unsaved people who are alive and thrown into Hades/Hell (Matthew 25: 41, 46). This judgment will happen shortly after Jesus returns to Earth in the Second Coming (Revelation 19: 11, Matthew 25: 31). There is no resurrection in this judgment. Saved people, in this case, Tribulation saints, will have earthly bodies and do not receive crowns of rewards. Only the people who died get rewards. The angels will gather together all the human beings who are alive (having earthly bodies) at the time of this judgment, after His (Jesus') feet touch down on the Mount of Olives, when He is seated on the throne of His glory. They will stand before the Lord shortly after He returns to Earth in Revelation 19: 11, but only after the events of verse 21 and Zechariah 14: 4, 5 have taken place. (Read Matthew 25: 31-33.). This is not a judgment of the dead in Christ. Nor is it referring to the lost of all Ages (the unsaved). There is no resurrection of the saved or unsaved when the Lord comes to Earth (Revelation 19: 11, Matthew 25: 31). Matthew 24: 31 is referring to the angels gathering together the living (Matthew 25: 32-33) not the dead. The saved Tribulation saints and the unsaved Tribulation people who survived the Tribulation period will be gathered together before Jesus when He is seated on the throne of His glory (Matthew 25: 31-34, 41). Matthew 25: 31-46 refers to what will happen after Jesus returns to Earth. When in Matthew 25: 32 it says "...before Him (Jesus) shall be gathered all nations..." it is referring to the saved and the unsaved people who are alive. Zechariah 14: 16 is talking about the saved, the sheep of Matthew 25: 32 - 34. Obviously, Zechariah 14: 16 is not referring to the unsaved. The entire group of enemy soldiers who fought against Jerusalem and the Jews will die according to Revelation 19: 21. So it is not talking about them either.

4. The Millennial Saints: Part of this group is made up of the Tribulation saints who did not die during the Tribulation period and were saved before the Lord returned to Earth (Revelation 19:11). They will be judged of the Lord (Jesus) as to whether they have the right to enter the Kingdom (Matthew 25: 34). He will place them at His right hand (Matthew 25: 32-34). Another portion of this group is the 144,000 Israelites of Revelation 7. In Revelation 12: 17 there is another group who are called the remnant. A lot of these Jews will be killed by the Antichrist. Those who survive the Tribulation period will be a part of this group as well. They are the Jews/Israelites who escape the Antichrist and are alive at the time of Jesus' return.

5. The Lost of all Ages: This group of people are dead and in the heart of the Earth in Hades/Hell and will be judged in Revelation 20:11-15 when the Heaven(s) and the Earth are destroyed (Revelation 20: 11, II Peter 3: 7). Those things will take place after Satan's and man's final rebellion and after the millennial reign of Christ.

Note carefully that the New Testament saints who are the dead in Christ and are saved will be resurrected and judged at the same time in Revelation 4: 1-4. The Old Testament saints will be resurrected and judged in Revelation 11:18. The Millennial saints will most likely be resurrected and judged some time after the Millennium reign of Christ and Satan's and man's final rebellion is over. The unsaved people of all ages who died without Christ and are lost will also be resurrected and judged at the Great White Throne Judgment.

Not all resurrections will happen at the same time, nor do all judgments take place at the same time. The resurrection of the dead in Christ (the saved) (Revelation 4:1), and the resurrection of the dead who are not in Christ (the unsaved) will happen at different times (Revelation 20: 11-15). The resurrection of the New Testament saints (at the time of the Rapture) and the Bema Judgment Seat of Christ, will happen before the Second Coming of Christ and the 1000-year reign of Christ takes place. However, the resurrection and judgment of the unsaved will happen after the Second Coming of Christ and after the 1000-year reign of Christ. Those resurrections and judgments have to be separate one from another. The saints (Christians) will go to Heaven in the Rapture with the Lord before the Second Coming happens; for we are wedded (married) to Jesus before we return to Earth with Him. (See Zechariah 14: 4-5, Revelation 19: 7-9, 11, 14.

Multiple Resurrections

Concerning resurrection, Jesus clearly taught that there would be more than one resurrection. In John 5:29 He refers to a "resurrection of life" and a "resurrection of judgment." The apostle Paul confirmed this concept in his defense before Felix when he stated that he believed the teaching of the prophets "that there shall certainly be a resurrection of both the righteous and the wicked" (Acts 24:15).

Of course, it could be argued that the two resurrections referred to in these Scriptures will occur at the same time. If they happen simultaneously, there is, in effect, only one resurrection. However, the Scriptures establish the fact that the resurrection of the righteous will occur in stages. In other words, the Bible does not teach one resurrection or even two resurrections in number. Rather, it teaches that there will be two resurrections in type which will be conducted in stages, resulting in several resurrections — at least four, to be specific.

The Resurrection of the Just

That the resurrection of the righteous will occur in stages is clearly taught in 1 Corinthians 15:20-24. In fact, the first stage of the resurrection of the righteous has already happened, for verse 20 says that "Christ has been raised from the dead, the first fruits of those who are asleep." Verses 22 and 23 go on to explain that all who have died in Christ shall be made alive, "but each in his own order: Christ, the first fruits, after that those who are Christ's at His coming." The imagery of the harvest that is used in these verses is a key to understanding the first resurrection, the resurrection of the righteous.

In Bible times the harvest was conducted in three stages. It began with the gathering of the first fruits which were offered as a sacrifice of thanksgiving to God. It proceeded with the general harvest. But not all was taken in this harvest. Some of the crop was left in the field to be gathered by the poor and the needy. This was called the gleanings (Leviticus 19:9-10).

Using this imagery, the Bible presents the resurrection of Jesus as the "first fruits" of the resurrection of the righteous. The gathering of the Church Age saints, living and dead, at the appearing of the Lord (the Rapture) is thus the general harvest stage or second stage of the resurrection of the righteous (John 14:1-3 and 1 Thessalonians 4:13-18).

But there is a third and final stage to this resurrection of the righteous. It is the gleanings, and it occurs at the end of the Tribulation when the Lord's Second Coming takes place. At that time two final groups of the righteous will be resurrected: 1) the Tribulation martyrs (Revelation 20:4), and 2) the Old Testament saints (Daniel 12:2).

Some people are startled by the thought that the Old Testament saints will not be resurrected until the end of the Tribulation. But keep in mind that the Rapture is a promise to the Church, and the Church only. Also, the book of Daniel makes it clear that the Old Testament saints will be resurrected at the END of the "time of distress" (Daniel 12:1-2) which is the Tribulation or the "Time of Jacob's Trouble". According to Jesus Christ, Israel's patriarchs Abraham, Isaac, and Jacob will be resurrected to enter and reign in their kingdom; obviously, their resurrection would have to be before the 1,000 years begin. Matthew 8:11: "And I say unto you, that many shall come from the east and west, and shall sit down with Abraham, and Isaac, and Jacob, in the kingdom of Heaven."

In addition, understand that Israel's 12 apostles also need to be resurrected before the Millennial Kingdom can begin, for they will sit on 12 thrones judging Israel's 12 tribes in her kingdom. Matthew 19:27-30, "Then answered Peter and said unto him, Behold, we have forsaken all, and followed thee; what shall we have therefore? And Jesus said unto them, Verily I say unto you, That ye which have followed me, in the regeneration when the Son of man shall sit in the throne of his glory, ye also shall sit upon twelve thrones, judging the twelve tribes of Israel. And every one that hath forsaken houses, or brethren, or sisters, or father, or mother, or wife, or children, or lands, for my name's sake, shall receive an hundredfold, and shall inherit everlasting life. But many that are first shall be last; and the last shall be first". Mark records similar statements in Mark 10:28-31.

Daniel 12:11-13 provides more information about the timeframe of the Old Testament saints' resurrection, "And from the time that the daily sacrifice shall be taken away, and the abomination that maketh desolate set up, there shall be a thousand two hundred and ninety days. Blessed is he that waiteth, and cometh to the thousand three hundred and five and thirty days. But go thou thy way till the end be: for thou shalt rest, and stand in thy lot at the end of the days."

According Daniel 9:27, the tribulation begins with the signing of a peace treaty between the Antichrist and Israel, intended to be for one "seven," that is, a set of seven years. But the "seven" is divided into halves: midway through the seven years, the Antichrist breaks the treaty and sets up in the temple a sacrilegious object (the "abomination that causes desolation"). The phrase "in the middle" indicates that the first half of the tribulation lasts for 3½ years (1,260 days, using a "prophetic year" of 360 days). Likewise, the second half of the tribulation lasts another 1,260 days (another 3½ years), for a total of seven years.

Revelation 11:3 specifically mentions 1,260 days, which corresponds exactly with Daniel's prophecy of the abomination of desolation. In Revelation, we have an added detail: two divinely appointed witnesses will preach and perform miracles for half of the tribulation—the first half, according to the chronology of Revelation. These two witnesses are killed at the midpoint of the tribulation; their bodies will lie in the streets for three and a half days as the world celebrates their demise; then they will be resurrected and taken up to Heaven (Revelation 11:7–13). The 1,260 days of the second half of the tribulation begins as the Antichrist breaks the treaty, occupies the third Jewish temple, and sets up a profane and sacrilegious object of worship. This 1,260-day period ends when the Antichrist is defeated at the battle of Armageddon upon Jesus' return to Earth. At that time, the tribulation will be at an end.

Daniel 12:11 mentions 1,290 days, however, which is 30 days more than the second half of the tribulation. Different ideas have been put forward to explain what happens in those 30 extra days. One likely theory is that the land of Israel will be rebuilt in that month after the devastation it endured during the tribulation. Then, according to Daniel 12:12, there will be an extra 45 days, on top of the extra 30 days, after which something else will happen. Daniel does not say explicitly what will happen, but he says those who remain until the end of that segment (1,335 days after the breaking of the treaty and 75 days after the end of the Tribulation) will be "blessed." The blessing here is entry into the Millennial Kingdom. What will take place during those 45 days? Very likely, this is when the judgment of the Gentile nations, described in Matthew 25:31–46, will take place. In this judgment, also called the judgment of the sheep and the goats, the Gentiles are judged for their treatment of Israel during the tribulation. Did they aid Jesus' "brothers and sisters" (Matthew 25:40), or did they turn a blind eye to the Jews' troubles or, worse yet, aid in their persecution?

So, those who survive the Tribulation and survive the sheep and goat judgment will enter the Millennium. This is a blessing, indeed. Also, Jesus fulfilled the four Hebrew Spring Feasts/Holy Days at His first coming. Likewise, I believe that He will fulfill the three Hebrew Fall Feasts/Holy Days at His second coming. As such, I believe a possible time for the Rapture or the awakening of the Jews to their Messiah is Rosh Hashanah or the Feast of Trumpets, the first of the three Fall Feasts. The next Fall Feast is Yom Kippur, the Feast of Atonement, which is a logical time for Jesus to return bodily for the atonement of the Jews from the Tribulation. Thus, by returning on a Yom Kippur for the Jews Atonement, Jesus will then tabernacle or abide on the Earth from then on thus fulfilling the third Fall Feast, the Feast of Tabernacles or Feast of Booths. Interestingly, on a calendar, there are 75 days from Yom Kippur to the first or second day of Hanukkah, the Feast of Dedication, which is a commemoration of the dedication of the rebuilt Jerusalem temple in ancient times which was a Fall Feast that Jesus, Himself, observed. Jesus' Second Advent (bodily descent) back to Earth is when the Millennial Temple will be constructed in Jerusalem, presumably by Jesus (Zechariah 6:12,13). It seems likely, then, that on the 1,335th day following the setting up of the "abomination that causes desolation" during the 70th Week, 75 days after the end of the Tribulation, the 1,000-year Temple will be dedicated. This would fulfill Daniel 12:12.

In summary, here is the end of the Tribulation timeline:

- Sometime after the Rapture of the church, could be up to 3 ½ years of the "In-Between" Times, the Antichrist enters a treaty with Israel (Daniel 9:27). This begins the seven-year Tribulation.

- At the midpoint of the Tribulation (1,260 days later), the Antichrist breaks the treaty, desecrates the Temple, and begins to persecute the Jews causing them to flee to the "wilderness".

- At the end of the Tribulation (1,260 days after the desecration of the temple), Jesus Christ returns to Earth and defeats the forces of the Antichrist at the "Battle" of Armageddon.

- During the next 30 days (leading up to 1,290 days after the desecration of the temple – Daniel 12:11), Israel is rebuilt, and the Earth is restored.

- During the next 45 days, the Millennial Temple is completed and dedicated corresponding to Hanukah.

- The Dispensation of the Millennium begins, and it will last for 1,000 years (Revelation 20:3, 5–6).

So, the first resurrection, the resurrection of the righteous, occurs in three stages, beginning with Christ, continuing with the Church at the Rapture, and culminating with the Tribulation martyrs and the Old Testament saints at the return of Jesus.

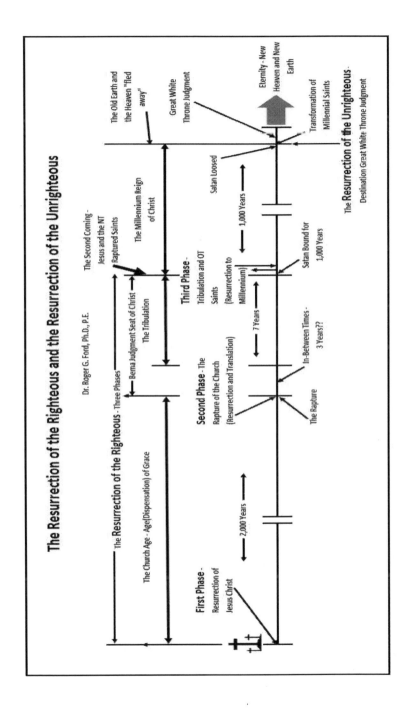

The Resurrection of the Righteous and the Resurrection of the Unrighteous

Dr. Roger G. Ford, Ph.D., P.E.

The Resurrection of the Unjust

The second type of resurrection, "the resurrection of the wicked" (Acts 24:15), will take place all at one time at the end of the Millennial reign of Jesus. This is at the time of the Great White Throne Judgment, the judgment of the damned (Revelation 20:11-15). Every person who ever failed to relate to God in faith will be resurrected at this time, regardless of when he or she may have lived and died whether before or after the Cross. This resurrection will also include the unjust who died during the Tribulation and the Millennium.

The Transformation of the Millennial Saints

There will be no need for an additional resurrection of the righteous at the end of the Millennium, because all those born during that time who accept Jesus as their Savior will live to the end of the Lord's reign (Isaiah 65:19-20). "'As the lifetime of a tree, so shall be the days of My people,'… says the Lord" (Isaiah 65:22,25). In other words, life spans during the Millennium will be returned to what they were at the beginning of time, before the flood. Those Millennial saints who are still alive at the end of the Millennium will never die, just be transformed into immortal bodies just as they have been made immortal spiritually in order to inhabit the New Heaven and the New Earth.

Conclusion

The Redeemed are judged of their works to determine their degrees of reward, the lost are judged of their works to determine their eternal destiny. And since no one can be justified before God by their works (Isaiah 64:6 and Ephesians 2:8-10), all will be condemned to Hell.

The unjust are also judged for another reason. There are going to be degrees of punishment (Luke 12:35-48; 20:45-47). There is a popular myth in Christendom that says, "All sin is equal in the eyes of God." That is not true. The only way in which all sin is equal is that any sin, whether a white lie or murder, condemns us before God and necessitates a Savior. But all sin is not equal in the eyes of God. For example, Proverbs 6:16-19 lists seven sins that the Lord particularly hates, including "hands that shed innocent blood." And the Bible makes it very clear that idolatry is a sin that is especially heinous in the eyes of God (Exodus 20:3-5). Because God considers some sins worse than others, there will be degrees of punishment (Revelation 22:12), and these degrees will be specified at the Great White Throne judgment.

So, where do you stand with respect to the inevitable judgment which you will face before the Lord? If you are a Christian, do you know what spiritual gifts you have been given? Are you using them to advance the Lord's kingdom? Is your motivation a love of the Lord?

If you have never confessed Jesus as your Lord and Savior, do you really want to participate in the Great White Throne Judgment – the judgment of the damned? Do you realize that the Bible says, "Every knee shall bow and every tongue confess that Jesus is Lord"? That means Hitler and every vile person like him who has ever lived will one day make the confession of Jesus' lordship. You will too.

I urge you to make that confession now so that you can participate in the resurrection and judgment of the righteous. As you consider your decision, weigh carefully the following words from the book of Hebrews: "Christ also, having been offered once to bear the sins of many, shall appear a second time for salvation without reference to sin, to those who eagerly await Him" (Hebrews 9:28). Notice carefully that this verse promises that for those who are ready for Him, Jesus will come "without reference to sin." That is a wonderful promise. And Jesus is coming soon meaning that hesitation could mean eternal separation from the Lord. So why not make the decision right now to spend eternity in the very presence of the Lord Jesus Christ and live forever in joy, peace, and righteousness?

CHAPTER SEVEN

SUMMATION, A TIMELINE, AND CONCLUSION

Introduction

We have now covered different areas of prophecy so that we can all grasp what the Almighty God wants us to know about our future while we are still on this Earth in corruptible bodies. We have covered: (1) What We Need to Understand Bible Prophecy; (2) Foundational Concepts to Understanding Bible Prophecy; (3) Old Testament References to the End Times; (4) Sequence of Events to Come and Why - New Testament References to the End Times; (5) Pre-Tribulation Rapture Explanation and Justification; and (6) Resurrections and Judgments in God's Word. In this last chapter in "Are These Days the End Times?", we will look at the Christian's necessary, sufficient, and Spirit-led attitude and approach to God's Word that we all need to understand fully what God has revealed to us through prophecy. We will examine what is the proper attitude last days Christians must have when reading, studying, and realizing prophetic Scripture and why many Christians do not understand and grasp what God wants us to know and understand. Last, we will present a comprehensive overview of the End Times recognizing that we have arrived there, in fact, we are in the last days of the last days of the End Times!

In order to fully and completely know how to do something and do it right, we all need to be sure we are very familiar with the subject. None of us would attempt to install a 220-volt range-top requiring connecting electrical power capable of killing us unless we knew what we were doing, had extensive experience, or had been trained by experts. The consequences of doing it incorrectly might ruin the new range-top, but our very lives might be in danger of electrocution. Because of the jeopardy of incorrect installation of high voltage equipment, care must be taken even if the knowledge is there. So, let me ask just why do we not see that our approach to God's Word, our respect for the God-breathed words of Almighty God, the acceptance of the inspiration, the inerrancy, the authority, the infallibility of each and every revelation of God in His Word can affect our eternal existence in either Heaven or Hell? Should we spend more time in studying God's Word? Should we be very careful to determine that we are getting understanding from the Holy Spirit and from what we read to be sure that we are not being misled? Should we be excited to learn what God is like, what He expects from us, what He has planned for us and for the rest of humanity? Of course, the answer is a resounding YES!

212

The Word of God

When we consider the Word of God that we call the Bible, where do we begin? The critical beginning point of any consideration of God's Word is God Himself. God is completely unique and different from us. Of course, we are made in His image, but He is not as we are. He is infinite, holy, just, sovereign, all powerful, present everywhere, all knowing, inescapable, and, most important to our salvation, God is merciful and gracious. But, do we really view Him this way, or do we see Him as a grandfather type with a long white beard looking down upon His Creation with a critical but loving eye?

It is a major mistake to visualize God as anything we can totally understand. Why? Because He is above us in every way. His power is never diminished, and neither is His Love. He is always just, expects obedience, but has forgiven confessed sin in all of us that He never remembers. But we cannot conceive of God as He really is because we are not as He is. What I mean by that is God is outside all that we know, therefore we cannot know all about Him because we are inside His Creation. Then there is the human fact that as we expend energy, we must rest and eat and sleep to restore ourselves. God does NOT have to do that because all that He is, is infinite and never decreasing! His love is always there, never diminished. His holiness is always there just as His expectation of obedience. When disobedience (sin) occurs, God is infinitely just and sin requires punishment. That's why we need Jesus so that God Almighty sees us through the shed blood of our Savior and we are kept from the wrath of God caused by His being holy and just.

One more thing most Christians and certainly most humans cannot conceive of is that God and all of His attributes are all in effect always. This means that God never makes a decision, never acts, never speaks, does nothing that all His holiness, all His love, all His Truth, all His Mercy, all His Grace are not fully involved. His being perfectly just is always working as well. God does not use one or two or a few of His attributes, He uses them all and all at once all the time. A.W. Tozer said, "All of God does all that God does!" Kind of makes you think, doesn't it?

So, if our merciful and gracious God is always just, always true, then when He wanted us to have His written Word so that we can know His Will, His commandments, His direction, His provision, His love, but also His power and might in holiness and righteousness that brings His Wrath to satisfy His justice, shouldn't we stand in reverent awe when we approach His Holy Word? Don't we, as saved sinners by the blood of Jesus Christ to an eternity with Him, owe God the respect and reverence to deem His very Word to us in the Bible with the same wonder and majesty and glory as we do to Him? To treat God's Word casually or not at all is to demean God Himself!

The Bible was written down by different human authors of varying backgrounds. Some were fishermen, others, shepherds. One was a tax collector! Yet behind each one of them was God the Holy Spirit who inspired what they wrote. "For prophecy never came by the will of man, but holy men of God spoke as they were moved by the Holy Spirit." (2 Peter 1:21). "All Scripture is given by inspiration of God, and is profitable for doctrine, for reproof, for correction, for instruction in righteousness, that the man of God be perfect, thoroughly furnished unto all good works" (2 Timothy 3:16,17).

We should respect the Word of God. Hebrews 4:12 says, "For the word of God is quick, and powerful, and sharper than any two-edged sword, piercing even to the dividing asunder of soul and spirit, and of the joints and marrow, and is a discerner of the thoughts and intents of the heart." Respect means "to regard with honor; to have a high opinion of; to place a great value upon; to reverence; to submit to the judgment or authority of another."

Current Conditions

Why does God give us prophecies in the Bible of things yet to happen? The simple answer is to show us that He has a plan for all of mankind that restores our fellowship with Him – the fellowship that was lost when Adam sinned because God cannot accept even one sin in His presence.

The more robust answer of why God gives us prophecies in the Bible is because He loves us so much that He wants us to know that He WANTS us to be with Him eternally. He wants us to have joy in THIS life as well as in eternity. He shows us that a great number of once-prophetic now-fulfilled prophecies certainly happened just as He said they would. The greatest of these is, of course, the birth of a Savior, in Bethlehem, Who died for our sins, and was resurrected on the third day. The next most important fulfilled prophecy is that Israel has, indeed, become a nation in one day (Isaiah 66:8), and celebrated its 70th anniversary on May 14, 2018! This fulfilled prophetic promise has ushered in the End Times in which we exist today. And, we see Jerusalem being the center of attention for the world just as Zechariah 14:2 clearly predicts.

Israel is the Key

Why is Israel so important to God? Why is there such attention on Israel? Zechariah 12:2 & 3 says, "Behold, I will make Jerusalem a cup of trembling unto all the people round about, when they shall be in the siege both against Judah and against Jerusalem. And in that day (the End Times) will I make Jerusalem a burdensome stone for all people: all that burden themselves with it shall be cut in pieces, though all the people of the Earth be gathered together against it." Are we not seeing this today? Anti-Semitism is growing at an alarming rate through social media. More than 2.6 million anti-Semitic Twitter posts including those aimed at Israel, were viewed an estimated 10 Billion times from August 2015 to July 2016 according to the Anti-Defamation League. More than 7 Million on Facebook follow the Hamas-affiliated Shehab News Agency. Is it any wonder that YouTube (owned by Google) bans pro-Israel videos from Dennis Prager, a Jewish radio talk-show host, and then allows anti-Semitic videos of viscous content?

Students of the Bible, both Old and New Testaments, know that God chose the Jewish nation for a specific purpose. "For thou art an holy people unto the Lord thy God; the Lord thy God hath chosen thee to be a special people unto Himself, above all people who are upon the face of the Earth" (Deuteronomy 7:6). God chose them according to His sovereign will so that He could bring from Israel the Savior of the world. Plus, God gave to the Israelites, the Jews, the Abrahamic Covenant found in Genesis 12:2–3, "And I will make of thee a great nation, and I will bless thee, and make thy name great; and thou shalt be a blessing: and I will bless them that bless thee, and curse him that curseth thee: and in thee shall all families of the Earth be blessed." Deuteronomy 7:7–9 makes it clear that God never has and never will give up on His people, "The Lord did not set his love upon you, nor choose you, because ye were more in number than any people; for ye were the fewest of all people: but because the Lord loved you, and because he would keep the oath which he had sworn unto your fathers, hath the Lord brought you out with a mighty hand, and redeemed you out of the house of bondmen, from the hand of Pharaoh king of Egypt. Know therefore that the Lord thy God, he is God, the faithful God, which keepeth covenant and mercy with them that love him and keep his commandments to a thousand generations". A thousand generations in time covers much more time than the biblical age of the Earth of 6,000 years, another way to say always!

And Israel's future is unique in all of history. First, it will be characterized by unprecedented suffering also known as the Tribulation to get Israel's attention turned to God. But, Israel's future will also be characterized by unequalled blessing starting with Jesus' Second Coming. Messiah will end global war and bind Satan for a thousand years, then set up His Millennial Kingdom where Jesus will rule from Jerusalem for a thousand years. Then, all nations will come to Jerusalem and seek out the Jews and their God to worship Jesus and to pay respect to Israel. Isaiah 55:5 says, "Behold, thou shalt call a nation that thou knowest not, and nations that knew not thee shall run unto thee because of the Lord thy God, and for the Holy One of Israel; for he hath glorified thee."

The restoration of Israel has begun. In fact, it became 70 years old, full maturity, on May 14, 2018. What does this mean for the Church since we are NOT Israel? It means that Daniel's 70th Week is about to start – the Tribulation. The first 69 weeks of Daniel's prophecy brought us Jesus Christ. But, there has been a pause in the prophecy because the 70th week has not taken place yet. God wants His people back worshipping Him and His Son as Savior. However, the hard-hearted and hard-headed Jews will require seven years of terrible wrath to wake them up spiritually.

How do we know that we are IN the End Times? Because Jesus told His disciples, "Now learn a parable of the fig tree; When her branch is yet tender, and putteth forth leaves, ye know that summer is near: so ye in like manner, when ye shall see these things come to pass, know that it is nigh, even at the doors. Verily I say unto you, that this generation shall not pass, till all these things be done" (Mark 13:28-30). The fig tree is Israel, "these things" refer to what Jesus had just told His disciples concerning the signs of His coming again (Mark 13:7-8, "And when ye shall hear of wars and rumors of wars, be ye not troubled: for such things must needs be; but the end shall not be yet. For nation shall rise against nation, and kingdom against kingdom: and there shall be earthquakes in divers places, and there shall be famines and troubles: these are the beginnings of sorrows.") And, what is a generation? Psalm 90:10 says a generation is threescore and ten (70) and maybe 80. If the generation that sees all these signs of Christ's Coming is also the generation that sees Israel becoming a nation again, then that must be the generation Jesus was referring to as not passing away entirely until He comes back. Plus, the number 70 is very important and has played a significant part in the Bible, for example: Daniel's 70 Week prophecy; seventy elders appointed by Moses to assist him; the seventy years of Jewish exile in Babylon; seventy of Jacob's family went to be with Joseph in Egypt; and seventy disciples were sent out by Jesus in Luke 10. Therefore, we ARE that generation since it has been 70-plus years since Israel became a nation!

The Church and Its Destiny

The Abrahamic Covenant specifically states that ALL the families of the Earth will be blessed through Abraham's descendant. Later in Isaiah, God speaks to His Messiah, the Lord said, "It is too small a thing for you to be my servant to restore the tribes of Jacob and bring back those of Israel I have kept. I will also make you a light for the Gentiles, that you may bring my salvation to the ends of the Earth." (Isaiah 49:6) It is clear that God does not limit His salvation to just the Church or to just the Jews but to all. But, the killing of Jesus was the sign that the time for His Kingdom had not arrived. Therefore, the Age of Grace began at the resurrection of Jesus Christ, and it continues today. That era of Grace now 2,000 years in duration will end at the Rapture, and it is sometimes called the Great Pause because of the 2,000-year postponement of Daniel's 70th week.

The purpose of the Great Pause is so the Lord can take from among the Gentiles a people for Himself. Of course, Jews that believe are included, but there will be but few Jews that accept Jesus as Savior because the need for the Tribulation still exists. Acts 15:14 says, "Simeon (Peter) hath declared how God at the first did visit the Gentiles, to take out of them a people for his name." The Greek word translated "take" in this verse is "lambano". A look at the primary meanings of "lambano" reveals that the intent of the word is to describe one who takes something for the purpose of carrying it away. Once the church is complete, the Lord will carry us away before turning again to Israel. This is consistent with Paul's statement in Romans 11:25 ("For I would not, brethren, that ye should be ignorant of this mystery, lest ye should be wise in your own conceits; that blindness in part is happened to Israel, until the fulness of the Gentiles be come in.") that Israel has experienced a partial blindness until God is ready. The phrase "come in" means to arrive at one's destination, as when a ship has "come in". According to John 14:2-3 ("In my Father's house are many mansions: if it were not so, I would have told you. I go to prepare a place for you. And if I go and prepare a place for you, I will come again, and receive you unto myself; that where I am, there ye may be also.") our destination is Heaven. Once the church has been carried away to its destination in Heaven, taken by Christ from Earth and received by Him in Heaven, the blinders will fall from Israel's eyes, the Great Pause will come to an end, and Israel will complete its final seven years of Daniel's 70 Weeks prophecy.

The Rapture has to happen before Daniel's 70th Week can begin, because the 70th Week is all about Israel and NOT about the Church. After chapter 4 in the book of Revelation, the church is never referred to until Christ's Second Coming in chapter 19. Daniel's 70th Week is the Jews final opportunity to be reconciled to God through the Messiah and prepare for the Kingdom He promised them so long ago. 2500 years before the fact, Zechariah prophesied that this would take place near the end of the 70th Week. "And I will pour out on the house of David and the inhabitants of Jerusalem a spirit of grace and supplication. They will look on me, the one they have pierced, and they will mourn for him as one mourns for an only child, and grieve bitterly for him as one grieves for a firstborn son." (Zech.

217

12:10) Therefore, many Jews will accept Jesus as Lord and Savior, but, sadly, many will not.

Darkness is Descending

There remain many prophecies unfulfilled. The nature of these unfulfilled prophecies centers on the Second Coming of our Lord and Savior Jesus Christ as King of kings and Lord of Lords. The Jews in the time when Jesus was on the Earth the first time wanted Him to be a conquering King, ridding them of the Roman conqueror. But the Bible was quite plain in saying that a suffering Servant had to come first to take away our sins (the book of Isaiah) which Jesus accomplished 2,000 years ago. The rest of Biblical prophecy is about to come true since Israel is back in their land.

We need to be able to understand the times from Scripture mainly because Jesus wants us to be able to do so. Why? Jesus scolded the Jewish leaders for not being able to "discern the signs of the times" (Matthew 16:3). Jesus said that they could read the signs of the weather but were oblivious to the signs of His first appearance on the Earth and why. So, why shouldn't we expect Jesus to be upset with Christians today if we are not understanding the times we are in or watching for and seeing the signs of His Second Coming and prepare for it? In fact, we are to be actively watching and waiting for the Lord's soon return. Luke 12:37 says, "It will be good for those servants whose master finds them watching when he comes. Truly I tell you, he will dress himself to serve, will have them recline at the table and will come and wait on them."

Since there are no signs that indicate the exact timing of the Rapture, which occurs first in the End Times plan, it is because the Rapture is supposed to be imminent ensuring those who anticipate it will remain pure. Then, since we cannot see signs leading up to the Rapture, we must look at the signs that we see today as signs of the start of the Tribulation. If the Tribulation is about to start, then the Rapture is about to happen since it **precedes** the Tribulation. The book of Revelation describes the Tribulation in great detail, and there are some other prophecies that I believe occur before the start of the Tribulation. Those signs, namely the Psalm 83 war and the Ezekiel 38 and 39 war, occur after the Rapture and before the Tribulation, so just what are the signs that Daniel's 70th Week is about to start?

2 Timothy 3:1-5 is very clear about the End Times and is a good measure for us to determine just how close we are to the Rapture and the start of the Tribulation. "But mark this: There will be terrible times in the last days. People will be lovers of themselves, lovers of money, boastful, proud,

abusive, disobedient to their parents, ungrateful, unholy, without love, unforgiving, slanderous, without self-control, brutal, not lovers of the good, treacherous, rash, conceited, lovers of pleasure rather than lovers of God, having a form of godliness but denying its power. Have nothing to do with such people." I can remember in my lifetime when these things were not very prominent. Life was much simpler when I was a kid, more people obeyed laws, more people respected their fellow man, there was less crowding and, hence, less tension and more calm. But, do we see these horrendous things given in 2 Timothy today, growing by leaps and bounds, with no end in sight? Astoundingly, Yes!

Consider this list that is indicative of our nation and world today: (1) Divisive and blatantly false cable and network news; (2) intolerance of free speech especially conservative free speech; (3) lack of parental training, incessant peer pressure through social media, and corrupt curriculums being taught our children; (4) an inexplicable rise in popularity of socialism indicating the failure of our schools to teach history; (5) the opiate, marijuana, and heroin epidemics; (6) governors and mayors, even the Justice Department and the FBI not obeying established law on immigration, privacy, and confidentiality; (7) Congress and its inability to accomplish any kind of bi-partisan government; and (8) Replacement Theology, the Social gospel, and Prosperity gospel accepted in our churches that many do not even mention the concept of sin or repentance.

Are we the generation that will see the Rapture? Do we see the signs of Christ's Second Coming? Consider these End Time signs that have become common in our fallen world: (1) "As it was in the days of Noah" is very clear today since most are oblivious to the End Times; (2) Mocking and scoffing that Peter prophesied in 2 Peter 3:3 is rampant; (3) there are worldwide calls for "Peace and safety" just as 1 Thessalonians 5 foretold just before sudden destruction; (4) strong delusion associated with the transgender nonsense and shared bathrooms of little girls with abominable men posing as women; (5) the meteoric rise in capability of technology, robotics, and the internet leaning to surveillance, invasion of privacy, and perversion; (6) the great and rising interest by the Jews to build a third Temple in Jerusalem; (7) the alignment of nations corresponding to prophecy, most notably Russia, Iran, and Turkey; (8) the prospect of "mystery Babylon" from Revelation or the rise of the Apostate World Church led by an unconventional Pope like the one now; (9) the globalist movement to nations without borders pointing to a world empire run by a "charismatic leader"; (10) the often-missed but real intensification, almost exponential growth in disasters, murders, terrorism, gang activity, earthquakes, hurricanes, death and disease, etc.; (11) the increased persecution of not only the Jews but Christians around the world and even here in the U.S.; and (12) the "convergence" of virtually ALL signs coming together and increasing in intensity and frequency as never before in recorded history.

The End of the Church Age and the Start of the End Times

Daniel 9:24 lists six things that must happen to Israel and the Jews before Jesus can make His Second Coming a reality, "Seventy 'sevens' are decreed for your people and your holy city to finish transgression, to put an end to sin, to atone for wickedness, to bring in everlasting righteousness, to seal up vision and prophecy and to anoint the Most Holy Place." None of these has happened with Israel or the Jews yet, so, they must be in our future. Is Israel ready to begin this transformation? I would say no since Israel today is very prosperous and in no immediate need from a worldly perspective. But, God does not prioritize worldly goals. He is interested in spiritual goals that will last eternally. Is Israel vulnerable for attack? Most certainly Israel is already under anti-Semitic attack, is unbelievably more hated than even North Korea or Iran, and even a faction of the so-called evangelical Christian groups espousing Replacement Theology, Amillennialism, Preterism (all prophecy has already been fulfilled), and Post-Millennialism (The Millennium has already occurred or is present today), discredit, despise, or ignore the Jews.

Jerusalem has been unified and under Jewish control for over 50 years now since the six-day war of 1967, and our President has officially recognized Jerusalem as the capitol of the State of Israel, something three previous Presidents failed to do since the legislation was signed in 1995. He has also gone on to recognize the Golan Heights as part of Israel and not Syria, as well as supporting the Israeli Prime Minister Benjamin Netanyahu's declaration that the so-called "Occupied Territories" of Judah and Samaria are also part of the nation of Israel and not disputed land.

Israel's enemies are aligning today amazingly just as Psalm 83 and Ezekiel 38 and 39 have told us. Remember, the Psalms and Ezekiel were written from 2700 to 3000 years ago, and their prophecies are happening today! The threat of Chinese emergence into world politics militarily, economically, and diplomatically is new and concerning when the kings of the east in prophecy is considered. Those kings of the east play a role in the Battle of Armageddon at the end of the Tribulation since they rebel against Christ at Megiddo.

The worldwide acceptance of the elimination of cash, the genetic editing and cloning work being advanced, the growth of clandestine surveillance and privacy invasions are all daily increasing in number and in intensity resulting in great anxiety. Many nations including our own are heavily in debt, their debt-to-production ratios are upside-down with debt being larger than income. This signals a worldwide economic collapse that will and must happen with all the unsustainable borrowing happening today by virtually every country. I believe this collapse is being supernaturally held back by God because of His timing of the Rapture. As soon as the Rapture occurs, all world markets and every country will collapse in an ocean of debt making world commerce stop dead in its tracks. This will lead to many wars and eventually to a world leader to "fix" the problem at least temporarily. Thus, the rise of THE Antichrist. Is he alive today? Because of the convergence and intensity of the End Times signs, I believe he is already a man of considerable political power or financial influence and is well known around the world.

These times just before the Tribulation are filled with godlessness. 2 Timothy 3:1-5 speaks of perilous times to come and they are already here. ("But mark this: There will be terrible times in the last days. People will be lovers of themselves, lovers of money, boastful, proud, abusive, disobedient to their parents, ungrateful, unholy, without love, unforgiving, slanderous, without self-control, brutal, not lovers of the good, treacherous, rash, conceited, lovers of pleasure rather than lovers of God, having a form of godliness but denying its power. Have nothing to do with such people.") But Paul's definition of perilous times does not include wars or earthquakes, it refers to the wickedness of man, the lawlessness and loss of love that is very easy to see in what is happening today. The left, the so-called caring and compassionate ideology that lies in such contrast to God's Word, dominates the media, state and federal government, and has as its base humanism, socialism, and an aversion to common sense and the morals of God's Word.

It is hard to accept that these kinds of things will grow even worse, but Paul has said that a sign of the times will be that the End Times will be just as the days of Noah and the days of Lot which are described as being exceedingly violent and wicked, so wicked that God destroyed the entire world save eight in Noah's day and four cities and all their inhabitants save three in Lot's day. We have already arrived at a time in our present day that the godless are mentally, spiritually, and physically unable to distinguish between right and wrong, sensible and loony, male from female, or even lawful from criminal. Are we in the last days? Seems unmistakable that we are simply because how could things get much worse or the divide between correct and incorrect be wider?

Then there is the element of convergence. What does this term mean in this scheme of the End Times? At virtually any time in Church history, we could find one or two elements of the End Times being displayed or evident in human culture. Over 2,000 years of the Age of Grace there have been many occurrences of wars, of earthquakes, of volcanic eruptions, of despots and millions murdered in the name of tyranny, but there has never been a time when ALL of the signs of Christ's Second Coming would be occurring at the same time – a convergence of signs simultaneously happening, dramatically comprehensive, increasing in frequency and intensity. Daniel told us that the end would come as a flood in Daniel 9:26, and those of us that are not asleep but are watchers can readily see the convergence of all the signs of the End Times occurring today. The intensity of the convergence is what is dramatic. Each of the signs seems to be getting stronger as the days go by making us wonder just how far away could the Rapture be?

Let's Consider Pentecost

First let me say I am not nor will I ever predict a date for the Rapture. That is disobedience since Jesus told His disciples and us that no man knows the day or the hour. But, we CAN know the season of the End Times which are preceded by the Rapture, and it is unmistakable that we are in the End Times because of Israel being back in their land for 70-plus years and the convergence of the signs of the Second Coming.

There is a belief that the Rapture will occur on a Jewish Feast day for the very clear reason that Jesus' death, burial, and resurrection all occurred on the first three Jewish Feasts of the Spring in order. Jesus died on Passover (Pesach), the perfect Lamb of God sacrificed for the sins of the world. Jesus was buried on the second Jewish Feast, the Feast of Unleavened Bread, a perfect picture of the sinless body of Christ laid in the tomb however briefly. The third Jewish Feast is the Feast of First Fruits which occurs on the first day after the Sabbath day following Passover. Jesus fulfilled this feast by being resurrected from the dead, a picture of the first fruits of the victory over death that Jesus demonstrated dramatically.

These first three Jewish Feasts occur in the Spring of each year. The last three of the seven feasts occur in the Fall of each year and are believed to also picture what comes in the future. The fifth feast is the Feast of Trumpets (Rosh Hashanah) occurring in late September usually, sometimes in October (remember the Jewish calendar is based on the lunar cycle which makes the dates of the feasts vary in our Gregorian calendar) and it is a picture of the Rapture to many because of the trumpet but could also be a calling to the Jews to recognize their Messiah. The sixth feast is the Day of Atonement (Yom Kippur) for Jews to seek the Lord for forgiveness of sins and a picture of the judgment of the Tribulation. The seventh feast is the Feast of Tabernacles (Sukkot) which is a foreshadow of the Millennial Kingdom when the Lord "tabernacles" or comes to live with His people in Person. All three of these feasts will, undoubtedly, be fulfilled with the End Times events we have been referring to, but the fourth feast is something special and worth of a little more study.

The fourth Jewish feast is the Festival of Weeks, Shavuot (Hebrew for "weeks"), what we call Pentecost, the Greek word for "fifty". This feast of all the seven feasts of Israel is the most mysterious, and it always falls on the fifth, sixth, or seventh days of the Jewish month of Sivan. Why three days? Because the moon's cycle around the Earth is 29 and a half days, the Jewish calendar has months of 29 and 30 days that vary from year to year to align with the seasons. In fact, they have so-called leap years that add a 13th month every few years to balance out the year with the seasons. So, fifty days after First Fruits varies from year to year as to the exact date it falls – therefore, the date of Pentecost is fluid. So, it is called the "festival without a date" by the Jews because it commemorates the harvest, the end of the grain harvest, when the High Priest would hold two loaves baked from the fresh grain ground into fine flour and leavened with yeast, and "wave" them before the Lord. These two loaves represent the completed bodies of the Church and spiritual Israel, two distinct entities in God's eyes.

Did you notice a couple of terms that sounded familiar? Harvest and the two loaves? Remember those. Now consider some additional interesting dates. The Dispensation of the Law preceded the Church Age or the Dispensation of Grace. It is interesting to note that the Law was given to the Israelites from Mt. Sinai (in Midian which is in Saudi Arabia and not in the Sinai Peninsula) by God to Moses on Pentecost marking the beginning of the Dispensation of the Law. This same dispensation of the Law ended on the day of "THE" Pentecost when the Holy Spirit descended on the apostles in Jerusalem marking the beginning of the Age of the Church or the Dispensation of Grace. The Feast of Weeks or Pentecost is also celebrated by the Jews as symbolic of the marriage of God, the Groom, and Israel, His bride, with the tablets Moses brought down from Sinai the marriage contract.

This also corresponds to the exact date that Ruth, at the time of the harvest, laid down at the kindred redeemer's feet, Boaz, on the night of Pentecost, and he claimed her and redeemed her as His bride. This is a perfect picture of the Bride of Christ being claimed by the Groom and being taken to the Marriage Supper of the Lamb in Heaven. David, Ruth and Boaz's son Obed's grandson, would have a descendent who would be the Savior Jesus Christ. David both was born on Pentecost and died on Pentecost some 70 years later, another interesting set of facts.

The Song of Solomon tells us of the Bridegroom coming for His Bride when Spring comes and the fruit is almost ripe (Song of Solomon 2:8-13), a notable Rapture passage. The prophet Micah in chapter 7 verses 1 to 6 tells us in the latter days Israel, at the time of the fruit harvest which is the time of Pentecost, is in distress because "the good man has perished out of the Earth: and there is none upright among men: they all lie in wait for blood; they hunt every man his brother with a net". Who are the good men? The Summer fruits have been "gathered" or harvested which is the Hebrew term "asaph" which means to "remove" or "take away". So, could this refer to the good men that have been identified as Christians by the Jews, their only good friends in the entire planet, and they have been raptured and are gone? A recent survey of evangelical Christians showed that 75% or more supported Israel being back in their land. The removal of Israel's Christian friends, the good men, is why Israel is in distress because everyone left is their enemy?

So, will the Church be "caught up" on a future Pentecost, perhaps this one this year in very late Spring? We'll see. God Willing! What about The Feast of Trumpets being the Rapture? After all, the trumpet sounds and the dead in Christ rise first, right? Could be, but look at Leviticus 23:24, "In the seventh month, in the first day of the month, shall ye have a sabbath, a memorial of blowing of trumpets, an holy convocation." Does the blowing of the shofar, the ram's horn, on the Feast of Trumpets (Rosh Hashanah) represent the final trumpet of resurrection? Or, does it represent a "memorial" of the heavenly Pentecost trumpet? Or could it be a call to the Jews that their Messiah is coming very soon and they need to turn back to God?

You know, it really doesn't matter whether the Rapture occurs on Pentecost, or Rosh Hashanah, or some other day, it is evident that it is near, it is imminent, it is next on the prophetic calendar since nothing has to happen before it, and we should be ready. Only five of the ten virgins had oil in their lamps, so the other five missed being with the Groom because they were not ready. We anticipate, we are excited at being "caught up", rising with the dead in Christ, receiving our heavenly, immortal, eternal bodies like that Jesus already has. So, the question really is, "Are you ready?" Is your family ready? Are your friends ready? Time is very short, even exceedingly short for the call to "Come up here" could come at any minute!

Conclusion

To say that we are in the End Times is abundantly clear to those spiritually attuned to Scripture and the Spirit's leading. The amazing alignment we see today of what the Bible says will be the conditions and the environment of the Earth just prior to His Coming is astoundingly apparent IF you are a watcher and you are familiar with Bible prophecy. To be ignorant of these things or to be disinterested or skeptical of what Jesus and the apostles have told us of the times just prior to His Second Coming is to be as the Pharisees were at the time of Jesus' first advent. And Scripture is very clear of Jesus' attitude toward the Pharisees and their "knowledge" of the Scriptures, yet their rejection of Him as Savior which they should have immediately recognized but chose to ignore and defy. (Of course, a few did accept Christ, but the majority did not.) Skepticism or rejection of biblical prophecy is very similar to the Pharisees' rejection of the known coming Messiah and puts those who are in that camp of rejecting prophecy in danger of the wrath to come, God's Wrath of the Tribulation.

John, in his little book of 1 John gives us Christians many tests to determine if we are truly saved and living the blessed eternal life of joy and peace that only God can give through Jesus Christ and His Holy Spirit. True Christians can see that John wanted us to be sure of our eternal destiny and be aware of the Antichrist to come as well as many other evil and wicked things. A little reflection on John's words can give us either confidence in God's Word and our sure salvation, or show us that we need to reevaluate our hearts in light of Scripture concerning Jesus' resurrection and our future in the soon coming Rapture of the True Church of Jesus Christ!

If vile things of the world we see around us today are not appalling to you as you see them grow and manifest themselves to you, if Christ's soon return is not thrilling to you causing your heart to leap at the very thought, if the immediate return in the clouds of Jesus to call us away to be with Him does not fill your heart with joy, your mind with wonder, if none of the convergence and intensity of the signs of the times means anything to you, then, perhaps, you need to examine your faith and seek God in earnest. Why? Because Jesus is near, even at the door. Our salvation draweth nigh, and we are about to leave this Earth to escape God's Wrath which He brings on the entire planet to convert His people Israel so that they will see that their Messiah Jesus is waiting for them to accept and worship Him. Then, Jesus can set up His Millennial Kingdom and reign for a thousand years. Let us all say, "Even so, come Lord Jesus!" Maranatha! Come save us!

The Fear of the Lord

At present, one of the most neglected teachings in many modern churches is the respectful fear of the Lord. At church conferences and meetings, in Christian magazines and television shows for churchgoers, the topic of the fear of the Lord seems to be mostly shunned as something from a past irrelevant era. One reason for this is the infiltration of humanism into the church. This infiltration has resulted in a dislike by many churchgoers of mentions of God's holiness, His wrath against sin, His future judgement, hell, church discipline, rebuking in preaching, correction, the fear of the Lord, repentance and a call to greater obedience to Him. Also, an excessive sub-dividing of the Bible which some Christians practice has encouraged the unbiblical attitude that these topics are better suited to the Old Mosaic Covenant than to the New Covenant. Ignoring or minimizing parts of God's Word while exalting other parts is dangerous to our spiritual maturity. It is also wrong to overemphasize some Biblical topics at the expense of the glorious teachings on God's grace, mercy, love, redemption, forgiveness of sin, our legal standing in Christ, knowing Jesus intimately and so on. And it is equally wrong to underemphasize or ignore the Old Testament and the fact that God is the same yesterday, today, and forever meaning that He is holy and rejects ALL sin regardless of the degree of it. We must maintain our awe of Almighty God and respect every single word in the Bible as the inspired, inerrant, authoritative Word of Almighty God because keeping that foremost in our minds is the basis for knowing and accepting our sinful natures which are unacceptable to God and the very reason for our needing the saving Grace of our Lord and Savior Jesus Christ!

Revealing Statistics of the Average American

An indication of how little real reverence, respect, and awe of God and Jesus Christ there is at present can be seen in the following from surveys of normal Americans (Barna Group – barna.com):

- sleeping 9 hours per day
- actual work per day – 4 hours
- watching screens of any kind – 6 hours per day
- eating, drinking, shopping, travel per day 3 hours
- sports or exercising about 30 minutes per day
- games/hobbies/arts/crafts 30 minutes per day
- religious activities like reading God's Word and/or praying average per day less than 15 minutes

To make it worse, 88% of American homes own Bibles with an average of 5 Bibles per home. But, only 37% of Americans read their Bibles once per week or more, only 11% have read through the Bible completely once, and only 9% of those more than once. Couple that with the average American spending less than 15 minutes per day on any sort of religious activity and you see how little devotion our country has to God and His Word.

Would it be so hard to carve out of those 9 hours of sleep or those 6 hours of watching screens to devote one simple hour to reading God's Word and praying to the Creator of the Universe?

Attitudes toward the Bible

There is much misunderstanding about the history of the Bible. For instance, according to Barna Research, four out of every ten adults (38%) believe that the entire Bible was written several decades after Jesus' death and resurrection. While this appears to be true for the New Testament, the entire Old Testament was written hundreds of years prior to the birth of Jesus Christ. Almost two out of three adults (62%) know that the Book of Isaiah is in the Old Testament. One out of ten people (11%) believe it is in the New Testament. One out of four (27%) don't know. It is always amazing that even when asked a question that only has two options, there are people who would rather claim ignorance rather than guess which makes them look ignorant anyway.

This is depressing information, but now we get to the ridiculous. 12% of adults believe that the name of Noah's wife was Joan of Arc. The Bible does not actually provide her name. One out of six people (16%) believe that one of the books in the New Testament is the Book of Thomas, written by the apostle Thomas. Another one-third of the population are not sure whether or not there is such a book in the New Testament of the Bible. Half of all adults (49%) believe that the Bible teaches that money is the root of all evil. One-third (37%) disagree with this contention. The actual teaching indicates that it is the "love" of money that is the root of all evil. Three-quarters of Americans (75%) believe that the Bible teaches that God helps those who help themselves (it is not in the Bible).

When we consider how relevant the Bible is to our lives today, we find out that most Americans really don't know or don't care. 60% of all adults agree that "the Bible is totally accurate in all of its teachings (44% agree strongly, 16% agree somewhat) Blacks are more likely than are whites to agree that the Bible is totally accurate in all of its teachings (75% to 58% respectively). 13% of born-again Christians disagree that "the Bible is totally accurate in all of its teachings."

While millions believe the Bible is accurate in its recording of information, a substantial number of adults do not believe that all of the information is relevant for today. One out of every five adults (18%) contend that one of the renowned portions of the Bible - the Ten Commandments - is not relevant for people living today. Most people take the Bible at face value when it comes to the descriptions of the miracles that took place. Three out of four adults (73%) believe that all of the miracles described in the Bible actually took place.

Evangelical Surprise

It's one thing for Americans in general to lack basic theological knowledge. After all, many of the 75 percent of the country who call themselves Christians don't take their faith that seriously, and the rest are either members of other religions, or have no religion. But what about those who wear their Christianity on their sleeve? Surely such a group, evangelicals, would perform much better.

In a survey only two years ago (Barna again), participants who called the Bible their highest authority, said personal evangelism is important, and indicated that trusting in Jesus' death on the cross is the only way of salvation, were labeled "evangelical." They totaled 586 survey-takers. Everyone expected them to perform better than most Americans. No one expected them to perform worse.

Seven in ten evangelicals, more than the population at large, said that Jesus was the first being God created. Fifty-six percent agreed that "the Holy Spirit is a divine force but not a personal being." They also saw a huge increase in evangelicals (28 percent, up from 9 percent) who indicated that the Third Person of the Trinity is not equal with God the Father or Jesus, a direct contradiction of orthodox Christianity.

The contradictory answers, not the outright heresies, should most concern us all. By definition, the evangelicals in this survey believed that "only those who trust in Jesus Christ alone as their Savior receive God's free gift of eternal salvation." Yet nearly half agreed that "God accepts the worship of all religions including Christianity, Judaism, and Islam." Two-thirds of evangelicals, more than Americans in general, said Heaven is a place where all people will ultimately be reunited with their loved ones. The most striking thing is how many of these folks evidently see no contradiction between their casual universalism and the evangelical creed that salvation comes through faith in Christ alone.

How, then, do we educate ourselves to God's Truth? We read, study, meditate, and repeat on a daily basis, continually, never missing a day, devoting time to God, for God alone, spending more time in personal prayer with God again daily. With this practice comes the Holy Spirit's wisdom, knowledge, and understanding of God's Will for us in our lives. Without

God's Word and the knowledge of it, we are blown by the wind of the world, signifying nothing!

What is the Bible?

The Bible is a collection of 66 books, 39 in the Old Testament or Old Covenant, and 27 in the New Testament or New Covenant. We can think of the Old Covenant as being the old contract or the old deal between God and men, while the New Covenant is the new contract or the new deal between God and man. The Old Testament contains the Law of Moses, books of history, books of poetry, books of wisdom, and books of prophecy, many of which are fulfilled today in amazing detail. The New Testament contains the story of the earthly life and ministry of Jesus Christ in the gospels of Matthew, Mark, Luke and John, the story of the early church in the book of Acts, letters written to various churches and church leaders, and a book of prophecy – Revelation.

All the books of the Bible, written over a period starting about 2,000 years before Christ and extending to about 95 A.D., give a consistent picture of who God is, who we are, what God wants, what His plan for mankind is, what we can expect depending on our choices in this life, and what we can expect in our future here on Earth and in the everlasting life to come. The Bible reveals the story of how God has dealt with mankind, His chosen nation of Israel, and His New Covenant people, the Church. The Bible speaks with the same authority and relevance today regarding who He is and what He is doing in our times. It speaks to us regarding what will happen in the future and how God will change everything.

The Bible is not just a book of rules and ancient history. It contains thousands of wonderful promises which are applicable to all who believe in all times. The challenge that faces mankind today is to know, understand and experience the wonderful things that God promises to do for those who believe. God's promises in the Bible guarantee us more than enough for all our needs in every area. The only condition is to trust and obey God and expect Him to do what He says He will do. If we do not trust Him, we are the losers with eternal effect. If we know the New Testament or the New Contract well, and apply it intelligently to our lives, we will be blessed both now and in eternity. If we reject its warnings and disregard its promises, we do so to our own hurt both now and especially for eternity.

The Old Testament begins in the book of Genesis with an account of the Creation of the world by God, and then continues with the story of the beginnings of human history. The rest of the Old Testament reveals mostly the history and the heart condition of the people of Israel in different periods before the coming of the promised Messiah. The New Testament shows us the most important events of the life and work of Jesus the Messiah, how many Jewish people rejected their own Messiah, and how from there God's offer of salvation began to go out into all the world. It uncovers more of God's promises and more information about our enemy, Satan, and how we can overcome his plans by trusting and obeying God.

The Message of the Bible

The Bible is God's Plan to bring mankind back into intimate relationship with Him. The Bible tells us about God and how we can come back to Him. It shows us the character and ways of God, the person of God in Jesus Christ our Lord, who we are, and how we ought to live. It tells us our origins, our identity, and our destiny.

Reasons to Believe in the Inspiration of the Bible

Large books have been written presenting in detail powerful evidences which give strong reasons for believing in the divine inspiration of the Bible. Here are some in very short form (from articles found at raptureready.com):

1. No other religious book has specific fulfilled prophecies that the Bible contains. We have today manuscripts dating well before the time of Jesus, containing Biblical prophecies which directly point to Him. In fact, Jesus fulfilled or will fulfill over 300 prophecies from the Old Testament prophecies in his lifetime and the time to come. Some of the strongest fulfilled ones are found in Psalm 22 and Isaiah 53. These passages are so strong that in Jewish synagogues today they are skipped over in the reading of the law since they point so directly and unmistakably to Jesus Christ.

   The emergence of the Persian, Greek, and Roman empires was prophesied by Daniel at a time when the Babylonian empire covered the world. The re-creation of the state of Israel in 1948 is a fulfilment of both Old and New Testament prophecy. Present world conditions were prophesied by Jesus almost 2000 years ago in Matthew 24. Large books have been written showing the detailed fulfilment of hundreds of Bible prophecies. No other religious or occultic book comes even close to the Bible when it comes to prophecy.

2. Events and places described in the Bible are confirmed more and

more by archaeology and other historical writings as discoveries are made. Ancient peoples such as the Hittites were believed to be a myth but were confirmed in 1887. Archaeologists have discovered ancient tablets and city sites which confirm time after time the historical accuracy of the Bible. Those who have speculated otherwise have been proved wrong again and again.

3. The internal consistency of doctrine right across the 66 books of the Bible, despite widely different authors in different periods of time, points to the common source of inspiration of the Bible. If we asked 20 people in this country to each write a separate book about God, we would certainly have conflicting opinions and doctrines. Yet because the Holy Spirit inspired the many human authors, this didn't happen in the writing of the different books of the Bible, even though the books were written at different times. They all reveal God as a God of mercy and justice.

4. One of the most important reasons for believing in the Bible is the fact that it works today. Hundreds of millions of people around the world today testify that Jesus Christ has changed their lives, and that the promises of God work when believed and applied. People have been healed physically and emotionally while reading the Bible or acting on its teaching. Thousands have been miraculously delivered from the effects of drug abuse or other harmful practices. The character of the man believing the Bible from the heart is changed from selfishness to love. All kinds of people from all kinds of backgrounds in all countries of the world will testify to the reality of all this. While not all have heard these testimonies, more and more are hearing and believing every day going on to experience the same things for themselves.

5. Then there is the historical evidence for the physical resurrection of Christ. The apostles preached this message right from the start, and most of them died for this faith. They knew what they saw. They would not all die for something they knew to be a lie of their own making. And the plain fact was, after many saw Jesus die and be buried, three days later, Jesus' grave was empty. Hundreds testified to seeing Jesus alive from the dead. Hundreds of thousands today, thousands of them formerly Muslims, testify to having seen him in a vision or a dream speaking to them in a way that changed their lives altogether. Miracles happen in Jesus' name today. All this shows that Jesus is alive. And if Jesus is alive, His book, the Bible, can be trusted. Since Christ rose, we should listen to him, believe his claims,

share his attitude to the Scriptures, and trust his ability to preserve his written Word to us.

6. Israel's 490 Year Cycles

Have you ever wondered why Christ commanded us to forgive our brothers "490 times" (Matt 18:21-22) or why "490 years" was the great prophetic timeline revealed to Daniel? God seems to have divided Israel's history into four 490-year cycles:

A. From Abraham to the Exodus (490 Years).

From Abraham's birth until the giving of the Law at Mount Sinai and the beginning of a new era (Galatians 3:17) are 505 years (Note: This time frame is obtained by simply adding the numbers of years given in Scripture). However, the 15 years when Abraham had lapsed from faith in God's promise and went in to Hagar (Genesis 16:3) until the promised seed was finally born (Genesis 21:5) must be deducted from this, leaving 490 years during which Abraham and his descendants were abiding under the covenant promise.

B. From Exodus to the Dedication of the Temple (490 Years).

From the giving of the Law at Mount Sinai in about 1446 B.C. until the dedication of Solomon's temple in about 956 B.C. are 490 years.

C. From the Temple to Ezra's finished projects of rebuilding Jerusalem, its walls and buildings (490 Years).

From the dedication of the temple in about 956 B.C. to Ezra's leading to build Jerusalem in 457 BC (Ezra 9:9) and the completion of the projects are about 490 years.

D. From Ezra's return to the fulfillment of Daniel's 70 Weeks Prophecy (490 Years).

The fourth cycle is actually stated in Scripture in the great "seventy week" prophecy of Daniel 9:24-27. The opening words of the prophecy make this clear: "Seventy weeks have been declared for your people and your holy city..." (Daniel 9:24). The phrase "seventy weeks" literally means in Hebrew "70 sevens"

(70 x 7), and the context demands that the sevens be reckoned in years-seventy sevens of years, which would be a total of 490 years.

Furthermore, Daniel's prophecy states that the 490 years are divided into three periods. After the first two periods (69 weeks or 483 years), the cycle terminates in the crucifixion of the Messiah (Daniel 9:25-26) as God breaks His covenant relation with His people. The cycle starts again when the last seven-year period begins-the so-called "70th week of Daniel" also known as the Tribulation (Daniel 9:27; Revelation 6-19). Thus, Daniel's prophecy is a major confirmation that God determines and measures the redemptive history of Israel in cycles of 490 (70 x 7) years!

But the most amazing part of the prophecy is that it pinpoints the year of Jesus' triumphal entry into Jerusalem-over 600 years before it occurred! In Daniel 9:25 we read, "Know therefore and understand, that from the going forth of the command to restore and build Jerusalem until Messiah the Prince, there shall be seven weeks and sixty-two weeks..." According to the prophecy, from the command to rebuild Jerusalem there would be seven weeks (49 years) and sixty-two more weeks (434 years), a total of 483 years, until Jesus' triumphal entry into Jerusalem (which is when Jesus publicly declared that he was the Messiah). We know from history that the command to "restore and rebuild Jerusalem" was given Ezra (Ezra 9:9). Adding 483 years to 457 BC gives 27 A.D. the exact year of Jesus' triumphal entry into Jerusalem!

7. Israel's 70/7 Year Pattern

As seen above, the numbers 70 and 7 are very significant numbers related to Israel (Dan. 9:2; 24). Throughout the Old Testament, Israel's inextricable link to the number 70 is unmistakable:

- Terah, the father of Abraham, was 70 years old when Abraham was born (Gen. 11:26)
- The Nation of Israel began with 70 Hebrews who migrated to Egypt (Ex. 1:1-5)
- The children of Israel camped at an oasis of 70 palm trees, following the liberation from bondage in Egypt (Ex. 15:27)
- Moses appointed 70 elders to be the governing body of Israel

(Num. 11:16)
- The Jews were liberated from captivity in Babylon after 70 years (Jer. 29:10)
- God's plan of redemption for Israel and Jerusalem is comprised of 70 weeks (Dan. 9:24-27)
- Israel's greatest ruler, King David, died at the age of 70 as well as his son, Solomon (2 Sam. 5:4)

Seeing the recurring pattern of 70's throughout Scripture relating to Israel, it's interesting that there are seven other instances of seventy (7 x 70) in Israel's history:

- Israel went into Babylonian exile in 606 B.C. and returned to Jerusalem in 537 B.C. (70 years)
- Jerusalem was destroyed in 587 B.C. and then rebuilt in 518 B.C. (70 years)
- The Second Jewish Temple was completed in 515 B.C. The wall around Jerusalem was completed in 445 B.C. (70 years)
- Jerusalem was destroyed by the Romans in 70 A.D.
- The first modern Jewish settlement in the Land of Israel (Petah Tikvah) in 1878 until the modern State of Israel was born in 1948 (70 years)
- The first [major] step in reestablishing the State of Israel (First Zionist Congress) in 1897 until the final step (restoration of Jerusalem) in 1967 (70 years)
- The UN vote in favor of the establishment of the modern State of Israel in 1947 until the first recognition by a foreign power (US) that Jerusalem is its capital in 2017 (70 years)

Have you noticed that the events occurring after 70-year intervals are restoration-themed? Given that the number 70 symbolizes restoration in the Bible, the odds against this occurring by chance are astronomical, suggesting divine orchestration. If the recurring pattern of 70's in Israel's significant historical events isn't uncanny enough, consider the following prophetically significant events that shaped the modern nation of Israel:

1897-First Zionist Congress (the intent to establish the   nation of Israel)
1917-Balfour Declaration (end of Ottoman rule in WWI)
1947-UN Partition Plan approved (declaration of Israel)
1967-Six Day War (reunification of Jerusalem)
1977-Camp David Accords (beginning of "Land for Peace")

1987-Temple Mount Institute founded
2017-Jerusalem recognized by Trump to be capital of Israel

Have you noticed that all these significant dates end in a "7"? Once again, the odds against this occurring by chance are astronomical, suggesting divine orchestration.

8. The Significance of 1948

We've seen that the numbers 70 and 7 are significant in Israel's history. But what about the date/number 1948? Surely, the year in which one of the most significant prophetic events in history took place, the rebirth of Israel, wasn't just some random date in human history. As it turns out, the significance of this date/number may be more than what you realize:

- The 19th book and 48th chapter in the Bible (Psalm 48) describes the rebirth of Israel. It's also interesting that this chapter has 14 verses. Is it a coincidence that the rebirth of Israel took place on May 14th?

- Not only is Psalm the 19th book of the Bible, but it is also the 48th book from the end of the Bible. This is interesting, considering the book of Psalms is right in the CENTER of the Bible and Israel is CENTRAL to God's redemptive plan.

- If you add 19 to 48 (19 + 48) you have 67. Is it a coincidence that the next most significant prophetic event since New Testament times, the liberation of Jerusalem, happened in 1967?

- Gold is heated to exactly 1,948 degrees Fahrenheit during the refining process. Interestingly, Scripture compares Israel's deliverance during Jacob's trouble to the refining and purification process of precious metal (Zech. 13:9).

- Even the sun and moon appear to point towards the significance of the numbers 19 and 48. Of the eight rare blood-moon tetrads since the time of Christ, three have been in the last 100 years, falling on feast days in 1949-1950, 1967-1968, and 2014-2015. Note the following pattern within this triad of tetrads:

    $$1968 - 1949 = 19$$
    $$2015 - 1967 = 48$$

- But that's not all-there was another span of three tetrads within 100 years falling on feast days, in 795-796, 842-843, and 860-861. Note the same pattern within this triad of tetrads:

    861 - 842 = 19
    843 - 795 = 48

- The number of years from the first man, Adam, to the first Hebrew, Abraham, is easily determined to be 1,948 years by simply adding up the years found in Genesis chapters 5 and 11. Coincidently, from the second man Adam, Jesus Christ (1 Cor. 15:45), to the rebirth of "Abraham's seed" (Israel) as a nation, there were also 1,948 years!

Has the Bible Been Changed?

Some people, especially those who don't like the moral constraints of the Bible, want to say that the Bible has changed since it was written. The textual evidence for the integrity of the Bible is better than for any other ancient book or document. Compared to other ancient writings, we have more manuscripts still in existence, and manuscripts whose age we know is much closer to the time of original writing, than it is in the case of other ancient writings like those of Julius Caesar or Plato. All variations which exist are of a very minor nature which do not affect any major doctrine of the Bible.

There are amazing mathematical patterns in Bible when looked at in the original Hebrew and Greek languages. Hundreds of facts based around the number 7 appear in every passage of the Bible when you look at the numerical values of the words in the original Hebrew and Greek texts of the Bible. Many of these patterns were discovered by Ivan Panin in the 19th century. This discovery turned him from being an agnostic into being a Christian. His subsequent research provides a virtually irrefutable evidence that the Bible is not simply the product of human minds. No computer today could create such a text. The conclusion is once again that the Bible is the Word of God.

There will always be people however who refuse to believe. This is basically because they are not willing to consider the evidence honestly. Human beings often believe things for reasons other than logic or persuasive argument. Many times, people believe what they want to believe, because it is convenient that way or too emotionally painful to recognize that they and their family have been fundamentally deceived all this time. People today are often "lovers of pleasure more than lovers of God." (2 Timothy 3:4). Hiding in their pride and communal ignorance, they do not want to consider the evidence for the Bible, in case they are forced to admit it is true and they have to give up their ungodly passions and pleasures. The Bible makes it clear that God is looking for a change in our lives. But that change will be good, because God is good, wise, and able to help us be what we were created to be.

Since God is manifest in Creation, in our consciences and our personhood, we are without excuse if we do not believe in a personal God. The Bible points this out in Romans 1:18-20. The truth is that a person who rejects the message of the Bible will often believe something very improbable or ridiculous from a rational point of view. This is actually part of God's judgment on those who willfully suppress the truth in unrighteousness (Romans 1:18; 2 Thessalonians 2:11,12).

The Authority of the Bible

Authority and author are directly related concepts. Because the Holy Spirit (who is God) is the author of the Bible, the authority of the Bible is the authority of God. That means, when the Bible speaks to us, then God is speaking to us. To disobey the New Testament is to disobey God. Jesus said, "If anyone loves me, he will keep my word; and my Father will love him, and we will come to him and make our home with him." (John 14:23)

"He who rejects Me, and does not receive my words, has that which judges him – the word that I have spoken will judge him on the last day." (John 12:48). The Word has authority to judge and will judge in the last day. Therefore, it is indeed wise to "tremble at God's Word" (Isaiah 66:2). "The fear of the Lord is the beginning of knowledge, but fools despise wisdom and instruction." (Proverbs 1:7).

Jesus said, "But why do you call me 'Lord, Lord,' and do not do the things I say?" (Luke 6:46). Lord means master, and just calling Jesus 'Lord' is not enough. In vain we call Him 'Lord' if by our lives we demonstrate that we do not know what we say, or we do not mean what we say. Jesus is Lord of your Life if and only if the true intention of your heart is to do what he says in His Word. We must come to Jesus, hear His sayings, and DO them. (Luke 6:47-49). We must dig past all the traditions, prejudices and errors of men. We must get to the solid rock of Christ's Word and put it into practice if our lives are to pass the test.

God has promised to preserve His words forever (Psalm 12:7). If we believe in the faithful God who causes the sun to rise every day, then we should believe He has preserved his Word to us also. "All Scripture is given by inspiration of God, and is profitable for doctrine, for reproof, for correction, for instruction in righteousness." (2 Timothy 3:16) The true doctrine of Christianity may never contradict the clear meaning of Scripture. We have the right to rebuke and correct people using Scripture, as long as we ourselves are being led by the Spirit as the Scripture commands us to be (Galatians 5:16).

Who Can Interpret the Bible?

Some religious leaders have the idea that only certain people have the right to read and pray to God in order to understand what God is saying to them through the Bible. For this reason, in some churches the Bible was kept for centuries untranslated in the language of the people. In this way religious leaders could claim to represent Christ and teach the truth without people being able to check them out. Just as Jesus said to the Pharisees, so we say to such leaders: "Hypocrites! For you shut up the kingdom of Heaven against men; for you neither go in yourselves, nor do you allow those who are entering to go in." (Matthew 23:13).

We do not need to have a perfect interpretation of all things in the Bible in order for God to able to speak to us through it. Those who want to do God's will shall be guided into all truth (John 7:17), step by step. We are commanded to be filled with the Word of God, and we must begin. "Let the Word of Christ dwell in you richly" (Colossians 3:16). All who want to be disciples of Jesus (true Christians, Acts 11:26) must remain in His Word. "If you remain in my word, you are my disciples indeed." (John 8:30-32; John 15:7; John 14:21,23). True believers must know what they believe and in whom. It is not just a matter of believing that Jesus existed and is somehow a savior.

Religious leaders who tell us not to read the Bible, as some prominent mega-church so-called pastors are doing today, are telling us to disobey Jesus. God has exalted His Word above all his name (Psalm 138:2). This means that the Word has the ultimate authority, not traditions of churches. Traditions can only be good when they don't contradict the Bible, and when they don't seek to replace the need for a personal dynamic relationship with God. Scripture is never superseded by man's tradition (Matthew 15:1-9; Mark 7:8,13). Jesus condemned those who put their own traditions before the written word of God. We are commanded to test all things (1 Thessalonians 5:21). How? By the Standard of God's Word, Scripture. "To the law and the testimony! If they do not speak according to this word, it is because there is no light in them." (Isaiah 8:20).

All church leaders and those claiming to be Christians who reject Christ's words will one day be judged according to the words of Christ which are recorded in Scripture (John 12:48). God reveals the truth about doctrine to those who want to do his will (John 7:17). We cannot trust those who willingly and consistently disobey God's Word to interpret the Bible correctly to us. Such men do not have the Holy Spirit. They are blind leaders of the blind. Thus, everyone who wants to follow Christ must seek first-hand knowledge of the Scriptures diligently. Laziness and indifference are not excuses - they are disobedience. This matter is critical! Our response to God's Word has eternal consequences and must be attended to now!

Principles of Interpreting the Scripture

Being the Word of God, the Scripture is consistent with itself and Scripture always interprets Scripture (2 Peter 1:21; Psalm 12:6-7). We cannot build a doctrine just based on one verse taken out of context. This principle gives us an important safeguard against false interpretations and doctrines. So, we must know all Scripture well. The Holy Spirit, as author, is the ultimate interpreter. No man can say that he is always right about Scripture and its application simply because he claims a position of religious authority. Even Peter the apostle was wrong at times and had to be corrected. See Galatians 2:11-14.

The Holy Spirit never contradicts himself. So, if an interpretation of Scripture contradicts another part of Scripture, taken in the context of the whole Bible, that interpretation cannot be right. Jesus said the Holy Spirit will guide us into all truth (John 16.13). We should therefore ask the Holy Spirit to guide us in our search for truth in the Bible, without being afraid. The Holy Spirit is given to those who obey God (Acts 5.32). Let us therefore seek to please God by believing and acting on what He has already revealed to us through the Bible and our consciences.

Daniel studied Jeremiah to understand it (Daniel 9:2). Likewise, we are commanded to study it (2 Timothy 2:15). We should ask God for wisdom in our study of the Scripture (James 1:5). God promises to give us the wisdom we need. Everyone must be fully convinced in his own mind about issues of importance (Romans 14:5). Much study, prayer and listening to Godly men will help us to know the Truth. We should not allow ourselves to be full of doubts on issues of major importance such as salvation.

The Nature and Power of the Word of God

"For the Word of God is living and powerful, and sharper than any two-edged sword, piercing even to the division of soul and spirit, and of joints and marrow, and is a discerner of the thoughts and intents of the heart." (Hebrews 4:12) God's Word is at work in the world today. It is an active force. It governs the spiritual activity in the Universe. It changes things, especially when spoken and believed, both in the hearts of men and in their circumstances. God is watching over his Word to perform it (Jeremiah 1:12).

God's Word is compared to a seed (Luke 8:11; Mark 4:14; 1 Peter 1:23). This seed produces new life if planted well. Like seed, it is growing in hearts and multiplying and spreading all over the world today. Satan, his demons and antichrist people cannot stop the inevitable progress of this seed. Every seed produces life after its own kind. The seed of God's Word, if planted well in soft hearts, open hearts, will produce the life, character and faith of God in its hearers. For hard hearts, the Word correctly applied will be like a hammer to break the hard heart open (Jeremiah 23:19).

The Word of God is compared to a fire, "'Is not my Word like a fire?', says the LORD, 'And like a hammer that breaks the rock in pieces?'" (Jeremiah 23:29). It can act as a fire (Jeremiah 5:14; 20:9). Fire spreads, gives light, warmth, energy and comfort, but it can also destroy. God's Word destroys the power of evil as it is believed and applied. It can break Satan's influence in our hearts and lives.

The Word of God is compared also to water (Ephesians 5:26; Psalm 1:1-3). Water brings cleansing, refreshing, life and encouragement and satisfies the thirsty. The Word of God can do this for us also. God's Word is also compared a mirror which shows us our true spiritual state (James 1:23; 2 Corinthians 3:18). It shows us how we need to be cleansed.

What the Word of God Can Produce in Your Life

In a world that is many times casual and uninterested in the things of God, the Word of God can produce conviction of sin (Romans 7:7). The Holy Spirit works through the knowledge of the law to show us how unrighteous we are and how we deserve condemnation. Preachers must, no, have to, preach the conviction of sin so that the Holy Spirit can perform His work on repentant hearts. By the Word of God also comes salvation (Romans 1:16). We receive wisdom for salvation through the Word (2 Timothy 3:15). "Faith comes by hearing, and hearing by the Word of God." (Romans 10:17). If you don't have enough faith, you can get it by paying attention to the preached

Word.

"Your Word has given me life" (Psalm 119:50). The Word gives a new spiritual life when received. It produces the new birth of the human spirit (1 Peter 1:23). The Word gives us hope (Romans 15:4; Psalm 119:49) both for this life and for the life to come. The Word acts to wash and cleanse us (Ephesians 5:25). Jesus said, "Sanctify them by your truth. Your word is truth." (John 17:17). So, the Word can produce in us true holiness. It gives us Truth. And that Truth, if we really know it, will make us free (John 8:31-32). Through the Word we can cleanse our way and keep sin out of our lives (Psalm 119:9,11). We can have victory over Satan through the Word, as Jesus did (Matthew 4:4,7,10,11; 1 John 2:14).

We can find wisdom in the Word when we don't know what to do. "The testimony of the Lord is sure, making wise the simple." (Psalm 19:7). To God we can truly say, "Your Word is a lamp to my feet, and a light to my path." (Psalm 119:105). So, in this way the Word gives guidance. God can "strengthen us according to His Word" (Psalm 119:28). His Word gives us comfort (Romans 15:4) The Word of God can work in our spiritual and emotional lives to produce joy and rejoicing (Nehemiah 8:12; Psalm 119:14; 1 Corinthians 13:6). Its purpose is to produce in us a true love, that we will live by (1 Timothy 1:5; Ephesians 5:2).

Paul commended the Ephesian believers to the word of God's grace, "which is able to build you up and give you an inheritance among all those who are sanctified" (Acts 20:32). So, the Word produces spiritual growth.

If we need physical healing, we should apply God's Words and promises. "For they are life to those who find them, and health to all their flesh." (Proverbs 4:22). Note that it is for the flesh, not just for the soul. Many times, God will send his Word and heal us (Psalm 107:20) if we need healing.

True prosperity and success will come to you if you consistently "meditate on the Word night and day, that you may observe to do according to all that is written in it. For then you will make your way prosperous, and then you will have good success." (Joshua 1:8; Psalm 1:1-3). If our souls prosper through obedience to the Word (3 John 2), then God wants our bodies to be in health too and for us to prosper. Concerning the works of men, by the Word of God, we can keep ourselves from the paths of the destroyer (Psalm 17:4). This means protection. It comes to those who obey the Word and abide in the presence of God (Psalm 91; John 15:10).

Everything that is really important for the man of God in his ministry can be obtained through the Word. The Word is given, "that the man of God may be complete, thoroughly equipped for every good work." (2 Timothy 3:17).

When the Word of God is spread to enough hearts, and put thoroughly into practice in at least a few, the Word will bring revival or spiritual awakening (Acts 19:20; Psalm 119:25; Nehemiah 9:3). The value of a true spiritual revival of God is beyond human calculation. This is because the salvation of even one soul is worth more to God than all the material things that exist that He made.

Different Attitudes of People for Prophecy

Many people have negative attitudes toward the study of biblical prophecy. For example, first, there are those who say, "I'm only concerned about the present, so don't bother me with ideas about the future."

Other people express a second negative attitude toward the study of biblical prophecy. It goes like this: "Nobody can understand the prophecies in the Bible, especially Revelation(S), so why bother to study them? Such effort is a useless waste of time." This negative attitude toward the study of the Book of Revelation (the Revelation of Jesus Christ which is ONE Mighty Revelation, not more than one) is tragic for at least two reasons. First, those who ignore Revelation will miss the following special blessing that Jesus Christ proclaimed in conjunction with that book, "Blessed is he that readeth, and they that hear the words of this prophecy, and keep those things which are written therein" (Revelation 1:3). Second, the very fact that the Book of Revelation and all other biblical prophecies were given by God to mankind through divine revelation and were recorded accurately through the means of divine inspiration (1 Corinthians 2:9-13; 2 Peter 1:19-21) indicates that God wants human beings to possess these prophecies and to pay attention to them. Otherwise He would never have given them to mankind. In light of this, those persons, who for any reason fail to heed them, will miss what God intends and desires for them.

A third negative attitude toward the study of biblical prophecy is expressed by some Christians. What these folks claim is that there are very few, if any, prophecies in the Bible concerning events that will transpire in the future beyond our present time. They say that almost all biblical prophecies were fulfilled by the end of the First Century A.D. For example, the great tribulation to which Jesus Christ referred in Matthew 24:21-22 was fulfilled by the events associated with the Roman destruction of Jerusalem and Israel as a nation state in 70 A.D. This was Christ's coming in judgment upon the Jewish nation that had rejected Him."

This sort of argument is easily seen as incorrect because, for instance, when was the last time you saw 70-pound hailstones falling from the sky? Revelation 16:21 tells us that will part of the seventh Bowl Judgment that occurs near the end of the Tribulation. And that has certainly never happened before nor could it since that would take a divine intervention since natural laws of hydrology make it impossible. There are many other prophecies that have never happened not the least of which Jesus coming back and setting foot on the Mount of Olives (Zechariah 14:4)

A fourth negative attitude toward the study of biblical prophecy is the result of the mishandling of the prophetic Scriptures by some Bible teachers and preachers. Some have erroneously and corruptly claimed that the prophetic Scriptures gave them information that enabled them to set a date for the Rapture or Second Coming of Christ, or to identify the personal name of the Antichrist. For example, during World War II Bible teachers and preachers in Great Britain and North America claimed that Bible prophecy indicated that Hitler or Mussolini was the Antichrist. In the recent past, a fairly well-known radio preacher claimed to know the exact date of the Rapture and made it very well known through many different means. Of course, since no one knows the exact date of either Christ's Second Coming or the Rapture, these dates and people came and went thereby destroying the credibility of the claimers and giving the unsaved more cause to ridicule biblical Christianity. Many weak Christians were turned off to Bible and prophecy study because of these charlatans.

Two things should be noted in conjunction with this fourth negative attitude. First, instead of learning from the past mistakes of teachers and preachers, some today continue the same mishandling of the prophetic Scriptures by setting dates for the Rapture or Second Coming of Christ, or by claiming that a certain prominent individual today is the Antichrist. Second, those Christians who are negative toward the study and teaching of biblical prophecy because of abuses should reject the abuses, realize that what the Bible says is true and no one "knows" the Antichrist by name or the date of the Rapture, and continue to study and teach the prophetic Scriptures. They should do so because there are significant reasons why the study and teaching of biblical prophecy is important.

Reasons for Studying Biblical Prophecy

The four negative attitudes that people have toward the study of biblical prophecy are unfortunate because there are four significant reasons why the study of biblical prophecy is important (adapted from articles found at raptureready.com and forty-five years of Bible Prophecy study). First, originally, almost a third of the Bible was prophecy when written and many prophecies are yet to be fulfilled. Those people who reject the study of biblical prophecy because of a negative attitude toward it choose to avoid the biblical revelation that God has given to mankind, revelation that God wants human beings to possess and heed. This avoidance amounts to willful rejection of a major portion of God's truth and, therefore, has serious implications. If God gave us His very Word about our future, then we have an obligation to Him to search out His Word to correctly and with understanding determine what He wants us to know and why.

Second, it is impossible to understand God's purpose for history apart from the study of biblical prophecy. Isaiah 46:9-11 quotes the following divine declaration, "I am God, and there is none else; I am God, and there is none like me, declaring the end from the beginning, and from ancient times the things that are not yet done, saying, My counsel shall stand, and I will do all my pleasure:…I have spoken it, I will also bring it to pass; I have purposed it, I will also do it." Isaiah 14:24, 26-27 states, "The LORD of hosts hath sworn, saying, Surely as I have thought, so shall it come to pass; and as I have purposed, so shall it stand:…This is the purpose that is purposed upon the whole Earth: and this is the hand that is stretched out upon all the nations. For the LORD of hosts hath purposed, and who shall annul it? And his hand is stretched out, and who shall turn it back?"

These Scriptures reveal that there is one true God, and that He has a sovereign purpose for this Earth's history. The evidence that He is the One True God, He exists outside of time, He is not as we are because He sees the past, present, and future all clearly, and He has a sovereign purpose for history. God's prophets declared to mankind what would happen in the future, even to the end of Earth's history. What this means is that God knows what will happen to our and Earth's history because He has planned it, is in full sovereign control, and His Will always comes to pass. The result will be the establishment of His Millennial Kingdom, then a New Heaven and Earth where His chosen will join Him in eternity to serve Him in joy and righteousness.

Nebuchadnezzar, ancient Babylon's greatest king, learned by personal experience that the God of the Bible has a sovereign purpose for what happens in history. Nebuchadnezzar's arrogance led him to claim all he had was a result of his own efforts and brilliance which caused him, by God's design, to eat grass like an animal for seven years until he came to his senses and gave recognition to God. Nebuchadnezzar wrote, "I blessed the most

High, and I praised and honored him that liveth forever, whose dominion is an everlasting dominion, and his kingdom is from generation to generation: and all the inhabitants of the Earth are reputed as nothing: and he doeth according to his will in the army of Heaven, and among the inhabitants of the Earth: and none can stay his hand or say unto him, What doest thou?" (Daniel 4:34-35).

The prophetic Scriptures are the written record of what God through the prophets declared to mankind would happen even to the end of this Earth's history. Since those divine declarations were based upon what God had planned and purposed for history, no one can understand God's purpose for history apart from the study of biblical prophecy. In light of the facts that God has a sovereign purpose for this Earth's history, that on the basis of that purpose He declared to mankind what would happen to the end of history, and that the prophetic Scriptures are the written record of that divine declaration, it is no mistake that the Book of Revelation was the last book of the Bible written. God intended it to be the capstone of His divine declaration to mankind, because it foretells how He will complete His purpose for history. Because of this, the person who decides to avoid the study of Revelation will remain completely oblivious to how God will complete His purpose. It is a tragedy to skip over, ignore, or say something stupid like Revelation cannot be understood. Besides, God promises a special blessing to all who read Revelation (Revelation 1:3).

Third, the study of biblical prophecy is an effective evangelistic tool. God had His declarations of future events recorded in written form in the Scriptures, not to satisfy the curiosity of people concerning what will happen, but to be a life-changing tool for people of every generation. God uses the study of biblical prophecy to serve as a warning to unsaved people: To warn them of the future wrathful judgment that He has purposed for this rebellious world and for all people who fail to receive His gracious gift of salvation through faith in His crucified, buried and resurrected Son, Jesus Christ. The Holy Spirit uses biblical prophecy to impress unsaved people with the urgency of their trusting Christ as their Savior now, before it may be too late for them. Any Christian who avoids the study and teaching of biblical prophecy thereby fails to use a very effective evangelistic tool that God has given to us.

Fourth, it is impossible to understand God's plan and purpose for Israel without studying biblical prophecy. The Bible reveals that God established a unique relationship with Israel as a nation thereby solidifying Israel as a separate entity from the Church and from unregenerate mankind. Moses made the following statement to the generation of Israelites who were to enter the land of Canaan years after Israel's exodus out of Egypt, "For thou art an holy people unto the LORD thy God: the LORD thy God hath chosen thee to be a special people unto himself, above all people that are upon the face of the Earth" (Deuteronomy 7:6).

In addition, the Scriptures indicate that God established this unique relationship with Israel forever. 2 Samuel 7:24 records the following statement of King David to God, "For thou hast confirmed to thyself thy people Israel to be a people unto thee **forever**." In addition, the Apostle Paul indicated that, in spite of Israel's unbelief, God's election or calling of the nation Israel for this unique relationship will never change (Romans 11:26-29).

The Bible also reveals that God did not establish this unique relationship with Israel because they were greater in number than any other people. Moses told them, "The LORD did not set his love upon you, nor choose you, because ye were more in number than any people; for ye were the fewest of all people" (Deuteronomy 7:7). Instead, God established it because He had a unique, sovereign purpose for Israel as a nation to be completely fulfilled in and during the Tribulation or Daniel's 70th Week.

God sovereignly purposed that the nation of Israel plays a key role in the fulfillment of His purpose for history. One aspect of that key role was that God determined to bring great blessing to the whole world through Israel. God promised to bless the world through Abraham's offspring, "And in thy seed shall all the nations of the Earth be blessed" (Genesis 22:18). God repeated that promise to Abraham's son, Isaac (Genesis 26:4), and grandson, Jacob (Genesis 28:14), whose twelve sons became the heads of the twelve tribes of Israel. This clearly shows how God works throughout many generations to accomplish His Will. He does the very same today.

God has already brought great blessings to the world through Israel. The Bible came to us through Israel which makes those that reject the Jews today with Replacement Theology seem very foolish indeed. The Apostle Paul wrote that unto the Jews "were committed the oracles of God" (Romans 3:1-2). The Messiah came to the world by birth through Israel and the Jews. Concerning the Israelites, Paul said, "of whom as concerning the flesh Christ came" (Romans 9:4-5). Since the Messiah, who provided salvation for all people, was a Jew in His humanity, then salvation came through Israel. Jesus Himself said, "Salvation is of the Jews" (John 4:22).

Biblical prophecy indicates that another aspect of Israel's key role is yet future. God will not totally crush Satan and his forces and establish His future theocratic Millennial Kingdom rule to the world until the nation of Israel repents by recognizing and accepting Jesus Christ as its Messiah.

Zechariah 12-14 reveals that, when the rulers and armies of all the Gentile nations of the world will come against Israel in the future (12:1-9), the remnant of Jews who are still alive will see the Messiah coming out of Heaven. When they see the evidences of His past crucifixion, they will repent, change their minds toward Him, and will mourn over His past rejection (12:10-14). God will cleanse them from their sin (13:1). Messiah will then go to battle and destroy the rulers and armies of the world (14:1-3, 12-15; Revelation 19:11-21) and have Satan imprisoned in the bottomless pit for 1,000 years (Revelation 20:1-3). Then He will establish God's theocratic Millennial Kingdom and will rule as "King over all the Earth" (Zechariah 14:9, 16-21; Revelation 20:4-6). In that theocratic Millennial Kingdom, Israel will be the spiritual leader of the world. The people of Israel will "be named the Priests of the LORD" and the Gentiles will call them "the Ministers of our God" (Isaiah 61:6). The Gentiles will take hold of the Jews, "saying, we will go with you: for we have heard that God is with you" (Zechariah 8:23).

Contrary to the divinely inspired statements of King David (2 Samuel 7:24) and the Apostle Paul (Romans 11:26-29), some professing Christians insist that God did not establish His unique relationship with Israel forever. They believe that, because Israel as a nation rejected Jesus Christ in His First Coming, God permanently removed Israel as a nation from that unique relationship and replaced it with the New Testament Church. This is found nowhere in Scripture but is very prominent in some mega-church ministries. They claim that God will save individual Jews, but that He has no present or future national program for Israel, again being completely unscriptural and ignoring major Bible Prophecies such as Daniel's 70 Weeks Prophecy.

This belief, referred to as Replacement Theology, affects their thinking concerning the right of Israel to exist as a national entity in the Middle East today, causes them to support the so-called two-state solution to the Israel-Palestinian issue, and fuels the abandonment of Israel over the support of the Palestinians who have NO right to any land in Israel. The Palestinians claim that there has been a "Palestine for many thousands of years going back so far as to even claim that Jesus was a Palestinian. This is historically absurd since the name "Palestine" only goes back to 135 A.D. and Hadrian when he was Rome's Caesar. Hadrian fought the last rebellion of Jews against the Roman Empire, killed all Jews left in the land, sowed the land with salt, and named the land "Palestina" and re-names Jerusalem "Aeolina Capitolina" after his middle name and the word capitol. This completely destroys from recorded history, the claim of the Palestinians. Also, Palestinians are descended from the dreaded biblical Philistines (same root word) who also had no claim to any land in Israel going back to well before Israel's first king Saul which dates to before 1000 B.C. This shows that the Palestinians have no right to any land anywhere near Israel since the Philistines supposedly came from the area surrounding the Aegean Sea which would put them near Greece or, perhaps, Western Turkey – NOT Israel.

Replacement Theology also causes adherents to reject the idea that God has purposed Israel to play a future key role in the fulfillment of His purpose for history. A significant part of the reason for this belief is the neglect or allegorical interpretation of biblical prophecy which is not only incorrect but very dangerous to those who teach it and to those who listen to and accept it (Genesis 12:3).

From all of this, it can be seen by those with Holy Spirit guidance that unfulfilled prophecy brings clarity of God's plan and purpose, provides blessing and joy in the knowledge of God's care for each of us in these troubling times when we seek righteousness and find very little, and encourages our hearts that God is in control! Without these, our lives would be filled with worry or, at least, concern for our futures, for our families, for our nation. When we study Scripture and prophecy, we find peace, reliance on God, and joy in the knowledge that He alone is sovereign. The conclusion of all of these appeals is one simple thing – respect God's Word, read it, study it, gain from it, apply it, rejoice in it because Almighty God gave it to us! What better gift could a loving and just God give in addition to giving us eternal life through His only Son?

An End Times Biblical Prophetic End of Days Current Timeline

We now need to put all of the End Times prophecies into a visual form so that we can better understand what God is saying. This interpretation comes from my many years of careful Bible study, but cannot be attested to as 100% accurate, just very close to that high standard and a reasonable and detailed compilation of Bible Prophecies. Can anyone know with perfect clarity exactly what and when and how any of these immediate future prophecies will be sequences and come to fruition? Of course not, but Jesus told us that we would know the general time of all of these things and to look because our redemption, the Rapture of the Church, is drawing near.

We will now take the chart of the End Times and endeavor to explain the interpretation of it.

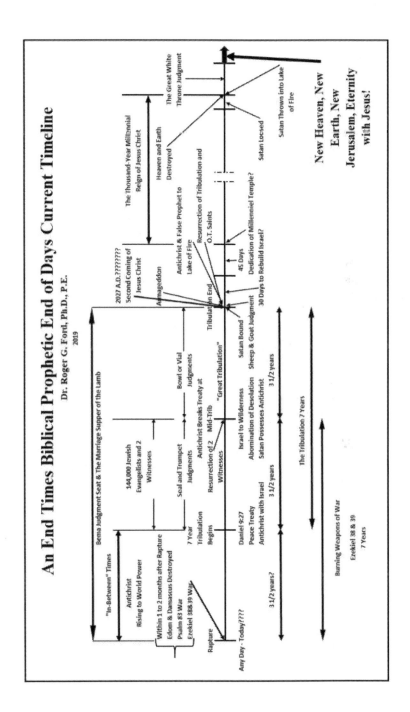

An End Times Biblical Prophetic End of Days Current Timeline

Dr. Roger G. Ford, Ph.D., P.E.
2019

New Heaven, New Earth, New Jerusalem, Eternity with Jesus!

The Timeline is meant to be a guideline only since we cannot be 100% sure of some of the detail of the chart. However, the general sequencing is purely from the Bible and free of wild speculation. There is much that will occur prophetically, and all of it, with little room for doubt, WILL happen AFTER the Rapture. That makes the Rapture THE key to the End Times for today because it happens before anything else. Those you know, your family members, some in your church need to see this timeline since it depicts what they will experience here on the Earth IF they do not know Jesus Christ as Lord and Savior.

The chart starts with the Rapture and assumes that it is a Pre-Tribulation Rapture which Scripture supports clearly. At the very bottom left of the chart, there is a reference to Ezekiel 38 & 39 and the burning of weapons of war for seven years. This is a result of God defeating the armies of Gog and Magog (Russia), Iran, Turkey, and others when God says Israel will be burning the weapons of that war for seven years, which occurs in the "In-Between" Times between the Rapture and the start of the Tribulation. It is for this reason alone that the "In-Between" Times exist because Israel will be hiding and protected by God from Satan and the Antichrist during the last half of the Tribulation (Revelation 12:4). This means the burning of the weapons (for seven years) of the Ezekiel 38 & 39 War must start three and one-half years BEFORE the Tribulation begins! This assumes that when the Antichrist comes to power, his ruthlessness at the Mid-Tribulation point will become so great that no one will continue burning these weapons of the Ezekiel 38 and 39 war for fear of him finding them, especially if they are Jews. The Bible says in Revelation 12:6 that the Antichrist, who is indwelt by Satan himself, will pursue all of the Jews to annihilate them but will be stopped by God's divine protection "in the wilderness" which we assume will be Petra.

There are other wars during this "In-Between" Time such as the Psalm 83 war in which God removes all of Israel's "close-in" enemies so that they can live in peace and safety which is the criterion for the Ezekiel war to take place (Ezekiel 38:11). Consequently, I place the Psalm 83 war in front of the Ezekiel war. The destruction of Damascus in Isaiah 17 comes at this time, and we can see this literally taking place as we look at the city today which is not quite yet fully destroyed. The Elam or Southern Iran area (where Iran's main nuclear facilities lie in Bushehr on the Persian Gulf) is to be destroyed

(Jeremiah 49:34-39) which also probably occurs during this time since it leads to Israel's peace. There could be further events happen at this time, but we will be gone in the Rapture and will not see them happen from Earth's perspective.

Another very important aspect of the "In-Between" years is that the world's objection to a one-world leader will disappear primarily because of the Muslims being all but eliminated through the Psalm 83 and Ezekiel 38 & 39 wars. Note that virtually all of the countries associated with the Psalm 83 war and the Ezekiel 38 and 39 war are Muslim countries except for Russia. Total devastation will result from the Rapture of the Church, of course, since the Christian influence is very strong on this world, but the sudden disappearance of many while driving cars and trucks, flying airplanes, controlling electronically enabled services, and many other essential aspects of daily life will cause utter chaos. Add to that the total destruction of all of Israel's enemies both near and far through the Psalm 83 war and then, soon after, the Ezekiel 38 & 39 war plus all the "islands" which is also translated "continents" associated with the Muslim and Russian nations, and you have a world that will be ready for a "messiah" in the form of a world leader to arise and gain control over the devastation. That person is the Antichrist!

After approximately three and one-half years, the actual Tribulation will begin with Daniel 9:27 and the Antichrist's emerging due to Jesus opening the scroll in Heaven and the first seal which contains the first rider of the Apocalypse or the Antichrist. The Antichrist will, as his first act, strike a peace treaty with Israel, again from Daniel 9:27. Most Prophecy students call this peace treaty a guarantee that Israel will not be attacked because the Antichrist will protect them (read that Satan will protect them). But, since God has been wiping out all of Israel's enemies causing world panic because of God's awesome power displayed on Israel's behalf, I believe the Antichrist draws up a treaty that Israel promises to plead with Jehovah to stop destroying the nations that are Israel's enemies so that the world can live in peace. Israel, now at peace themselves because of God's intervention, naturally signs the peace treaty with the Antichrist thus starting the actual Tribulation period of seven years otherwise called the Time of Jacob's Trouble or Daniel's 70th Week. Great worldwide joy and peace will ensue because of this "remarkable" and "miraculous" peace treaty that the Antichrist gets Israel to sign. But that peace is short lived due to the megalomaniacal Antichrist and his thirst for power and war with righteousness.

What also happens in the first half of the Tribulation is Jesus anoints 12,000 Jews from each of the twelve tribes of Israel to be an army of 144,000 Jewish evangelists for Christ to proclaim the Gospel for three and one-half years. Jesus also sends His Two Witnesses, could be either Moses and Elijah or Enoch and Elijah or even two others we do not expect, to reside at the Temple in Jerusalem, proclaim Jesus Christ as Lord and Savior, completely enraging the Antichrist because he cannot kill them nor the 144,000 because they are divinely protected. These Two Witnesses and the 144,000 expand the Gospel all over the world untouched and safe until the Mid-Tribulation point where God allows them to be martyred. The most dramatic display of all that completely astounds the whole Earth and makes the Antichrist raving mad at the Jews is the three days the Two Witnesses lie dead finally at the Antichrist's hand in Jerusalem. All of a sudden, a voice from Heaven tells them to "Come up here" in the same manner that the Church was called to Heaven some years before in the Rapture, and the three-days-dead Two Witnesses, in front of the world's cameras and everyone's cell phones, rise to their feet and ascend to Heaven spiting and spitting the Antichrist in the eye in front of the world!

So, what is happening to the raptured Church during this "In-Between" time? The Bema Judgment Seat of Christ. Judgment? Yes, but NOT for sin, for works done in Jesus' Name! We all will face the Bema Seat, "bema" means judgment, where our works, deeds, thoughts, and actions are all evaluated as to whether we did them for Him or for some other reason such as self-promoting reasons. 1 Corinthians 3:9-15 describes the difference in works for Jesus (gold, silver, precious stones) or for selfish reasons (wood, hay, stubble). All these works will be subjected to the Lord's fire of Judgment, and the works done for selfish reasons will be burned up, but those done for Christ shall remain. This is the Bema Judgment Seat of Christ from 2 Corinthians 5:10 and Romans 14:10-12. Then, the Church of Jesus Christ, purified, will experience the Marriage Supper of the Lamb. The Bema and the Marriage Supper will occupy the time between the Rapture and the Second Coming of Christ to the Earth where His Church, that's us, will accompany Him back to Earth from Heaven to witness Jesus end the Battle of Armageddon, bind Satan and his hordes of fallen angels and demons for a thousand years, throw the Antichrist and the False Prophet into the Lake of Fire alive, and conduct the Sheep and Goat Judgment to separate out the believers who will inhabit the Millennium from the unbelievers who will be sent to Hell.

Back on Earth before the Second Coming, the Tribulation has to take place to bring the unbelieving Jews, Israel, back to their God, Jehovah, and fulfill Daniel's 70th Week. The Wrath of God is contained in the little scroll of Revelation Chapter 5 that only Jesus is worthy to open because of the terrible wrath it contains. That scroll contains ALL of the Wrath of God that the entire Earth will be subject to, the seven Seal Judgments, the seven

Trumpet Judgments, and the seven Bowl Judgments. The Seal and Trumpet Judgments occur during the first half of the Tribulation, and the Bowl Judgments during the second half. The middle of the Tribulation is significant for several reasons.

The Antichrist grows in power and influence during the first half of the Tribulation because of the False Prophet's efforts to make him look special, even divine. A talking statue or anthropomorphic robot is made in the Antichrist's image, and people are made to bow down to it. It even speaks! Because of all of this adulation, at the Mid-Tribulation point, three and one-half years after the Peace Treaty which started the Tribulation, the Time of Jacob's Trouble, the Antichrist is quite literally possessed by none other than Satan himself, goes into the Tribulation Temple in Jerusalem which had been built as a result of the Peace Treaty, and declares himself to be God thereby committing what is called in Daniel, the Abomination of Desolation (2 Thessalonians 2:4). The possessed Antichrist then declares he is going after the Jews to completely destroy them which sends the Jews into hiding "in the wilderness" (we think to Petra, although that is not specified in the Bible) to be protected by God Himself for the last half of the Tribulation (Revelation 12:6,14). This protection by God of the Jews throws the Antichrist into a rage that turns against all Christians causing him to seek them all out and beheadings begin that last the rest of the Tribulation time (Revelation 12:17).

The second half of the Tribulation is filled with the despotic rage of the Antichrist and Satan aimed at God's people who accept Christ during the Tribulation (Revelation 12:17). But God's Bowl Judgments come upon the Earth which are unlike anything ever seen or ever will be seen. All in the seas die because all salt water is turned into blood, mankind gets covered with boils, all fresh water becomes blood so there is nothing to drink, the sun increases in intensity and burns all men, the Antichrist's kingdom is plunged into a darkness that can be felt, the river Euphrates dries up allowing the kings of the East to proceed to Armageddon, and an earthquake never seen before levels all mountains, makes all islands disappear, 70-pound hailstones fall everywhere killing many, and the rest blaspheme God for all the devastation. This all ends with the Battle of Armageddon which takes place in the Valley of Megiddo, a flat plain surrounded by low mountains in Israel that is 50 miles wide and 200 miles long. In this valley, this so-called battle of Earth's armies against the King of kings and Lord of lords takes place when Jesus returns with His Church at the very end of the Tribulation. Jesus defeats the millions warring against Him with the Sword of His Word! All Jesus has to do to defeat these enemies is utter a Word and it is over. Jesus then proceeds to Jerusalem where His foot touches down again on the Earth in the same place He left from so many years before – the Mount of Olives. At that instant, the mount splits in two, separates toward the North and the South creating a valley running East and West where living water from Jerusalem will flow toward the Mediterranean to the West and the Dead Sea to the East.

The Sheep and Goat Judgment takes place at this time also to separate the believers in Christ (sheep) to the right from the unbelievers (goats) to the left because only the sheep get to walk into the Millennial Kingdom as human beings to live throughout the Millennium of 1,000 years! The goats get to go to Hell. Then, according to Daniel Chapter 12, there is a period of 30 days and then 45 additional days before the Millennial Kingdom begins. The Bible does not explain these "extra" days that go beyond the three and one-half years or 1,260 days. We have to speculate here, but the 30 days could be for the restoration of Israel and Jerusalem, and the 45 days leads up to the Feast of dedication which could be for dedicating the Millennial Temple.

What also occurs at this time is the resurrection and transformation into new, immortal bodies the Old Testament Saints and the Tribulation Saints that died during the Tribulation. The living Tribulation Saints will populate the Millennium, but those that died in Christ during the Tribulation get their immortal bodies just like Jesus' Church did at the Rapture. We get this knowledge from Daniel 12:2 and Revelation 20:4. Now, the Millennium reign of Christ begins! Try to envision a restored Earth with no devil, everyone is a believer (at least at the start), and Jesus ruling and reigning "In Person" in Jerusalem in a new Millennium Temple for a thousand years! What a different Earth will result. Questions answered, long lives of purpose and fulfillment, worship direct and awesome! But sin is still very present, and many will reject Christ in spite of His magnificent presence in the flesh! Isaiah 65:20 suggests that if a person born during the Millennium reaches an age of 100 years and does not accept Christ as Lord and Savior, they will be accursed and be sent to the Lake of Fire. But that does not stop the final rebellion.

Something that has never happened will also happen at the end of the Tribulation and after Jesus sets foot on the Mount of Olives. Satan is bound for a thousand years! Revelation 20:1-3 tells how an angel (maybe Michael) comes down from Heaven with the keys to the bottomless pit and a great chain in his hand. He grabs Satan, the old serpent, the dragon, and binds him and casts him into the bottomless pit with a seal of no escape. He, his fallen angelic horde, and the demons will be powerless for the thousand-year Millennium until just before the end of the Millennium when Satan will be loosed again (Revelation 20:7). The result of his being loosed is very difficult and sad to imagine. What he does in a very short time is go throughout the world and gather literally millions of humans to rebel against the very presence of Jesus Christ, God Almighty, who has been visible on the Earth for the entire thousand years. This rebellious army surrounds Jerusalem, then is destroyed with fire that descends from Heaven. The devil is then thrown into the Lake of Fire to join the Antichrist and the False Prophet for ever and ever.

The next event is one that will never be repeated nor has anything like it ever happened. First, Christ must destroy the present Creation. Why? The Creation has been cursed ever since the Fall of Adam. The sin of man has caused the Earth and the Universe to be accursed which simply means that God's entire Creation is in travail or agony because of man's sin. In order to restore Creation, all of it, to its original state of being "very good", as God declared it to be in Genesis 1:31, God will re-create everything. Revelation 20:11 tells us that, "…the Earth and Heaven fled away; and there was no place found for them." While there is no more Earth or Universe, the Great White Throne Judgment takes place. This is the time when all the unredeemed dead are brought before Jesus Christ on His Great White Throne of Judgment and all the books are opened that contain records of everything ever said, thought, or done in every ungodly persons' life who has ever lived from Cain to the last person born in the Millennium. There is no excuse for anyone without God, so all who come before Jesus at this Judgment will not be able to explain away their selfishness or their sin against Almighty God. They will individually be examined by Jesus, found wanting, and then thrown into the Lake of Fire to be punished for eternity. At the culmination of that horrific event, Jesus as Creator God will remake a new Heaven and a New Earth.

Then, a most spectacular event will take place. The New Jerusalem in all of its splendor and majesty will descend from Heaven (Revelation 21:10) with the Glory of God shining like a jasper stone completely enveloping its cubic shape and 1,500-mile width, its 1,500-mile depth, and its 1,500-mile height! The Throne of God and the Lamb are in it from which a pure river of water of life flows clear as crystal. On either side of that river is the tree of life which produces twelve different types of fruit, one per month. And the Face of God and the Lamb will be seen there in perpetual light with no more darkness ever. There, in the New Jerusalem, we will dwell and serve our Lord Jesus for eternity, learning from Him, worshipping Him, being ever joyful in His presence!

Conclusion and Challenge

The purpose of this little book on Bible Prophecy has attempted to accentuate, enlighten, stir up, and encourage all who heard or read what has been presented. The Bible is God's gift of enlightenment to us so that we can know Him better, understand His expectations for us, know how to please Him, and how to be guaranteed to be with Him for eternity. All of God's Word is God-breathed which means that God is speaking directly to our hearts from His. He tells us the Truth, God's Truth, so that we can be sure of what He tells us. And, we know that almost a third of the Bible was prophecy when it was written, foretold future events before they happened, and most of those prophecies have come to pass exactly as the Bible said they would. But there are many prophecies that still lie in OUR future that have not taken place yet, but soon will!

How do I know that they will take place? Because God never lies and never misleads. So, what He says will happen and what He tells us is the Truth. How do I know that these future events will happen soon? Because Jesus gave us signs to look for which tell us that He is going to come back to Earth in the very near future. The most significant and often overlooked by many in the Christian Church today is the Nation of Israel. Israel is a nation once again after over 1,800 years of "wilderness wandering". Their language is again alive and being used, they are continuing to return to the Promised Land where almost 7 million reside out of the 14 million Jews worldwide. Israel is an exporter of vegetables to Europe and other countries, has one of the top 5 militaries in the world, is a nuclear power, and is truly a "cup of trembling" to all, a "burdensome stone" for all the people of Earth as Zechariah 12 tells us.

Jesus told His disciples, which includes us, that the signs of the end would be like birth pains in a woman about to give birth. They start out relatively low in pain and occur infrequently. So have the wars and rumors of wars, nation rising against nation, kingdom against kingdom (read ethnic or racial group against ethnic or racial group), famines, pestilences, and earthquakes – all of which we have seen and heard happening. But, as a woman approaches the point of giving birth to a new baby, the birth pains gain in intensity, become more and more painful, and they increase in frequency, getting closer and closer together. The signs of the times are coming together in what Bible Prophecy Watchers call "Convergence" which simply means ALL OF THEM are happening more and more with little space between happenings.

The condition of our planet today is one that is out of control due to financial upheaval, a return to the often failed and always deadly socialism/Marxism/communism philosophies where, for obvious selfish reasons, people think that there is the ability to get something for nothing and someone else has to "pay the piper"! Worldwide economic disaster is at the doorstep with almost all countries borrowing so much money to maintain a sinful lifestyle that there is no way to ever pay it all back. The U.S. says it is $22 Trillion dollars in debt when the actual number due to retirement plans, unfunded entitlements such as Welfare and Hospitalization (read Obamacare), Medicare/Medicaid and Social Security, the proposal of the Green New Deal, unending and seemingly unwinnable wars in such places as Syria, Afghanistan, many in Africa, and others, illegal immigration both here and in Europe, the drug wars, human trafficking, just an unrighteous lifestyle outside of God, and a lenient justice system, is closer to $200 Trillion dollars which is a number inconceivable to any mind and definitely unpayable ever! (Just to make a trillion a little more understandable, if you spent a million dollars a day, every day, seven days a week, 365 days a year ever since Jesus was born, you would not have spent a trillion up to today, just only about ¾ of a trillion!) All of this is a loud confirmation of the nearness of the Rapture! As soon as the Rapture happens, I believe the entire world will be thrown into financial collapse leaving no foothold for even the very rich. Again, this is just a necessary set-up for the Antichrist to rise to power and to gain control over everyone left behind!

Our challenge, each and every true Christian who believes in Jesus Christ and has made Him both Savior and Lord, is to be a watchman! What does it mean to be a watchman? Ezekiel 33:7 says, "So thou, O son of man, I have set thee a watchman unto the house of Israel; therefore, thou shalt hear the word at my mouth, and warn them from me." God appointed Ezekiel to be a watchman to Israel. We should be watchmen to not only watch Israel and care for Israel but watch out for the signs of the times so that we can relate the Gospel of Jesus Christ to everyone we know or meet so that they will not have to endure the very Wrath of God that is coming soon. In order to watch out for the signs, to be a watchman for God, we must KNOW the Scriptures and Prophecies! And we do that by reading, studying, memorizing, meditating, sharing, and teaching God's Word as often as we can so that the Holy Spirit can complete the work and bring those that will listen into His Kingdom.

One of the obstacles that the enemy has placed in our path to clarity and understanding of the Scriptures is false teaching. There are many spouting unbiblical half-truths on radio, cable, and on DVD and CD. Many preach a prosperity gospel which leaves out the true nature of man being sinful in need of redemption. Others avoid prophecy claiming the subject unnecessary as some say applies to the Old Testament as well (probably because their study takes away from the false teachers' pleas for money and attention). Others are deep into self-promotion and audience building because there are mountains of money to be extorted to uneducated minds. Then there are those false teachers that claim to have all the answers and persuade their followers to listen to them and never read God's Word for themselves since it is too difficult to understand with an "uneducated" or "un-initiated" mind.

I have found over the years that there are reliable Bible scholars and theologians that can be trusted to augment our understanding of God's Word. This clarity comes through commentaries that explain the culture and times of the writers of the Bible which clarify difficult areas, from understanding of the original languages and the increased clarity of the knowledge that brings, from those that are gifted in their ability to cross-reference subject matter in the Bible with all the many times the Word covers the subject in other books of the Bible, and much more. The resources that I have found to be very reliable start with John MacArthur and GTY.org, The Institute for Creation Research (Henry Morris) and ICR.org, Answers in Genesis (Ken Ham) and answersingenesis.org, David Jeremiah and DavidJeremiah.org, RaptureReady.com, Bruce Malone and Searchforthetruth.net, and many others. A general rule of thumb is to avoid the mega-churches and rely on the local church if it is sound and has a Bible-preaching Pastor as mine does (see the Forward of this book).

So, my challenge to every one of us is to continue to make God's Word PRIORITY in our lives, to read God's Word every day, pray every day, repent of our sins daily, and be filled with the Holy Spirit's Wisdom so that our lives will be pleasing to God through the works His Spirit leads into! And, as I always tell you, "Even so, Come Lord Jesus!"

CHAPTER EIGHT

"...BEHOLD, NOW IS THE ACCEPTED TIME; BEHOLD, NOW IS THE DAY OF SALVATION" (2 CORINTHIANS 6:2b)

Prophecy, eschatology, or the study of things to come from a biblical perspective are all very exciting even from a non-believer's viewpoint. Everyone is interested in their future to some degree. Many ever since Saul sought out the witch of Endor have pursued the future through mediums, gypsies, horoscopes, astrology, tarot cards, magicians, palm readers, and so forth, all evil, flawed, and satanic. There is but one source of knowledge of the future and that is God's Word which is 100% accurate all the time. Why seek out man's opinions when God has told us exactly what will happen and that if we trust in Him, He will give us assurance, guidance, and eternal life? Of course, and unfortunately, there are people who claim to know the Bible and still pursue these evil resources when looking to the future.

It is surprising the number of people that are fairly well versed in the Bible and know quite a lot about the Bible. By that I mean they know many Scriptures, they are familiar with the basic doctrines of the faith, they have distinct opinions on many aspects of Christianity and the Jewish people and their country of Israel, but they exhibit no charity, seem to have no understanding of world affairs, do not know how God's Word is consistent and uniform from Genesis 1:1 to revelation 22:21, or that God is the same yesterday, today, and forever (Hebrews 13:8).

It is certainly not for any human to condemn any other human, especially for their beliefs. But it is our responsibility to discern motives and veracity in other humans if we are to function successfully in this world whether biblically or not. We have to make decisions about daily occurrences and people with which we have to do so that we can survive, be gainfully employed, raise families, and function on an acceptable level in our rather complicated if corrupted society.

But how do we accomplish that decision-making without drawing conclusions or being tempted to condemn really bad behavior so we can avoid it? We first make sure that we correct the bad behavior and thought processes we have within ourselves before we start criticizing others. Jesus said, "Do not judge (condemn) so that you will not be judged (condemned). For in the way you judge, you will be judged; and by your standard of measure, it will be measured back to you. Why do you look at the splinter that is in your brother's eye, but do not notice the log that is in your own eye?

Or how can you say to your brother, 'Let me take the splinter out of your eye,' while there is a log in your own eye? You hypocrite! First take the log out of your own eye, then you can see clearly how to remove the splinter from your brother's eye." (Matthew 7:1-5)

Of course, this applies to everyone since God is not a respecter of persons. But it certainly applies to Christians, that is those who have accepted Jesus Christ as Lord and Savior. It is nonetheless quite proper in behavior so that we are not thought to be hypocrites. This also goes for the acceptance as the True Truth of Scripture, and especially Prophecy and its reliability, veracity, and accuracy.

Many have decided that the Bible is too hard to understand, and this applies to Prophecy specifically because there is so much cross-referencing from one book to another, from one Testament to the other, that the understanding of it all even at a rudimentary level is just too daunting a task over too long a time for most to even want to tackle it. We must all realize that there are two kinds of people and only two. Saved and unsaved. Regenerate and unregenerate. Believer and unbeliever. Christian and non-Christian. There is no gray area, it is indeed black and white. Unfortunately, however, there are many that either think that they are Christian when they are not, many that know they are not Christian but would like others to think they are, some who want to convince others of their Christianity but teach heresy and opposition to God's Word, then there are those that do not care one way or the other. Interestingly, most if not all of these are really unbelievers who still have a desire to know the future, so they are probably interested in Bible Prophecy at least a little.

It is to these folks who greatly outnumber true Christians that I would like to address. Some of you who know who you are have read this small treatise on Bible Prophecy with some understanding, but probably have many questions simply because you do not have the Holy Spirit to give you the understanding that you need to fully understand. Would you like to get increasing understanding the more you read and study the Bible, God's very Word? There is a very easy way to accomplish that, but it will take giving up something very precious to you that you will be reluctant to release forever. What is that? Your pride! You must think greater of others than yourself. You must put others ahead of yourself. You must realize that it is NOT about YOU! It is about Jesus Christ and His Will for your life, not your will for your life. YOU are the cause of your unhappiness, your discouragement, your unfulfilled desires, not God or anyone else. God wants you to be joyful and complete because He loves you better than any other human ever could. Plus, He can grant you the distinct honor and pleasure of spending eternity with

260

Him in a New Heaven and a New Earth that is free from all unrighteousness and evil! Doesn't that sound glorious, especially in this crazy world of liars, leakers, politicians (but I repeat myself), death, illness, catastrophes, and uncertainty?

All you have to do is accept the free gift of salvation from death and eternal punishment by believing that what Jesus Christ accomplished on the cross was the payment for your sins so that Almighty God will not hold you accountable for them. Then, you must make Jesus Christ the Lord of your life, follow His commands in His Word, then the Holy Spirit will come inside of you to guide and direct you into His Will for your life. The Holy Spirit will also give you wisdom, God's Wisdom, knowledge, and understanding so that your life will have meaning and a real future to look forward to. Then Bible Prophecy will start to make sense, you will know where you fit, and you will be able to share God's Truth with your family, your friends, and all you meet so that they, too, can be free from this world of sin, death, disappointment, and regret not to mention eternal damnation in the Lake of Fire!

I would also like to address the Christians who are struggling to understand Bible Prophecy. You already have the Holy Spirit in His full manifestation living within you. He has already given to you of His fruit – love, joy, peace, patience, kindness, goodness, faithfulness, gentleness, and self-control. But you have not tapped into these wonderful gifts because you have not asked to be made aware of them. You are standing in YOUR own way even though you are a true Christian. Pray that the Lord will open your eyes to His Wisdom, His Knowledge, His Understanding, and the Holy Spirit will open you up to a world where the Bible comes alive with meaning and applicability and assurance that you never have realized before. Bible Prophecy will be clearer, more impactful, easier to share, and ever so sweet when you realize that the Holy Spirit, Who is Very God Himself, is part of you, living within you, and will help you with whatever your life brings your way. All you have to do is ask!

Bible Prophecy is such a wonderful expression of the Love of God for His people. We should all feel the blessing of Revelation 1:3, "Blessed is he that readeth, and they that hear the words of this prophecy, and keep those things which are written therein: for the time is at hand." Do you? Pray that the Holy Spirit will invade your thoughts, lead you to Truth, open the door of Revelation, and clear the narrow road ahead to the Glory of God. He will do it, guaranteed. The Bible tells me so!

May your life be complete in the Lord, may you be blessed in the knowledge that you are the child of the Almighty God, the Blessed Savior,

Jesus Christ our Lord. Maranatha! Even so, Come Lord Jesus! The Rapture could be any second! Are you ready?

BIO

With over 40 years of industrial and academic experience, I retired to be with my beautiful wife of over 50 years, Mary. After engineering work, consulting, being a tenured professor, a global vice president, and extensive world travel of which I am very grateful, my time to step away from the work-a-day world finally came. Now, we spend our time with our friends in Bible Study, Church, and leisure with trips to visit our two boys and our five incredible grandchildren.

I have studied Bible Prophecy for over 45 years ever since my first reading of Hal Lindsey's "Late Great Planet Earth" back in 1972. Since then I have voraciously read everything I could from hundreds of sources and authors which, along with personal, Spirit-led, in-depth Bible research and study, has led me to the point of putting all of this information together into this little book. I know this is more of a course than a book, however, I am not surprised, frankly, that there is so much here to grasp because God wants us to know what He has in store for us. My prayer is that what is written here will be a help and possibly a revelation to anyone willing to look into it.

May God lead you to increased desire and dedication to His infallible Word because it is the source of peace, security, and eternal life. The basis for this incredible desire and dedication in me and, hopefully, in you? The Word of God is, indeed, Jesus Christ, King of kings and Lord of lords, the Alpha and Omega, Wonderful, Counselor, Prince of Peace, and my Lord and Savior! John 1:1 says, "In the beginning was the Word, and the Word was with God, and the Word was God." Maranatha! Even so, come Lord Jesus!

CHAPTER RESOURCES

I believe that all Christian authors write and share their studies and writings in order to evangelize, teach, train, encourage, exhort, share, educate, and many other reasons. Because of this realization of the real reason for writing about God, we should all use each others' information. But, if we do not give proper attribution to the original authors, the possibility of others being able to use those resources for future reference and possible additional knowledge is lost, not to mention giving proper acknowledgment to originality. There is a wealth of information available, but everyone needs to be very careful because there are still false teachers, ravening wolves out there. That is why I have listed the sources I have used because I recommend them after careful study and experience.

For these and other reasons, I have chosen to give the resources that I have used in each chapter so that further information can be sought out by readers from those resources which makes the resources that I have chosen all the more important to be trustworthy for further use.

In each chapter, I have listed the names of people, ministries, and internet sites that I have used to make my points. Much that I have written comes from the over 45 years of Bible study with concentration in Bible Prophecy being the key area in relation to this book, but not exclusively since all Bible study relates to all Scripture in the entire Bible. This is not the traditional method of attribution I realize, but most of my Prophecy knowledge has come from my over 45 years studying, writing, teaching, and researching the Bible in its entirety. So, forgive me if I do not remember the specifics of exactly where I have gained some of my information and knowledge. Here's to hoping that some benefit will be realized by reading what I am offering. God Bless!

45940072R00159

Made in the USA
Middletown, DE
22 May 2019